Robin Knox-Johnston was born in Putney in 1939 and joined the Merchant Navy at the age of 17. After successfully completing a non-stop solo circumnavigation of the globe on *Suhaili* in 1969, he took on numerous other sailing challenges and became a successful businessman.

RUNNING FREE

THE AUTOBIOGRAPHY

ROBIN KNOX-JOHNSTON

**SIMON &
SCHUSTER**

London · New York · Sydney · Toronto · New Delhi

A CBS COMPANY

First published in Great Britain by Simon & Schuster UK Ltd, 2018
This edition published in Great Britain by Simon & Schuster UK Ltd, 2019
A CBS COMPANY

1 3 5 7 9 10 8 6 4 2

Simon & Schuster UK Ltd
1st Floor
222 Gray's Inn Road
London WC1X 8HB

www.simonandschuster.co.uk
www.simonandschuster.com.au
www.simonandschuster.co.in

Simon & Schuster Australia, Sydney
Simon & Schuster India, New Delhi

A CIP catalogue record for this book
is available from the British Library

Paperback ISBN: 978-1-4711-7765-1
eBook ISBN: 978-1-4711-7764-4

Typeset in Bembo by M Rules
Printed and bound by CPI Group (UK) Ltd, Croydon, CR0 4YY

Contents

1

ARE SEAMEN BORN OR BRED?

I first took a serious interest in the sea aged eight, but I am sure that my father's job in a shipping company had some influence. I suppose that once an enthusiasm has been expressed it makes it easier for people to find birthday and Christmas presents that appear to suit your interests so that was that. I was destined for a career at sea in one form or another. When I was nine I saw a small pram sailing dinghy for sale costing £13, I spent the next three years saving every penny I could to buy it. By the time I had sufficient funds the price of the boat had risen to £18 so it was not to be, but, if anything, this increased my determination to buy a boat and get afloat somehow. So an eight-year-old decided the course of my life.

I was born in 1939 in Putney in south-west London but my first recollections are of Heswall on the Wirral. We had lived in New Brighton for a time while Dad was working for Ellerman Lines in Liverpool, but Hitler dropped a bomb on the flats where we lived so we moved further out to Pipers Lane in Heswall. From the kitchen we could see the River Dee and there I launched my first attempt at a boat, a raft made from an oranges box. Disappointingly, it sank under my weight – an early introduction to Archimedes' principle, had I known it!

You could not possibly be unaware of the war going on, but growing up in it you took it as normal. Most families seemed to have someone serving in uniform and we were aware of the danger from bombers. On one occasion, visiting my mother's Aunt Betty in Putney, a 'buzz bomb' was heard and then the engine stopped. 'That's all right,' said Mother, not appreciating that this meant it was about to come down. In seconds Aunt Betty had us awake and in the middle of the house wrapped in eiderdowns to avoid any splintering glass from the impending blast.

On Mother's side her father, Arthur Thomas Crawford Cree, a barrister, was killed while serving with the Durham Light Infantry at Ypres in 1915. We had no cousins on Father's side but 11 on Mother's: the Irvings and the Platts-Mills. Grandmother Cree was a Williams and grew up at Pendley near Tring in Hertfordshire. Father's parents were both from Ulster, Grandfather from Macosquin near Coleraine and Grandmother was a McHenry from Derriaghy near Lisburn. They had that hard Ulster Protestant work ethic that was to influence me when I lived with them at Berkhamsted to save the cost of boarding fees at school and for which I have always been grateful. My DNA indicates my heritage is 42 per cent Fermanagh and 9 per cent Scandinavian, the remainder being largely the Scottish Lowlands, very typical of people known as the Scots-Irish.

Dad volunteered for the army in 1940 and went into the Royal Engineers, ending up commanding a dock company that went over to France six days after D-Day to take over the Port of Courseulles and then move with General Montgomery's rapidly advancing 21st Army Group along the coast as far as Antwerp to keep the supplies coming in. Posted briefly to Palestine he spent his last two years in Greece and was de-mobbed in 1947. By then we had moved down to Beckenham into a family-owned house at 124 Bromley Road with the Irvings and for a while I went to the infant school at St Christopher's across the road before moving on to prep school at Clare House in Oakwood Avenue. When Dad eventually came home he was a stranger who I had really only seen for the odd week throughout my short life. He returned to Ellerman Lines but they were not too pleased he had left a reserved job to join up and reinstated him in the same position and on the same salary he had had seven years earlier. This was not sustainable as he now had four sons – Christopher and Michael had followed me and Richard. So he left and joined Grandfather in the Irish linen business of William Adams & Co. in Belfast. For two years we shuttled between England for school in Beckenham and Northern Ireland for the holidays, not far from Whitehead in County Antrim, as Dad picked up a new career.

Those were happy days, fishing on the Belfast Lough or visiting Bangor for its annual regatta and playing along the side of the Lough just above White Harbour. My younger brother Richard and I used to beachcomb. Christopher and Michael were a bit too young to be allowed to roam loose with us but Mother had no qualms about allowing her eleven- and eight-year-olds out on their own. On one occasion, after finding nothing of interest our attention was drawn to a rowing boat pulled up on the beach. 'Let's go for a row, come on, help me launch this,' I ordered, in the way elder brothers speak to their siblings. We heaved and hauled until we got the craft into the water. Richard jumped in, I gave it a push and joined him. The first thing we discovered was that there were no oars as we turned slowly within ten feet of the beach. Then we noticed that water was filling the boat at an alarming rate. We looked for a leak and found it – the empty bung hole. Using the bottom boards we struggled to row the boat back to the beach but she sank before we could quite get her there. We jumped into the sea, hefted and slowly moved it closer. The tide was ebbing and its increasing weight was making the task impossible. We gave up temporarily and retired to the railway embankment to strip off and lay out our clothes to dry. We were lying there when the owner arrived. He was remarkably good-natured about it all as the three of us hauled the craft above the high water mark and then he walked us back to the bungalow we lived in on the main Whitehead – Carrickfergus Road. I have never forgotten to look out for bungs since. We remember the lessons from our mistakes more than our successes.

In the meantime we had moved to a large Victorian house at 28 The Avenue in Beckenham, in those days a gravel road, where the family was to stay until 1961 when we moved out to The Rookery in Downe, close to Biggin Hill. Dad took an interest in local politics in Beckenham, becoming a council-lor and then mayor in 1956. More significantly for me, across the road in Raleigh Court was another family, the Singers, whose daughter Suzanne soon became a part of our group. We remained just friends until I was nineteen and she seventeen and our interest in each other became more romantic.

Back in 1952, Common Entrance, the examination for public schools, approached. My workup was hindered by a torn car-tilage, which meant I missed weeks of school during the final preparations, but I just managed to squeak through. My father had been to Berkhamsted Boys, and five of my aunts to the sister school, and wanted us to go there too. The school accepted me and I went to live with my grandparents at their house named Craigavad in Cross Oak Road during term times to save boarding fees. Their no-nonsense attitude meant I did my homework properly and was expected to help in the garden. In my spare time I designed and built a canoe in the attic with a wooden framework covered in canvas which I then painted. It was not a thing of beauty, but it got me afloat, first on the Grand Union Canal and later at Selsey where we usually spent our summer holidays. Granny Cree lived in Hillfield Road in Selsey, after one of her many moves. Moving had become her hobby since she had left Pendley near Tring to get married.

Dad transported my canoe on top of our venerable Morris 12 to get it to the sea. Our annual seaside holiday was a major expedition and required a trailer for all our gear by the time parents, nanny – the lovely and long-suffering Carrie Richards – and four boys were jammed into the car. On arrival I could not wait to get launched and paddle out beyond the Bill itself where the rocks extend out to near the Owers Buoy and are almost dry at low water. Pagham Bay was another interesting place to paddle among the mud banks. I relished this freedom to be able to go where I wanted on my own. It was no reflection on my family, as my brothers Richard, Chris and Mike and I have always been able to cooperate when it suited us and they had goes in the canoe, or helped me to set up night lines on the beach, but I was discovering for the first time the magic of being able to explore by sea and to visit places otherwise out of reach. I even made a mast in the school craft shop and created a peculiar frame that could bolt onto the gunwale and allow a keel to be slung beneath the hull. These attempts to sail were supported by occasional trips to Blechley with the Pollocks, another Northern Irish family living in Berkhamsted, who had built a car top dinghy in their sitting room. But I had much to learn and the experiments to sail the canoe were not very successful.

Berkhamsted School, situated just behind the church in the middle of the town, was civilised compared with some and on balance I enjoyed my time there although I was not one to join any particular group. It was not pretentious but very sound. Interesting teaching of history, maths and geography has benefitted me all my life and I wish I could have managed a better grasp of the sciences, but that came much later. Perhaps the best known Old Boys were the Greenes, Graham and Hugh Carlton, but for me the most fascinating was Bill Tilman, mountaineer and sailor, who had won two Military Crosses before he was 21 years old in the First World War.

The school was forward-thinking and the first to have a science lab and an indoor swimming pool. My best sport was boxing where I represented the school in my weight three years running with only one defeat, in my first year. Under Chris Jay, the gym master, we had a diminutive RAF Sergeant as a tutor, who had been a professional flyweight and trained us remorselessly. How many people have you seen throw a left and their right? Their guard goes off to the right exposing your jaw unless you are a southpaw. He put a strop around our necks to hold our right where it should be, protecting the face. I am slightly ambidextrous, which threw him at first as I could switch to leading with my right (southpaw) if I thought my opponent needed unsettling. He solved that with his strop around my left arm! If he thought you were getting cocky he would take you into the ring and for three rounds dodge every punch you aimed at him while softly picking you off. It was frustrating but made us try even harder.

Inter-school boxing was judged by service people and they quickly stopped a fight if it was uneven. The only knockdown I saw was to one of our team who was winning but got caught by a wild haymaker punch. Boxing is a very athletic sport and taught me not to pick fights as you can never be certain of another person's ability until maybe it is too late. As you sat on your stool looking at your opponent before the first round you seldom knew what to expect. The lanky one might have a long reach and pick you off, the short one might be quick and a scrapper. You only found out in the first round as you sounded each other out. But while boxing taught me not to pick fights it also gave me the confidence not to walk away when pushed. I was also a distance runner but not quite good enough for the school team. Neither is a team sport, which is interesting considering my later adoption of solo sailing. I did play for my house at rugby, on the wing and later as a flanker as I was small in those days, and was used as a longstop in cricket where my performance would do least harm.

Hanging over us was the spectre of a future that was dependent upon how well we did at O- and A-levels, but eventually we all faced the unavoidable choice of whether to do National Service before or after university. The perceived wisdom was that university first meant a worse degree but a better chance of an officer's commission. Most chose to get National Service out of the way before university. We did not debate the rights or wrongs of the service, it was there and had to be done. This might seem strange today but our earliest memories were of our nation being involved in out and out war, which affected everyone in one way or another. Britain was still fighting wars all over the globe; Korea may have gone quiet, but there were revolutions in various colonies and communists to fight in Malaya. The demand for manpower to fight these wars was still there so we had National Service for all fit males while we withdrew uneasily from our colonial past, trying to maintain some sort of order in the process.

Like all my generation the Second World War had left an enormous impression on me. As children we were imbued with the concept of shortages, rationing, fathers being away, air raids, for some even the arrival of bombs or the sound of cannon fire from aircraft above the countryside, vast military convoys of British, American and Canadian trucks and tanks and safe Prisoners of War helping in the fields. Shortages meant old steam traction engines heaved reapers across fields of corn, which was especially exciting for a small boy, and some deliveries were made in steam trucks. This was the only life we knew until quite long after the war ended. I can still remember being allowed up for the celebrations on VE night, Victory in Europe, with a bonfire onto which an effigy of Hitler was thrown accompanied by loud cheers. We still did not know when our parents might come home as the war against Japan continued, but fortunately the atom bombs on Hiroshima and Nagasaki brought that war to an end, saving the lives of millions of Allied soldiers and of even more Japanese people if their suicidal defence of Okinawa was anything to go by. Even when peace arrived it took some years for rationing to disappear and the most fun places to play were bombed-out houses, despite the justified strictures against it as many were unsafe and awaiting demolition when the country's manpower was demobbed from the forces and returned to civilian life.

In the summer of 1954, when I was fifteen, I drove to Kessock on the Black Isle, north of Inverness with my aunt Maureen to stay with her sister Aileen, who had married Sir Kerr Fraser-Tytler. Kerr had retired to a small estate after service in the Indian Cavalry in Tanganyika during the First World War, the Indian Civil Service, then as British Minister to Afghanistan and subsequently Britain's Red Cross representative to the USA during the Second World War. Largely retired now, he took pains to make me safe with a shot gun and then allowed me to roam to reduce the number of pigeons. Fly fishing on a beat on the River Beauly was another great treat and although I never hooked a salmon he allowed me to play and land those that he had hooked. In the meantime the aunts heated stones on the bank to cook the trout I had caught. His book *Afghanistan* is still relevant today and anyone reading it will appreciate why you do not want to interfere with that country.

The holiday came to an abrupt end when we learned that my grandmother Johnston had died and we drove back hurriedly to Berkhamsted. She had been a huge influence in my life. She did not accept anything but the highest standards and any success was treated as expected, not a surprise. When I obtained my school boxing colour, the first in my year to gain a school colour, she made me wait three weeks before she deigned to sew the badge on my blazer. Her whole philosophy could be summed up in two adages: 'Do as you would be done by' and 'The Lord helps those who help themselves' – pretty good advice for life that I have tried to follow ever since, not always successfully.

I became a boarder in St John's House when my second brother Richard arrived at the school and he took my place with our grandparents. By this time I was in the sixth form and my sudden arrival in a boarding house at a senior level was resented by some who felt I had missed out on the fagging stage as a fourth former. It came to a head one weekend when I had to fight a larger boy but luckily for me it quickly became apparent that a member of the school boxing team should not be picked on casually.

As seniors we were allowed slightly more freedom, but not much. Shopping in the town was permitted provided one had a chit from one's house tutor, who knew perfectly well we did not need a tube of toothpaste every Saturday but were going to wander around the shops between twelve and one o'clock with the objective of meeting the senior girls from our sister school on similar errands, from whom we were otherwise rigorously segregated. The day boys and girls might meet socially with their families, but for the boarders such trysts were almost impossible. Not that this worried me too much at the time. I was focused on sport more than anything and my interests lay with which of the numerous maritime openings that were available to a young man leaving school I should choose as a career.

The autumn term was rugby, spring was athletics and the summer cricket or tennis. Not being very good at cricket I put myself down officially for tennis on Saturday afternoons. I took to leaving St John's dressed for tennis and when out of sight doubling back to my grandparents where I had a 1927 Austin 7 I was restoring. The captain of tennis, Michael Meacher, later an MP, was untroubled by my absence as I was not a very good player. Working on the car had the added benefit that I was fed one of Grandmother's fabulous teas. On returning one day from an afternoon working on the car the head of the house, Ajaz Fakir, hauled me in and said, 'Knox, we know you are no good at cricket, and we know you don't play tennis, and we know you go to your grandparents to work on your car, but would you please get the grease out from under your finger-nails before coming back to the house!' Ajaz and I were to meet again many decades later when I went to stay with him for a few days in Karachi on the understanding he provided tickets for an England v. Pakistan one-day cricket match. England were slaughtered and Ajaz, remembering my lack of interest at school, was puzzled as to why I had become such an enthusiastic England cricket supporter even if our team had not shown well.

Like many my age I had some experience with a rifle and Bren and Sten guns since we were trained in the Combined Cadet Force (CCF) for about four hours each week. Cadet Corps Camps were mandatory. We had a school tradition going back 50 years that we marched to these camps, so the first year I attended, aged 15, we marched 53 miles in three days with rifle and pack. It was meant to be a lesser distance but heavy rain flooded one of the camp sites. On arrival we were fighting fit and always showed off by carrying one item of kit more than ordered, to show we could hack it. In 1953 we went to Thetford where 2,000 delighted schoolboys watched the then brand new Hawker Hunter speed overhead followed by a Canberra Bomber, but the high point of the day was when parachutes holding a jeep failed and it fell to the ground with a devastating crash. The camp lasted ten days, during which we all took turns on the rifle ranges, did map reading exercises, rode in armoured cars and crawled all over Centurion and Conqueror tanks. I loved it.

The next term we took a newly introduced examination, known as Certificate A, where the examiners were supplied by the regular army. Only 16 out of 94 passed, and I am convinced I was mistaken for someone else as during the drill test I marched my squad straight into a brick wall! However, that pass got me a Lance Corporal's stripe.

I joined the RNVR, the Royal Navy Volunteer Reserve, in 1956 once I was seventeen years old, while still at school. I joined out of interest and also to ensure that when the time came to do my National Service it would be with the Royal Navy. I had intended to go to Summer CCF camp that year, my third in succession, but the Navy expected its recruits to start early so I put myself down for 15 days' basic training instead and awaited orders. When they came I was over the moon at my luck. I was to join the battleship HMS *Vanguard* in Plymouth at the end of July. A rail warrant bought my ticket to Plymouth where a bus took me and some 120 others to the Devonport dockyard where we were checked and then taken to stores to be issued with our kit. The standing joke was that nothing ever fitted and the recruits had to lump it, but in fact some sort of an effort was made to see that we would not look too ridiculous. Then we were marched down to a jetty to board a boat to take us out to our ship, which was moored in the harbour.

Even at a distance *Vanguard* was impressive and dwarfed the anchorage, even the 39,150-ton battleship HMS *Howe* that lay alongside looked small in comparison. *Vanguard* was our newest battleship, the largest of its type ever built for the Royal Navy at 44,500 tons and the last battleship to be built in the world. She had been completed in 1946 at a cost of £9 million and was armed with eight 15-inch diameter guns each capable of hurling a shell weighing three quarters of a ton almost 38,000 yards. Her secondary armament was the equivalent of two cruisers, sixteen high-angle 5.25 guns and she carried more than 80 other lighter pieces.

Like all of her type she was built to slug it out with her own kind and to withstand 15 and 16 inch shells she carried 18 inch thick armour along her sides to protect her engines and magazines. Her steam turbines developed 120,000 horse power and gave her a maximum speed of 32 knots. To me she represented the ultimate expression of Britain's sea power, but greater examination of the lessons of the Second World War would have shown that the days of the battleship were gone, we were in the era of air power, and she and her sisters were all to be scrapped within the next six years, the only exceptions being the slightly larger US Missouri Class which lasted another 40 years in various roles, not least because most missiles at the time would bounce off a battleship's armour.

However, that was in the future and the immediate excitement was of boarding this leviathan, being taken to the Marine Gunners' mess below X turret, traditionally manned by the Royal Marine Gunners, stowing our gear and being quickly shown how to rig our hammocks. Seventy of us, known as S & U's or school and university entrants, were jammed into three small metal compartments. We were told it was designed for 120 men and wondered how on earth that could be possible. The war complement of the ship was more than 2,000, but there were only about half that number aboard at the time, although rumours abounded that she might be put into commission and sent to the Mediterranean as a result of the Egyptian nationalisation of the British and French-owned Suez Canal. These rumours were strengthened by the ejection of a number of half-painted frigates from dry dock to be replaced by landing craft. Landing craft meant troops and tanks and that in turn meant just one thing: amphibious invasion. I don't think at that age any of us considered the rights and wrongs of the situation, the canal had been owned by the British and French for more than 80 years so if the governments decided to take back their property that was their political decision. As young men we obeyed orders and saw it as another adventure for the British armed forces.

For two weeks we were taught basic knots, drill and marching, not so easy for those of us from army Cadet Corps as the navy gives orders on the right foot whereas the army gives them on the left. The lectures included the organisation of the navy, how a ship was divided and sealed off and the basics of the nuclear bomb and how to protect ourselves against radiation. The last lecture broke down when one of our number, who was studying nuclear physics at Cambridge so knew rather a lot about the subject, questioned the petty officer on a particular fact and was told to be quiet or be put on a charge, which rather sapped our confidence!

Each day we were called on the tannoy at 0600 hours, and had to be washed, dressed and have our hammocks lashed and stowed away by 0630 when we 'turned to' until 0745. This time was spent on routine tasks, such as scrubbing the decks or paintwork, but after cutting my hand I was told to replenish the Captain's motor launch with diesel each day, allowing me to roam the ship. The supply tank was in one of the eight huge generator compartments where I filled a five-gallon jerrycan and carried it up three vertical ladders. Below the main deck there were no doors in the bulkheads so all access was vertical. I carried my 50 pounds of full jerrycan to the weather deck and climbed out along the boom and down a rope ladder to the boat. If I was lucky there was someone else about to lower the 25-kilo container, if not I found a way of slinging it on my back and hoping not to fall. There were no such things as safety lines; you were expected to be sensible and look after yourself.

Divisions followed breakfast. This was where the entire crew paraded on the quarterdeck, wet or dry, were brought to attention and inspected by a succession of increasingly senior officers until finally the captain himself acknowledged we were paraded and then we were dismissed for the day's programme. Although there were bright moments, such as when our classmate leader for the day while parading us yelled 'God Damn your eyes!' after a raggedy movement, made worse by his comment which caused us to collapse laughing. I thought it a bit of a waste of time and was quite pleased when I was able to avoid it by attending sick parade instead for the cut in my hand. This was caused by playing with my new sailors knife and the cut proceeded to come out in a rash because the doctor did not believe me when I said I was allergic to plasters. Filling the captain's fuel tank was infinitely preferable to drills on the quarterdeck.

After a day in the classroom, or touring the dockyard or ships of various types, or of learning evolutions of various kinds – and evolutions came to mean anything that demanded lots of hands and plenty of heaving, including 80 of us one day heaving up a whaler weighing 27 hundredweight – we were allowed shore leave. Cocky and swaggering in our bell bottoms, we made our way ashore to Union Street or the nearest pub to be Jolly Jack Tar ashore. Union Street, with its lines of pubs, nightclubs and dance halls, was the centre of this activity, reached by a bus, and there was no point in travelling further as the city centre, 11 years after the war had finished, was still a bomb site.

We were rich after our first pay day, nearly £5 for the week, which rose the following week to £7 5s as I was over 17½ years of age and thus automatically moved from being a boy to a junior seaman. This was a fortune, and as much as I was to earn in a month once I joined the Merchant Navy a few months later. Pay was drawn in cash, in a special parade on the quarterdeck. We paraded by mess and when your name was called you marched up to a small table, removed your hat, acknowledged who you were when your name was read out with the amount due, counted by a sub lieutenant in the supply department and you scraped the money into your hat and marched away. You were allowed about 30 seconds to empty the money from your hat into your pocket, then 'On hats and fall in!' Saturday was for rugby or rowing and our mess petty officer had us out in a cutter pulling up to a pub near Brunel's bridge where he kindly allowed us to buy him a few pints.

The fortnight passed all too quickly. It was a brief insight into an organisation that still maintained most of the customs and traditions that had seen it manage to fight in three theatres during the previous war instead of the one that the politicians had planned and the Treasury paid for. It was uncompromising,

16

expected very high standards, knew what it wanted and how things should be done. We would buckle to it or clear out as far as they were concerned. Above all, it was proud and left us with no doubt that it had every reason to be so. One thing it did teach me was that officers were to be avoided by junior rates as they always found something wrong with your salute and if you wanted to join up, the only way to have a half-decent life under your own control was as an officer.

Back at school I was made sergeant in the Cadet Force in the autumn term of 1956 but we were focused on forthcoming A-Levels. The following summer I took the Civil Service Commission examinations, but only put down the navy. My results put me 27th out of 1,200 in overall marks as I did very well in history and geography, which interested me, but I was one vital mark short in physics for the navy, and although I would have been passed for the army and air force they did not appeal to me. I could have taken the exam again but I had heard about the Merchant Navy in the meantime. I went to London for an interview with the British India Steam Navigation Company and was accepted as a cadet. I left school at the end of that term aged 17½, infuriating the headmaster who did not approve of my chosen career. University was his choice but I had found a different calling.

2

LEARNING THE ROPES

The British India Steam Navigation Company opened its office at One Aldgate in the City of London on 4 February 1957; prior to that its headquarters had been in Calcutta. Dad had signed my apprentice indentures but I don't think he had to pay the normal £50 indenture fee. I was bound to the company for four years and in return for my work, the company would teach me my trade. The indentures stated that I was not to visit ale houses or places of ill repute, but how was a 17 year old to define 'ill repute'? My joining instructions told me to report to the offices that morning and with four other new cadets we climbed into a station wagon in our brand new uniforms and were driven round to various points to collect our trunks containing our clothing, blue working gear, tropical white uniforms, white mess kits, oilskins, duffle coats and so on. The wagon took us to the Royal Albert Docks, a long journey as the Commercial Road was thick with traffic, mainly lorries heading towards the docks.

The company had been established in 1856 in Calcutta as the Calcutta and Burmah Steam Navigation Company to bid for the mail contract between those two ports, but its founders, two enterprising Scots, changed its name to the British India Steam Navigation Company in 1862. A few years later when Sir Henry Bartle Frere became Governor of Bombay, he concluded an agreement to subsidise a service of coasting steamers calling at all ports from Calcutta to Karachi. It expanded rapidly, providing services to, from and around the Indian subcontinent. At one stage it operated 180 vessels, the largest single fleet in the world. Calcutta and Bombay were still home to a good number of the company's ships when I joined in 1957 and many of the officers took their wives with them to India for their two-and-a-half year contracts.

Like all merchant shipping companies BI had suffered badly in the Second World War, losing 52 of its 103 ships. The merchant navy had lost more than 2,400 ships during the war and a fifth of its manpower had died in service, but by 1957 most of the war losses had been replaced and things looked back to normal with the British fleet being by far the largest in the world, employing some 150,000 seamen. With its war replacement tonnage BI was just short of 80 ships at the moment I joined, and one of the largest in the UK. Some exciting and fast new ships were being delivered and if dramatic changes were on the horizon, such as the independence of the colonies and their desire to have their own shipping instead of being dependent on British ships, as well as containerisation just around the corner, these were not obvious to we enthusiastic 'First Trippers'.

The shipping companies were rather like the regiments of the British Army. Each had its own traditions and routes. The different lines could be recognised instantly by their hull colours and funnel markings, in the case of BI a black funnel with two close white bands. Uniforms, badges and insignia varied from company to company although on the whole they were similar to the Royal Navy. Many of the officer corps were recruited from specialist schools like Conway, Worcester and Pangbourne, others, like myself, were from public or grammar schools, although anyone could rise through the ranks if they made the effort. It required four years' sea time, whether you were an apprentice or an able seaman (AB), to be eligible to take a Second Mate's Certificate. Once you passed there was not much movement between companies and most officers stayed with one company throughout their careers.

The MV *Chindwara* was one of a class of 13 shelter deck cargo ships but was fitted out with additional accommodation in the upper 'tween deck where 39 cadets were berthed. The usual crew of Indian seamen, traditional in the company, were removed and the cadets had to man the ship instead. She was in an unloading berth on the south side of the busy Royal Albert Docks as our station wagon drove up. Here was my new home. I looked up at the deck, above the black funnel with its white bands, at the mast and derricks with their bewildering arrays of wires and ropes.

The docks were a hive of noisy activity. Each hold was being served by electric cranes and cargo was being swung ashore to be manhandled into the adjacent warehouses by shouting dockers. We were warned to avoid walking beneath a load as it swung between ship and shore, good advice because occasionally items did fall and a serious injury would be the least of your problems if it landed on you. A long gangway ascended from the docks to the main deck and we climbed up to be greeted by a bored-looking cadet quartermaster in faded working gear who was manning it. We were unceremoniously conducted down from the main deck to a section of the upper 'tween deck, which was where the cadets lived, and met three other new boys. After stowing our gear we changed into embarrassingly new working gear for lunch. The interrogation began: where were we from? What previous experience had we? And so on. For our first afternoon's work we were told to wash paintwork with 'sugee', a mixture of soda and soft soap, something we would become very familiar with over the next couple of years.

We quickly learned that First Trippers were the lowest form of life, used for all the menial duties just as fags had been at school. This was my third crash from senior to junior, so I shrugged and got on with it. However, the next morning as we cleaned and scrubbed out the cadets' accommodation, known as 'peggying', another word for house work, I wondered whether I had made the right choice in life and thought enviously of what my contemporaries would be doing back at Berkhamsted. But the die was cast. I had made my choice of career.

The Royal Naval Volunteer Reserves threw me out the moment I reported I had joined the merchant navy and I had to return my sailors uniform to HMS *President*, the drill ship on London's embankment. I was informed I could apply to rejoin in four years' time when I had my Second Mate's Certificate if I was still interested and they would then decide whether I was up to becoming an officer. There was no encouragement – there did not need to be, they had all the manpower they required. Even as the *Chindwara* sailed, Britons not much older than me were fighting in Malaysia, Kenya and Cyprus and on standby in Korea and we were all starting at the bottom again.

Two days after joining we sailed for Holland to continue our discharge of cargo. I was put on forward lookout with another cadet and quickly learned how to signal the bridge if another ship was sighted. Three strokes on the fo'c's'le bell if it was right ahead, two if it was to port and one if it was to starboard. After a brief stop we headed back to load for our next voyage, which was to East Africa. The senior cadets were not happy about the change from their usual run to Australia and took it out on the First Trippers. That was all right until the bullying became physical. Being hit with a tightly-rolled towel whose end has been soaked in water can remove skin and the first time it landed on me I swung round and punched the person who had delivered it. People piled in but as I was underneath no one could get at me for a while! One accepted this treatment as a rite of passage, but it was sadistic and indicative of the type of person who relies on their term of service or age to feel superior rather than their ability. No one hit me with one of those towels again though.

The Suez Canal was closed as a result of the Anglo-French invasion the previous year so our voyage to East Africa went around the Cape of Good Hope. But first we had to get through the Bay of Biscay where we encountered a gale. This was the first time I had been seasick and fortunately it was the last. We bunkered in Las Palmas and then had 14 days at sea before reaching Cape Town. A ship settles down on long voyages and a comfortable routine is created. On average we spent three days working on deck, doing the work that would normally be carried out by the crew, and then a day in study where we began to learn the rudiments of navigation, stability, cargoes and the mathematics required for calculating the loads on derricks from the Cadet Instruction Officer, a company second officer especially appointed for the task. In the evenings we started to learn Semaphore, the Morse code and the meaning and use of flags. On average, every three nights one had an hour on lookout on the fo'c's'le, a pleasant experience in the tropics with clear skies and warm winds and one could enjoy the solitude. Deck work was supervised by the senior cadets but under the watchful eye of the seamanship instructor, Bertie Miller. Not particularly tall, but immensely powerful, he had come from being a bosun in the New Zealand Shipping Company. He only had one standard, the best, and if your work did not reach that standard you did it all again. It taught us to get things right the first time.

Bertie was incredible. At thirty-five years of age he was as strong as an ox, possibly stronger, with arms thicker than most of our thighs. His methods did not always make sense to us, but he got results. It took him about four square yards of deck space with a piece of chalk to work out a complicated calculation using a formula that even our mathematicians could not crack to calculate the diameter of a canvas vent cover we were about to make, but he got the answer right and he did not want to know anything about pi. He could come out with some wonderful malapropisms such as, 'Son, move that contraceptive down the deck' or 'Yes, I've circumcised Africa five times now'. But he was pure gold when it came to teaching, not just the sailors' skills of canvas work, splicing, painting and all the myriad tasks that a sailor is asked to take on, but also how to work. Woe betide anyone caught slacking if he was on deck, and working consistently became a habit, possibly the greatest gift he gave me. On one occasion, when four of us were trying to get our hands around a 45-gallon drum full of Presomet, a tar-like paint used for painting the decks, he came up, asked us why we were skiving, put his huge arms around the drum and with a heave lifted it onto no. 1 hatch and told us to catch up with our work! You did not argue with Bertie. Later he came to work for me and remained a good friend until his death. I owe a great debt to him for all the seaman's skills he taught me.

As we moved south we held the ceremony of crossing 'the Line', the equator, and it was a rumbustious occasion. The First Trippers were allowed an hour to hide and then were hunted out and dragged before King Neptune after being coated with a nasty and very smelly mix of oil, dye and goodness knows what else. The trial was brief. Everyone was found guilty, and thrown into the swimming pool to be set upon by the bulls which at least removed some of the sticky mixture.

A ship is a self-sufficient organism. At sea it is alive, the ceaseless throb of its enormous diesel engines penetrating from bow to stern, keel to bridge. Even if its main engines are the almost-silent steam turbines, the turning propeller thrusting the water aside creates a slight vibration as a reminder of the force being exerted. The modern ship's life force comes from deep within, down in its engine room, where the generators and pumps take it in turns to provide the services necessary to support its functions at sea or in port, month in, month out, sometimes for years at a time. But it must be constantly served and tended like some primitive god by members of its crew. These men, and at the time I went to sea, the crews were almost universally male, formed what seemed a complex society to the outsider where each member knew his position and task and applied their varying and specialised skills to ensure a smoothly running machine designed and ready to fulfil its purpose. The water that comes through the taps, the lights and fans in the cabins and public rooms, the winches, galley stove, radar are all there and taken for granted just as essential services are ashore, but on a ship they are mobile, sourced from within.

A stranger climbing a varnished teak gangway seldom questions how it got there or who cleaned and varnished it, but the seaman knows the work that went into it, the special knots used on its manropes, the splices and servings on its falls and lashings and inspects another vessel's work with a critical eye. It is only when you stand back and look at a ship towering above a wharf that you realise what a vast, wonderful and complex creation it is. The seaman's job is to understand its complexities, make them work in port or at sea and navigate it safely in fair or foul weather wherever it is ordered to go. Some of the knowledge needed for this task can be learned ashore or in a classroom, but it is experience and tradition that make the difference between a well or badly run ship or a safe or an unsafe one. So many of the tasks aboard demand experience so training for a career at sea at the time put enormous emphasis upon hands-on teaching in order to achieve the high standard that was expected on British ships. The BI cadetships were a very logical and efficient method of providing this thorough and wide-ranging experience for a large number of trainees at one time, turning them into competent officers in due course.

The captain, Ben Rogers DSC, was a distant figure that we saw when we were on the bridge learning to steer, understudying the officer of the watch or at Sunday divisions and divine service. If he came onto the bridge you cleared out to the bridge wing. During the war, as a member of the Royal Naval Reserve he commissioned the first of the Loch class HMS *Loch Fada* and then joined Captain Walker's 2nd Support Group, credited with the destruction of 32 U–boats. Ben sank U1018 and assisted in the destruction of U1279. He was the ideal person to command a cadet ship, firm and fair but insistent on very high standards. Towards the end of the first voyage we had to go before him and recite the first nine of the International Regulations for Preventing Collisions at Sea. It was rumoured that if you failed to be able to recite and understand them perfectly you would lose your end of voyage leave so a great deal of memorising went on as we got closer to home.

On the outward voyage we stopped briefly in Cape Town to top up the water tanks and take the opportunity to climb Table Mountain, and then it was round the Cape and on to Mombasa to begin our discharge. Ships did not enter Mombasa at night, so we were called to our 'stations' at 0530, mine being on the fo'c's'le. As we stood in line, dressed in our blue shorts and shirts, with the mandatory sun hat, the ship approached the entrance channel. The early morning rain was refreshing, a 'docking shower', because they last just long enough for you to get wet but not long enough to justifying going below for waterproofs.

A romantic, earthy smell came off the land as we turned into the channel and made our way into Kilindini port. As the tugs pulled us into our berth we threw heaving lines ashore, attached our large sisal mooring lines to them and, once they were on the shore bollard, heaved in on the windlass. As a First Tripper I was not to be trusted on the winch drum end and was delegated to coiling down the surplus rope as it came in, all the time watching and learning. Next we raised our derricks and hauled them out of the way of the hatches so the shoreside cranes had easy access. Eventually we got our breakfast. Mombasa was far less developed than Cape Town and an exciting place to roam ashore. The other side of the island held the old port and time appeared to have stood still as it was filled with Arab dhows and sweating wharfies manhandling cargo to and from them in a scene that had not changed for hundreds of years.

Departing Mombasa we cruised down to other exciting and fascinating ports for which our cargo was consigned – Zanzibar, Tanga, Dar es Salaam, Mtwara and Beira in Mozambique – and took the opportunity when possible to go ashore and explore or visit beaches.

Because the company made a big effort to educate their cadets by letting them see the world as much as possible, we were on a charter that had been arranged with Harrison Line for the return voyage. Known as two-of-fat-and-one-of-lean after the thin white, red, white stripes on their black funnels, Harrisons traded with South Africa, which was not one of our regular countries except for the two-deck passenger ships that connected with India for the large population of people from the Indian subcontinent who had settled in Natal. This charter gave us the chance to visit the ports in South Africa, an opportunity we relished.

We sailed from Beira to Durban, picking up the Agulhas current as we sailed southwards, which increased our speed by more than two knots. This did not help us much in the long-term because we found we had hastened only to wait. Durban was congested so we remained at anchor for five days in a nasty rolling swell just off the city. Some were seasick and, although I was pleased to find that I no longer felt any qualms, nevertheless it was a relief when our berth was eventually ready and we could enter by far the largest port we had visited since leaving London. The extent of trade and the variety of shipping at that time can be appreciated by the number of movements while we were in port. A French troop ship came through on its way to Vietnam, then a Portuguese one going to Mozambique, both full of young conscripts of our age being sent to fight and die in doomed colonial wars. The P&O liner *Carthage* made a short stop, plus four Russian ships, one Egyptian and numerous British. Even three BP tankers sailing in one day left three of their sisters in port.

The cargo, in the form of tinned fruit, tobacco, sugar and other raw materials, was brought down to the docks in railway trucks hauled by huge coal-powered steam engines, lifted aboard and then stowed by hand. The stevedores doing this heavy work in the holds were all well-muscled Zulus, chattering and chanting cheerfully among themselves in their clicking language, heaving the weighty cartons, cases and sacks effortlessly and tightly into place so they would not move when the ship rolled and pitched at sea. There were no mechanical aids for this job, it was done in a manner that the Phoenicians would have recognised from three thousand years earlier,

Our stay culminated with a dance on board, for which we holystoned the boat deck until it gleamed. This involved dragging sandstones across the deck in a slurry of sand, leaving the deck planking clean and even. Awnings were rigged over the whole of no. 3 hatch and then flags hung inside so that the cargo winches disappeared and it was hard to recognise it as a part of a working cargo ship. During the afternoon we pressed our mess kit and polished our shoes. None of us had girlfriends, so we were all looking forward to meeting girls of our own age.

Music was supplied by a gramophone, one of the cadets acting as disc jockey, and the dance tunes were mainly quicksteps but interspersed with jives to the likes of the Everly Brothers, Ricky Nelson and, of course, Elvis Presley. The jive was as international as the waltz and we had one or two among us who were up to exhibition standard. In the interval our skiffle group, consisting of two guitarists, a washboard, drums made from large paint tins and a double bass constructed from a tea chest and broom handle, performed many of the songs at that time on the hit parade. I occasionally took part, but as fourth guitarist, and was only brought in when quantity rather than quality was required as I had only mastered three chords! Our guests, drawn from the families of businessmen and farmers, departed at midnight but many returned the next day to collect their partners and take them home for the day with the family.

A busload of us were invited up to a farm near Pinetown to spend the day swimming and riding, a lovely setting and the first chance for most of us to begin to see the interior of Africa. Durban was a large city but although the roads were better, the buildings larger and there were a lot more of them, once away from the built-up areas the countryside was like Kenya, except more lush and there were fewer signs of man's influence. But it did not matter where you were in Africa, there was always an exciting feeling of the promise of opportunity and something more to see just over the neighbouring hill.

Exploring ports could also be an eye-opening experience, introducing us rather unworldly cadets to walks of life and cultures hitherto unknown to us – sometimes in an alarming fashion, which served to remind us that we could be seen as easy prey to some. In Durban, having an afternoon free I went to the Seaman's Institute to see a film. I was in uniform, which was not unusual and the end of my row was soon occupied by three large well-dressed men. The lights went out and the film began. After about half an hour a hand started to fondle my leg and I knocked it away, but it persisted. The man was a good four inches taller than me, broad and athletic. To punch him was asking to be beaten up or at least become involved in an unpleasant incident. Fortunately there was a break in the film shortly afterwards – in those days the reel had to be changed halfway in a feature length film – and I pushed my way past the three, ignoring the wandering hands as I did so. I made for the toilets but, just as I was about to enter, I noticed they were all following me. Not wishing to get trapped I spun round and headed for the door and out into the street. They followed and I took to my heels, only pausing when I came across another cadet from the ship. The incident shook me as I realised how vulnerable I had been and it was some months before I ventured ashore alone again.

Cape Town is one of the world's great ports, not because of its size, which is medium in international terms, but on account of its strategic position at the southern point of Africa and its incredible setting beneath Table Mountain. It stands out – tall, magnificent and dominating, shadowing the whole town, the docks and Table Bay and can be seen from thirty-five miles away out at sea on a clear day. Unfortunately, we came in through mist and anchored off the port, which was frantically busy with additional traffic caused by the Suez Canal closure, most of which was calling only for bunkers, water and mail. Next morning dawned clear and the view was breathtaking.

Because we had arrived to collect cargo, we berthed in the Victoria and Alfred Basin the next day and began loading. The port provided a fascinating study of the various types of vessels and their specialisations. Not for nothing is Cape Town known as the Tavern of the Seas. An evening passed quickly, walking round the docks viewing the boats ranging from huge Australia-bound passenger liners to a large Russian Antarctic research vessel with two aircraft lashed on the deck. The sea knows no national boundaries and the South Africans saw nothing strange in allowing Communist bloc ships to call for supplies, even though they were the Cold War enemy at the time and indeed had recently threatened Britain with a missile attack. We found the Russians strange, but had little to do with them as their crews were not allowed ashore to fraternise with the cosmopolitan mix of nationalities using the Cape Town Mission to Seamen just outside the docks.

Laid up, with their crews back home on leave awaiting the next season, was a small fleet of Norwegian whale catchers: sleek, functional hunters, with high bows and distinctive harpoon gun platforms at the bows. We now understand that had sensible controls been applied to whaling in the 1950s some species would not have become so threatened with extinction, but that risk was not known then and the whale catchers were thoroughbreds, a mercantile equivalent of the destroyer and an aura of romance hung over them. To some extent this was based on the fact that these comparatively small vessels operated deep in the south, in the maelstrom of the Roaring Forties where the crews gambled with their lives for the whales. The sea takes no prisoners.

Being on quartermaster duties again meant that I had free

time during the day so I was able to explore the docks and the town and climb the mountain for the first time. I have never lost that first rush of attraction to this mountain, nor the desire to get to the summit. In the intervening forty years I have climbed it twelve times, used the cable car on three other occasions and each time I sit on the summit and look out to sea there is a strange feeling of being at home, which I cannot fully explain. It has all left an indelible impression and Cape Town is still my favourite foreign port.

We took aboard a small number of passengers for the voyage home. Like many of the general cargo ships of the time, the *Chindwara* had accommodation for a dozen passengers and it was a favoured method of travel for many people working on contracts in the colonies. Their leave did not begin until the ship arrived home, so they took advantage of a cargo ship's longer stays in port to do sightseeing at their employer's expense.

One soon discovered that passengers could be divided into two categories: some were pleasant and friendly, others keen to get their money's worth by making constant demands and complaints. Whether there was any justice in their complaints I was far too junior to know, but I could not help wondering why they bothered us young cadets with them, until I realised that they never worked up the courage actually to speak to anyone in authority, they just wanted to beef to someone. On balance we found them a bit of a nuisance and left them alone, but it was good experience in a company that operated fourteen passenger liners and three troop ships to which we might be appointed later in our careers.

*

When we sailed, loaded almost to our Plimsoll mark, it was out into the northern edge of a Southern Ocean storm and, although the winds were not serious, the swell was considerable and caused heavy rolling, so when it was my turn to take the helm I found it hard work as the vessel was yawing a lot. There is a knack that comes with experience of anticipating the swing of the bow and so reducing the amount of rudder used to hold the course. Since any use of the rudder creates resistance to the forward motion, the less the rudder has to be used the better. While this has only a small effect on a large cargo ship, it has a noticeable effect on a sailing vessel or yacht and this was where I began to pick up the secret. Despite the steering being transmitted through hydraulic pipes to a steam telemotor, the constant turning was hard work and one's concentration began to go towards the end of an hour's spell. Upon being relieved you reported the course and the name of your relief to the officer of the watch, who would usually come and check the course recorder and comment on how well or badly you had done.

When the trick on the helm was over we went on standby and this hour off duty was not spent idly. Fire rounds had to be made, taking a clock and turning a key at various points around the ship to show that the rounds had been carried out properly. The brass work on the bridge was polished daily. Then tea would be made for those on duty, lookouts called, the log read each hour, flags hoisted or lowered as required, and any spare time would be spent cleaning and polishing around the bridge by day or as an additional lookout by night. Even when the decks were quiet there was always something to watch from the bridge. Albatrosses were with us for the first two days, wheeling effortlessly in our wake searching for food as we headed north-eastwards towards warmer climes. I was ticked off for being a few minutes late calling the next watch because I had become absorbed by the grace of a particular albatross with a wing span of perhaps eleven feet, who did not flap his wings for what seemed like five minutes.

Learning the stars – finding them at a glance in the sky, using them to check the accuracy of the compass – were skills that were picked up as a matter of course. It is not difficult. You establish where the star is at that moment in the celestial sphere, the imaginary sphere set at an infinite distance surrounding the earth. Then you calculate what the bearing should be from your own position on the earth's surface and compare this with the actual bearing. The difference between the two is the error, a vital piece of information even in these days of gyrocompasses.

Since we were on our way home every effort was made to paint the ship in readiness for arrival back in London. The company expected returning vessels to look clean and smart when they entered the docks, and the marine superintendent, a senior captain responsible for the operation of the ships, would have strong words with our captain and chief officer if we did not come up to standard. The rattle of chipping hammers reverberated every morning as we sailed through the tropics as party of cadets, stripped to the waist, hammered away at rust to free it from the steel plates which were then wire-brushed and primed quickly to keep the sea air from starting the whole oxidisation process again. Everything else was washed down with the ubiquitous sugee before paint was applied. The tropics were ideal for painting, and the chief officer made full use of the opportunity. But it was not all deck work, we had exams to prepare for, an essay to write, and finally each of us had to go before the captain and be tested on the international collision regulations.

Dakar was our re-fuelling stop on the way home, a port on the north-west African coast run by the French. The chief officer did not miss the chance of being able to swing out the six lifeboats while it was safe and having the steel decks beneath painted. On the brighter side, two of the boats were lowered to the water and the inter-watch rowing race took place. Lifeboats are bluff and heavy, not designed for speed rowing and it takes a great effort just to get them moving. Being small I was not included in the team and as a spectator saw the starboard watch win by a foot, so my watch, the port, had lost both this and the tug-of-war, which hurt.

After Dakar we were on the final run home and thoughts of leave were on everyone's minds. The tension was relieved a little by the traditional 'Channel's Dinner', held to celebrate reaching soundings in the English Channel, where the depth fell to less than 100 fathoms or 600 feet. The Channel's Dinner was followed by inter-dormitory ruckuses involving a combination of rugby and all-in wrestling, allowing everyone to let off steam. It was late June, and the Channel seemed altogether brighter and less grey than it had in March. The pilot came aboard off Dungeness and handed over to the river pilot at Gravesend, a hive of activity, and then we were locking into the Royal Docks and those of us on first leave packed, collected our balance of pay and left for home. There were stories to tell, new skills to show off and one could almost start calling oneself a professional seaman.

*

Everyone had hoped the ship would return to the Australian run, but the next voyage was back to East Africa again. Those of us who had not been to Australia did not mind as much as those who had and had girlfriends there. Their frustration was expressed in a number of ways, not least against my fellow First Trippers, who were considered to have got off lightly because our first voyage was about half the length of an Aussie trip. We did not realise the nasty turn this was taking until one of our number suddenly appeared with rope burns around his wrists and ankles. He had been strung up between the gangway davit and the stanchion rail and the davit callously kicked to stretch him out. Of course the lashings had bitten into his skin and torn it away. There was no motive for this torture, the cadet concerned was mild-mannered, it was just sadism of the worst sort: for the sake of it.

I was next, cornered by eight cadets all bigger than me and similarly triced up. It hurt like hell but I was determined not show the bastards they were succeeding. My cuts turned septic and I reported to the doctor, explaining that I had caught a rope badly as the strain came on. Whether he guessed or not, I do not know, but another cadet, sickened by this needless bullying, reported it to the cadet instruction officer and there were no follow-ups. But it left an uneasy, ominous atmosphere until we had grown large enough to feel unthreatened. I had joined the *Chindwara* at a height of 5 feet 9 inches, but within a year I was over 6 feet and two stone heavier with hard-working muscles and prepared to fight back.

We were rumbustious but there is a line to be drawn between rough amusement and bullying. On a later voyage an Australian cadet, John Briggs, known inevitably as 'Abbo' was working overside on a painting stage and at lunchtime decided to climb the stage rope rather than the ladder. Watching him climb the rope, I found it impossible not to start paying out at the same speed. There was nothing personal in it, it was just a good joke. It was some time before he realised that although he was climbing energetically he wasn't making any progress. His query as to what was going on turned to a yell as I let go of the end, shouting 'End Oh!' as I did so and he fell six feet into the harbour. He surfaced and began to shout abuse up at me but turned and swam at high speed for the nearest ladder when I asked him what the big grey fish with the wide head just behind him was . . . Thirty years later in Australia where he was Sydney Harbour's port captain, Captain John 'Abbo' Briggs and I met up again and enjoyed an evening out.

Rivalry between different companies' cadets was strong and although a cadet ship was an obvious target incidents were rare. Only a fool would take on a tribe of 39 young and fit men, but occasionally someone decided to live dangerously. In Durban a small group of us were returning from the cinema ashore and found someone climbing down our after-mooring lines. We naturally assumed it was one of our own and went to shake the lines to see if he would fall into the harbour. But the yells that greeted this treatment were not familiar. Curious, we allowed the climber ashore and then wrestled him to the ground to find out his identity. He turned out to be from a neighbouring Clan Line ship, caught in an attempt to hoist a bra to the mainmast truck. He was allowed free after being rolled in a puddle on the quayside, but this softness was a mistake and sent the wrong message as the next night we found 'Clan and Union Castle

Lines' painted in white lead on our bow. The trouble with white lead paint is that, rather like tar-based paints, it will show through a number of coats and our hull was black.

Retaliation was immediate and almost the entire cadet complement was mustered, given tasks and sent round to counter-attack the Clan *Robertson*. It was an uneven contest from the start. The main group rushed the gangway and were swarming all over the ship in no time. Their cadets' cabin was attacked first, its occupants stripped and hung up by the feet and sensitive spots suitably decorated with aeroplane dope. Their second officer, who made the mistake of trying to interfere, received similar treatment. My small group had been dispatched up the forward-mooring lines hand-over-hand, past the rat guards, to remove the fo'c's'le bell. We reached the fo'c's'le all right, but the bell's bolt was rusted in place, so we went to the bridge to collect that one instead but found it already taken.

A whistle announced that the time for withdrawal had arrived and 36 cadets poured down to the main deck, carrying various items that had attracted them, and returned to our ship with the rearguard, led by someone who is now a respectable senior captain, holding off the half-hearted resistance. As far as we were concerned honour had been satisfied, but it was not left at that. One of our number, who was small in size, was kidnapped and roughed up the next evening, so, angered, we attacked again, this time the Clan *Urquhart*, and with little finesse. She was one of the war-built fast cargo ships and had just been painted up for her homeward voyage. When we left her she was a mess. A high-level complaint led to everyone being warned that any future operations would result in the senior participant being sacked from the company. We were attacked again from the same quarter in Lourenço Marques on the next voyage and, unable to respond, morale fell. The Clan Line cadets responsible wisely stayed aboard their own ship while we remained in port.

A writer in *The Times* in 1928 stated, 'Going down to the sea in ships has been deprived of almost all its terrors and most of its romance ... The fear that the sea once inspired, except in rare cases, has vanished ... the mysteries of the deep have lost their attraction.' It might have lost its terrors from the safety of the newspaper's pages, but if a reminder was needed that the sea was thoroughly dangerous, it came on my third homeward voyage as we were heading into the Bay of Biscay in a strong gale.

Up on the fo'c's'le on lookout duty, the bow was rising and falling heavily in the big seas, so much so that water was coming out of the hawse pipes behind me – where the anchor chain ran from the windlass to the anchor – like enormous fountains. It was a gloriously wild scene, so dark that only the luminescence of the breaking waves close to the ship was visible and the ship was occasionally rolling so heavily that waves came in over the bulwarks on the main deck and washed against the hatch coamings. When my hour was up no one appeared to relieve me. I tried the phone to the bridge but it was out of action. Eventually I was blinded by the Aldis signalling light sending me the message, in Morse code, to report to the bridge. I made my way down to the main deck and then, holding firmly onto the life lines that had been rigged earlier, made a rush for the ladder two holds away that led up to the boat deck. A wave broke behind me over the deck as I leaped up the steps.

The captain was on the bridge, in earnest conversation with the sparks, the mate and the second mate. The standby quartermaster explained that an SOS had been received and we were waiting to hear if we were required to assist in the rescue. There was little information available, but by the time we turned to a couple of hours later, we knew the vessel in trouble was the German four-masted barque *Pamir* with 52 cadets aboard, which had gone on her beam ends during Hurricane Carrie 600 miles south-west of the Azores, but being more than 500 miles from the scene we were not asked to help. She sank quickly and although three of her lifeboats floated free in the end only six of the entire crew of eighty-six souls were saved.

The subsequent enquiry blamed the tragedy on the way she had been loaded. She had a full cargo of grain from Argentina which can shift easily if not properly stowed. The usual method is to load a number of layers of bags on top of the loose cargo to hold it in place and rig shifting boards down the middle of the hold so that even if the cargo does move, it can only go halfway across the hold which reduces the effect on the stability by four. But apparently this had not been done properly. It was the end of sail-training in the German Merchant Marine, and the *Passat*, the sister ship of the *Pamir*, was taken out of service. This knee-jerk reaction in response to a press-orchestrated public outcry was understandable, although made for all the wrong reasons. People will always make mistakes but just because there has been a human failing does not mean the system is all bad. This left only the Russians, Japanese and the US Coastguard using large square-riggers for merchant navy training

On average, each round trip was taking four months so on my third voyage we were in Mombasa for Christmas 1957. We were a long way from home and had nowhere to go, apart from the

Mission to Seamen, so most of us went ashore in groups on Christmas Eve. After a few beers we inevitably became rowdy and on this occasion took over the band's instruments in the Star Bar. Our music was not to the taste of some Union Castle Line ABs, traditional rivals, who started to complain. The management was, not unnaturally, worried at the possibility of furniture being broken, but since we were not in an aggressive mood we gave up the instruments and went elsewhere.

We had barely ordered a beer when the ABs followed us in, grabbed bottles in a workmanlike manner by the necks and told us to leave. The two sides fanned out since we felt we had backed down enough and saw no reason to leave a second time. The numbers were the same and we were probably pretty evenly matched. I tentatively picked up a bottle as I heard of the nasty use of them as a weapon, although I had never seen one in use and looked for something to break it on, since it was obvious that this might get very dirty. Just as things were becoming extremely tense, a British police inspector with his Kenyan constables marched in, apparently at the behest of the bar owner. He ordered our group to one bar and the ABs to another and ensured we departed. It was a very fine piece of police work and we wisely kept out of trouble until it was time to go to the cathedral for midnight mass. Why become involved? We were young, fit, confident and cocky, as young males are at that age when they consider themselves immortal. Partly it was pride that prevented us backing down, but also we just did not see why we should be pushed around and were prepared to stand up for ourselves.

The Suez Canal had re-opened by this time so our return voyage was via the Red Sea, which frequently meant calls in places like Massawa, Port Sudan, Jeddah and Assab. My memory of them is the boiling heat – suffocating temperatures in the dormitories, where the cadet accommodation, being below the main deck, was inside a black hull which absorbed the heat, five portholes giving insufficient ventilation. As a result, while we were at anchor off Massawa there was a rush to make hammocks which could be slung on the boat deck, the mate giving out the canvas but the sewing having to be done under Bertie's supervision. This meant if you did not get the stitching neat and even you unpicked it and did it all over again. But no one slept well in those conditions, even in a hammock beneath the stars, and we were glad to get underway again when at least the ship's movement provided the relief of a small breeze.

There were some compensations, however. In Port Sudan the Mission to Seamen was next to the port and on the beach. If you walked out through the shallow waters to the reef 500 feet away you suddenly found a 600-foot drop and the view faded into the blue. Floating beneath were sharks, turtles, rays and fish of every colour and description. It was the most magical sight I had seen, and on the East African run we were lucky to be able to explore coral reefs through much of the Tropics.

As trip followed trip we progressed professionally. The advantage of cadetship training, as opposed to spending time in schools ashore, was that we got into the rhythm of life at sea and learned the sailors crafts hands-on. The saying that a sailor is jack of all trades (and master of none) has some justification as the training was practical, but eventually we would become Masters of Navigation and Watch-keeping. Exams came and went. We had to pass the Lifeboat Certificate, which showed our ability to launch and take command of a lifeboat and this was followed by the EDH (Efficient Deck Hand) examination, which qualified us as ABs in the merchant navy, a necessity on the cadet ships as there were no other qualified crew. Every ship has to comply with the government manning scales stipulating the minimum number of qualified seamen for a ship of a certain class and tonnage. In the *Chindwara*'s case this was seven, which we easily exceeded.

We were introduced to the mysteries of the basics of astronavigation, working out the position by the bearings and altitudes of the sun and stars, how to calculate latitude by meridian altitudes and longitude by chronometer, and then, when we were two years into our apprenticeships, we started doing bridge watches under the supervision of the officers and practising what we had learned in navigation, collision avoidance and signalling. As we progressed, the tasks we undertook became more interesting and although there was still plenty of paintwork washing, chipping away rust and painting, we spent more time on splicing, derrick gear overhauls and canvas work.

The demand for officers meant that at the end of 1958 the number of cadets was increased from 39 to 52, which gave the chief officer more labour to work on deck. I was particularly fortunate to spend one voyage as the lamp trimmer which meant I was also the storekeeper. This gave me an insight into some of Bertie Miller's mysterious brews, such as his own tallow-based treatment for lubricating the runner wires on the winches, and how to make proper sugee. With larger gangs to work the ship two of us were needed to prepare paint and brushes and could not knock off until all these had been cleaned and carefully stowed. Failure in this respect earned Bertie's wrath, betraying a lack of ambition as far as longevity was concerned.

My spell in the store coincided with a keep-fit urge, so I removed the ladder down to the forepeak and put a rope in its place so that we had to shin up and down if we wanted anything from the lower forepeak store below. This had the unforeseen benefit of delaying a cuffing when Bertie discovered that his precious shark-fishing line had been cut and used for a paint line by my predecessor. It was useless to explain that I was not responsible. I saw Bertie coming towards the store with a face like thunder and dropped down to the lower peak and hid behind a spare coil of 8-inch sisal hawser. Bertie's voice bellowed down to me, telling me he knew I was there (he could probably see the coil of rope trembling in sympathy), but eventually he went away. This only put off the evil moment, though, and later that day he returned before I could hide. I took to my heels, shot down the deck and climbed the mainmast shrouds hand-over-hand, pausing only when I was twenty feet above the deck. Bertie, who had been sprinting after me, slowed to a saunter, leaned against the bulwark below and looked up at me. 'All right, son, I can wait here longer than you can hang there.' I hung on a while, hoping he might be distracted, but he wasn't moving. What the hell, I thought, I might as well get it over with as he would catch me sooner or later. He did not punch me, it was a gentle bash on the shoulder – which sent me staggering 15 feet down the deck!

The Lebanese crisis of 1958 led to the sudden arrival in Mombasa of aircraft carrier HMS *Bulwark*, the cruiser HMS *Gambia* and eight assorted destroyers and frigates. While this flotilla was in port they held a whaler race which we entered. We managed second, being fairly beaten by *Gambia*'s crew. Life was enlivened by HMS *Ulysses* misjudging the currents off our berth and hitting our stern, an impact preceded by the abrupt and unceremonious arrival on deck of a dozen cadets, who had been busily painting the ship's side on stages until someone noticed the knife-like bow of this frigate heading towards them. No one was hurt, although the frigate hit the quay at 10 knots and subsequently did not last long in service.

Variety is the spice of the sailor's life and we certainly had a very wide range of weather that year, varying between Arctic cold in the Siberia Dock in Antwerp to desiccating heat on the Red Sea. In Antwerp it became so cold that we had to wear gloves, normally frowned on as they can get caught in a snag on a wire, as without them our skin stuck to anything metal we touched. Heaters had to be placed beneath the ship while in dry dock to prevent the double bottom tanks, which were full of water, from freezing and rupturing. By contrast, in the late summer when we called at Port Sudan it was so hot that all but seven of us were laid flat with heat stroke or exhaustion.

BI was a very successful company, its average annual profit was more than £4 million, enough to buy four new ships a year, and at some stage someone in head office had the bright idea of spending a small amount of this to give each ship a sailing dinghy. The *Chindwara* received two lovely mahogany clinker-built jobs, and Bertie set about making special chocks, gripes and lifting gear so they could be slung overside by means of a cargo derrick. I watched them come aboard with interest and when volunteers were called for to help Bertie with the work, I was in like a shot. The first port of call where they could be used was Port Sudan and being a senior by then I managed to get one for an afternoon. Despite a capsize, my crew enjoyed himself as much as I did and we became a regular team, taking the dinghy away whenever it was permitted.

Jan Simon, whose father was chairman of the Port of London Authority, was only a year younger than me but he had delayed coming to sea even longer. Together we explored ports, anchorages, bays and rivers whenever the ship was moored and we were able to get time off. Inevitably, it was hard to keep in contact after I left the ship and it was 38 years before we met again in the unlikely environs of the House of Lords where I had gone to give a talk. As I was walking out a quiet surprised voice said 'Knox!' and there was Jan, instantly recognisable, who had recently inherited his father's title. He accused me of capsizing him in all the ports of the Near East and I would be guilty of perjury if I denied it.

My final trip aboard the *Chindwara* came in 1959 for which I was made petty officer of the port watch of sixteen cadets. Although on the previous trip I had started to oversee gangs on deck as a leading hand, as a PO I was in charge of the deck one day in four which was invaluable experience. We had a good bunch in my port watch and won the inter-watch competitions quite easily. I signed off in Avonmouth in the autumn of 1959, having earned five months remission of sea time for the two and a half years spent on board which brought forward the time when I could sit my Second Mate's Certificate to the beginning of September 1960. This meant, in effect, I could go ashore to study at the beginning of June that year as the three months' preparatory course at the nautical college was allowed to count as sea time.

The time on board *Chindwara* was one of my most formative experiences. I had arrived as a bumptious, small and rather innocent schoolboy. I left as a young adult who had developed a social, physical and mental self-confidence that is invaluable in life. Thanks as much to Bertie Miller as anyone, I was totally unafraid of hard work, in fact the habit of working has never left me since, a priceless attribute. There is much talk about people being born to lead, rather than trained, and undoubtedly there are a few people helped by lucky genes. But real leadership, which might be defined as giving the aura of confidence that others feel willing to follow, is owed to attitudes, habits, examples and expectations which are picked up from home, school and surroundings.

I am not sure that I would still have been attracted to the merchant navy faced with the career it offers today. In the past 60 years the tasks of the merchant navy officer have changed completely. Back then, we decided how and where we would load the cargo, today it comes in containers, pre-loaded and the responsibility for loading the cargo has gone and with it the pride in a good out-turn at the destination. The ships are no longer maintained by the crew, removing the satisfaction in their appearance. Finally, the skill of navigation is no longer needed when a black box gives an accurate position to within yards every three seconds. It has removed the pride in an accurate landfall using a sextant and chronometer. This is progress of course, cargo arrives quicker and probably in better condition, but in removing some possibilities of human error taken away is the challenge of avoiding them that made the career so attractive. The type of person who relishes surmounting problems, the person who is invaluable in an emergency, will seek their challenges elsewhere and the shipping industry is the poorer for it.

3

SPYING ON THE IRAQIS

I studied hard at the King Edward VII Nautical College, working late nights memorising everything that might be asked and within three weeks felt sufficiently confident to put in my application for the second mate's examination. I was helped by sitting next to a boatswain from another company who had decided to improve himself and was having difficulty with some of the more technical subjects. Explaining things makes you think and is a great way to learn oneself. Forty-two of us sat the exam on 3 October 1960 at the Dock Street offices of the Mercantile Marine department in London; seven of us, including all three of us from BI, passed.

I could have changed career then. There is no fortune to be made from a life at sea working for other people. The big money is made by the few with the gumption to risk all in a business, plus, for some peculiar reason, those non-wealth-generators, the lawyers and accountants. I was too young to realise this but in any case I was enjoying the life at sea and was not that money-motivated at the time, you probably need to mix with City people to understand the opportunities. During the last four years I had diverged from the life ashore and was no longer familiar or interested in career patterns away from the sea. I had lost touch with most of my school friends, and those I still knew were at work or university when I was on leave and did not relish a few days helping me have a good run ashore. In addition I was proud and wanted to succeed at the career I had chosen and that, for the immediate future, meant returning to sea until I had at least obtained my Master's Certificate. I was also totally entrapped by the life at sea, the security of the life aboard a ship and the constant variety in ports, peoples and cargoes. I was seduced by the feel of a warm breeze on my skin, the glitter of the sun on the sea's ever-changing surface, the warm smell coming off the shore of Africa, India or Arabia as the ship waited, sleepy crew at their stations, for the sky to lighten and a fresh port to open for us.

There was more to it, though. I was responding to an inner need to get away from the crowded land and back to the open spaces where there are no roads, no signposts, but where the navigator is never lost. I had those navigational skills now. I had worked hard to obtain them and was proud of my Board of Trade Certificate. I wanted to exercise those skills almost as much as I wanted those clean, uncluttered horizons and the comfort of a well-ordered, disciplined life.

While ashore awaiting an appointment I applied to join the Royal Naval Reserve, which was a source of qualified navigators and watch-keepers the Navy wanted to keep available in case of the need for a sudden expansion in an emergency. The interview went well. The commodore at one stage asked me whether I had enjoyed my visit to Shanghai, so he knew I had been busy with my camera while there. At the finish I was accepted as an acting probationary sub-lieutenant, which dizzy rank I held until I returned from eastern service and obtained my Master's Certificate four years later.

BI offered a bonus if one returned to the company after passing the Second Mate's Certificate and I spent it on an engagement ring for Sue. A couple of years before, I had noticed that the tomboy friend from my youth had become a very attractive blue-grey-eyed brunette and our relationship changed from friendship into something more romantic. We were young, I was 21 and she 19, but I was going to be away for the next year on Eastern service and this gave our relationship a future and stability.

In November 1960 I joined the SS *Nyanza* as third officer in the Royal Albert Docks in London where we were loading. Sue managed to get down there for a few days, which was her first experience of the life we lead on a ship, and fortunately it did not put her off. As we sailed out, heading for Suez and on to Karachi, Sue and I knew we would not see each other for a year, which started me wondering again whether I had chosen the right career after all. It is one of the problems of life at sea. It is great while one is single, but the moment you get married the long absences from your family are hard to bear.

My first watch as a qualified officer took us down channel from Dover and past Dungeness. The ship was making 18 knots and here was I, aged 21, racing along in charge. It was a sobering moment, but then I took a deep breath. I was qualified now, I knew the job, so it was time to just get on with it. Check the other shipping nearby – the English Channel is a busy area but traffic tended to go in lanes so most of the shipping nearby was going the same way. We were a fast ship so the main concern was to make sure that when overtaking we were clear of the other vessels. Then get a bearing of the sun to check the accuracy of the compass. I was kept busy and scarcely noticed that my four hours were up when my relief appeared. Later I discovered that Captain Robson, knowing it was my first watch, had deliberately left me alone to allow me to settle myself down, but he watched our progress from his cabin one deck below just to be certain. I have always been grateful to him for this as there is nothing more damaging for one's confidence than someone breathing down one's neck. His thoughtfulness helped me to develop my confidence.

As I had chosen to go on Eastern service, where more than half the BI fleet operated providing the commercial links that had developed trade throughout the British Empire – although most of the countries that had made up that Empire were either already independent or soon would be – the trip out was working my passage. The Eastern service fleet was largely operated out of Bombay and the ships never came home throughout their lives. Our contracts were for two and a half years, but the advantages were that the pay was higher and there were no tax deductions either. This enabled me to start saving for our future married life.

I had been advised that I would be joining the Bombay to Basra passenger, cargo and mails service and I signed off the articles of agreement from *Nyanza* and onto those of the *Dwarka* in Karachi. *Dwarka* was one of four BI vessels built post-war that operated a weekly mail and passenger service from Bombay to Basra and most of the Gulf States in between. I joined as extra third officer as on this run, with its frequent stops in port, the chief officer did not stand a watch. The officers' accommodation was just below the bridge on the boat deck, the deck and radio officers forward and the engineers aft, and most of the passengers lived on the decks below, amid their trunks. We were licensed to carry 720 deck passengers in a 4,500 ton ship and we often sailed at full complement with people and families going to the Gulf states where the wages were higher than on the Indian subcontinent and their labour was welcomed. There was also accommodation for a number of first- and second-class cabin passengers.

It was lively and clamorous. There were Indians, Pakistanis, Arabs from the towns of all the states around the Gulf and occasionally proud and stately Bedouins from the desert interiors. The one group banned were Somalis. Some years before two had gone on a rampage killing one officer and maiming another until finally subdued by the chief engineer firing a soda acid fire extinguisher into the face of one of them and following up with a bang on the head with the heavy extinguisher. We were supplied with stab-proof vests thereafter although I never wore one. The Indian women wore their bright saris, the Pakistanis their kameezes and shalwars and the Arabic Muslim women were usually all in black. Children ran about everywhere. Deck passengers could either cook their own meals or buy from contractors, known as *vishiwallahs*, who supplied some delicious curries at a very low price. There was an inherent fire risk with Primus stoves all over the decks for those who wished to cook for themselves, but I do not remember a serious fire. The aroma of spices floated up as far as the bridge from the decks below, and one of the treats was to get the standby quartermaster, known as a secunny, to go and get a hot freshly baked nan bread from the *vishiwallahs* mid-morning.

There was a romance about the Persian Gulf at the time. BI had been providing this service for almost 100 years and had done much of the early surveying of the Gulf so it was real company territory, handled in the ports by the agents Grey Mackenzie whose personnel we got to know well. It was also a time of considerable change as small Gulf states were suddenly finding they were sitting on vast reserves of oil and gas but investment in infrastructure had yet to get going noticeably except in Kuwait and Saudi Arabia. Change was on the horizon too for passenger services by sea, as air travel was becoming cheaper, but it was still too expensive for most at that time and even when it did become available not everyone used it. However, within ten years falling demand reduced that route to one ship, the *Dwarka*. She kept going, the last relic of the Imperial services that had straddled the world, right through until the 1980s when spares for her ageing Doxford diesel main engine could no longer be sourced – she was scrapped in 1982. She went out on a high, though, appearing briefly in a background shot in Richard Attenborough's film *Gandhi*.

On our normal schedule after Karachi we sometimes anchored at Gwadar or Pasni along the Pakistan Makran coast to collect or deliver a small amount of cargo. We also collected the large and impressive Baluchi tribesmen for the Sultan of Muscat and Oman's armed forces, then fighting a war with communist guerrillas. Muscat itself was a small bay, with two old Portuguese forts at its head, still inhabited, one serving as a prison. As there were no quays to take large vessels we anchored in the middle of the bay so passengers and cargo were transferred by motorised dhows to the shore. From there we sailed through the Straits of Hormuz to Dubai, where we anchored off what was then a small town on a creek. Umm Said in Qatar followed, again an anchorage far from any signs of habitation, and then on to Bahrain where we anchored off the north coast.

Bahrain was home to the Royal Navy in the Gulf where Britain had treaties with many of the states and there was usually a battalion of infantry based there so the shops were better stocked. It provided the best shopping location in the Gulf at the time so I usually stood in on duty for the married officers allowing them to go ashore to buy little extras for their families not available in Bombay. Bushire in Iran sometimes followed, again an anchorage quite far out from the coast.

Kuwait was more developed than most ports at the time and had modern quays where we berthed alongside. A new city was being built which included all the upmarket shops you might find in London or New York. We were now at the head of the Persian Gulf and heading for Basra in Iraq. We picked up a pilot off the Shatt al-Arab river, the confluence of the Rivers Tigris and Euphrates, and motored up to Khorramshahr in Iran, sometimes berthed alongside but more often anchored, before finally reaching Basra where we had a wharf to tie to and usually remained for one or two days. This was the end of the outward passage – we finished discharge and in the season might take hundreds of tons of dates back to India, but there was not much other cargo. The return voyage mirrored the outward one, in all 19 ports in 21 days.

Dhows, the traditional Arab wooden-built sailing craft that had dominated trade in the Indian Ocean from before the time of Sinbad, were still a frequent sight. Most of these graceful vessels we saw were motorised, but we still came across sailing ones out at sea with their huge lateen rigs. With a good wind they could sail very fast. The greatest concentration came each year at Basra and there might be as many as 200 moored up there as they awaited the date harvest. Tacking, to bring the wind onto the other side of the sail when altering course, was a huge manual task and it was not surprising that they had crews of 20 or more, lean, hard-muscled and suntanned.

Even with no accommodation they could make long voyages. We had seen dhows on the east African coast as far down as the Rufiji River and the rulers of Muscat and Zanzibar were of the same family. Most of the trade between these two countries was still carried in dhows. A different type of vessel, known as country craft, were still to be seen trading around the Indian coast, the main difference being their lower freeboard. With experience we could tell where the different style of vessels had been built and I managed to get to a boatyard where they were still being built in Bahrain. Once built they were coated below the waterline with a mixture of lime and shark oil, which I was told seemed to work as pretty efficient antifouling. Our main problem with all these traditional craft was their habit of not showing lights at night and with unreliable radar sets on our own ships this called for keeping a sharp-eyed lookout.

I loved being on watch at night. My watch started at 2000 and by 2200 the ship was largely asleep. Standing on the bridge under a clear starlit sky, enjoying the warm wind created by our movement through the water, the only sounds coming from the thump of the diesel engine and the waves passing down the ship's side, I felt no envy for those who had to commute morning and evening to and from an office. My companions on the bridge were two secunnies, who relieved each other every hour on the wheel. There was plenty of shipping around in the Gulf, but along the Makran coast lights from ships were rare. Apart from plotting the ship's position at regular intervals when there was something to take a bearing of or checking the magnetic compass error with a convenient star, my job was to keep a lookout, and alter course when necessary if another vessel was coming close. At midnight the senior third officer, Danny Goswell, would arrive to relieve me. We would chat for a while as I handed over and he drank his tea that a steward had brought to the bridge, and then I would go down and make rounds. This involved checking around the ship and walking quietly through the passenger decks, where up to 700 people were asleep, murmuring, shuffling, some lightly snoring. Rounds completed it was back to my cabin and sleep until 0730 when tea arrived to wake me up to go on watch at 0800.

Occasionally the rulers of the various states would come aboard with a colourful retinue and take passage. On one occasion Sheikh Al Thani of Qatar boarded to join the Sheikh of Dubai and go on a hunting expedition near Bandar Abbas in Iran. All the cabin accommodation was taken over on the promenade and main decks, hooded hawks sat on the ping-pong table on the promenade deck and the Sheikh settled into the main lounge with his servants and advisors – one of the few areas with air conditioning.

On one such occasion, late on the first evening out of Qatar while I was on watch, I heard a noise above the bridge on the monkey island and going up to investigate found an Arab man staggering around having obviously got some alcohol. How he got there I don't know, he must have slipped past while I was writing the log, but I suggested he came down as sparks were probably using the radio and if he touched the aerials he might get a shock. 'Dangerous to you,' he responded, 'But I am an Arab, it cannot hurt me.' I persuaded him to come down nevertheless and to keep him quiet, as I assumed he was part of the Sheikh's entourage, chatted to him for a while. Then he made an unfortunate suggestion as to what he would like to do with me when I came off watch. Furious, I picked him up and flung him down the companionway. He lay there for a moment and then lurched away and I thought no more about it. Then about ten minutes later all hell broke loose from the first-class lounge.

The man had gone down, climbed over the sleeping bodyguards and started to strangle the sheikh. The bodyguards, keen to make up for their failure to protect their chief, were now trying to kill the aggressor. I missed the action but we managed to get him away and locked him in one of the *vishi-wallah* galleys where he spent what was probably his last night on earth cowering from the knives of the bodyguards trying to get at him through the iron bars. Next day the Dubai police boarded and took him away and I don't like to imagine his fate. The Sheikh of Dubai joined with his equally colourful retinue and we landed them without further incident in Iran. As was customary, the captain and chief officer received gold watches from the sheikhs and even at my lowly level I received 200 Gulf Rupees, or about £15, almost a week's pay.

BI ships traditionally had a shaded walkway around the accommodation to reduce the effect of the direct sun and a permanent awning above the bridge. It undoubtedly helped to keep our cabins cooler, but in July and August the Gulf could be like a furnace. Temperatures rose above 50 degrees Celsius and the humidity varied so it could be very dry in Basra and then unbearable at the southern end in Dubai when a shamal was blowing. This dry north-westerly wind blew in from Turkey and collected water vapour as it crossed the waters of the Gulf. We did not have air conditioning, with the exception of the captain and chief engineer's cabins, the saloon, lounge and engineers' mess room. To get to sleep at night when it was really dry it sometimes helped to sprinkle water onto the sheets on one's bunk and wait for it to start to evaporate and cool the sheets. Then you got into your bunk and hoped to drop off before the sheets heated up again. How the engineers on our ships coped with the added heat in the engine room during those months was always a mystery as at least we might have a breeze on the bridge.

Our small vessels carried a total of 12 lifeboats, one fitted with a motor designed to tow the remaining lifeboats away from a sinking ship as they were only equipped with oars. The motor boat was exercised regularly and I took to asking the chief officer if I could take it away in Muscat and Umm Said so some of us could go swimming or spear fishing. I had also taken up underwater photography, making a housing for my camera with a form of epoxy known as Thistle Bond and the camera controls controlled by water taps bought in the Bombay markets.

On one occasion while we were swimming over a rocky outcrop in Muscat I looked down and saw a large moray eel making its way aggressively towards our group of swimmers. I took a breath and went down to meet it as I was the only one with a harpoon gun. My harpoon went in behind its head, but it was so angry it started to work its way along the harpoon line towards me. I waited until it was halfway and let go of the gun and picked up the harpoon at the other end of the line. We landed it in the boat and it slithered beneath the bottom boards out of sight so we forgot about it. As our Indian crew were securing the boat in its chocks back on board, the boat suddenly erupted seamen. We had forgotten to tell them about an eight-foot-long moray eel lurking in the bottom, which had decided to work its way back up from the bilge. They recovered quickly and probably cooked it for supper.

We could swim from the ship if we could not take the motor boat away for any reason. Diving off the main deck into the sea by the gangway was a blessing when temperatures were high. Then sometimes, with a deep breath, I would swim underneath the ship to the other side. Since I did not smoke in those days, holding my breath underwater for more than three minutes was not a problem. There could be unexpected surprises though as once, off Dubai, as I was coming back up to the surface, I found myself surrounded by yellow-and-black-striped sea snakes. Fortunately, although venomous, they are not normally aggres- sive and they swam away, but I was always a bit more careful to check the waters before diving there in future. We occasionally came across rays and sharks, not particularly large sand ones, perhaps eight feet, and they showed little interest.

To give myself more freedom if the motor lifeboat could not be taken away, I built another canoe (the style was improving). I took up scuba-diving, my interest stimulated by Barry Young, a fellow third officer from South Africa who sold me an early Cousteau Gagnon set. He taught me its use and the safety rules, particularly the tables for diving at depth and the time needed to surface to avoid embolism or nitrogen narcosis, which gave me confidence to explore the magical world below the surface in places like Muscat where the water was incredibly clear. I still find diving magical today. I used to hunt and spear rock cod and grouper and then sell the fish I caught to the chief steward for a rupee a pound, about eight pence in modern money, and this business covered all my diving and fishing costs – sometimes bringing in as much as 700 rupees on a good day. When our ships coincided and we were in Bombay together, Barry and I used to go and swim a mile in the Breach Candy swimming club pool, which improved my style and speed enormously, but however hard I tried I could never beat him – a constant source of frustration!

The canoe could also be launched in Bombay harbour where the attractions were the Arab dhows and local country craft anchored off Darukhana further up the harbour discharging or awaiting cargoes. Although BI had been operating a coastal service for more than a century, it had not been possible to remove all the sailing competition. In the early BI days, the steamers used to cruise down the coast on the lookout for a man waving an umbrella at obvious points. This was the signal that there was cargo to be collected and the ship would stop or anchor and send in a boat to collect whatever it was that needed shipment. Although the service competed with the country craft it never fully replaced them and this practice lasted until the Indian Railways provided a more convenient option. Although the BI service had discontinued the country craft still managed to operate.

Our regular routine was further shattered on 7 April 1961 when we learned that a bomb had exploded in the passenger decks of our sister ship the *Dara*. As news came through it got worse and we learned that the fire had quickly overwhelmed the resources of the crew, whose attempts at an orderly abandon ship were hampered by passengers trying to save their belongings and flinging trunks into the lifeboats. People were jumping from the decks above into one lifeboat as it was being lowered and so overloaded it that it turned turtle on being released from its falls.

The bomb, thought to be a trunk full of Egyptian-manufactured Russian anti-tank mines, probably put aboard by Omani rebels attacking anything British at the time, had gone off on the deck above the fuel settling tanks in the engine room, blasting a hole into the engine room and through the three decks above. Burning fuel in the engine room meant the fire pumps were not activated and the order to abandon ship was given 20 minutes later when the fire had got out of control and was spreading rapidly. The captain and some of the other officers trapped on the bridge escaped by jumping into the sea. Despite the efforts of three Royal Navy frigates about 238 people were killed in all and the ship, fire still raging, eventually capsized just north of Dubai.

The company responded by transferring one of the larger S Class from the Calcutta to Japan service and providing an additional third officer to improve security. Since most of us were in our early twenties, spoke limited Hindi at that stage and no Arabic, this was not going to work. A quick course in how to defuse a bomb from a bomb disposal sergeant in Bahrain did little to encourage us to go anywhere near a suspected bomb. His shaking hands as he placed a detonator into a lump of plastic explosive had us nervously eyeing the nearest exit! Security was eventually improved by recruiting men who had served in the Palestinian police force during the war and some other colonial police forces since. They were no-nonsense and did a far better job, plus they had a fund of stories from their experiences of colonial policing and anti-terror operations from Nigeria to Malaysia and all places in between, including Cyprus. Despite their efforts we still had a succession of bombs. You can check all the passenger trunks and baggage in advance and run random checks aboard, but there were so many passengers some explosives got through.

Fire and emergency stations, known as Board of Trade Sports, suddenly took on renewed urgency after the *Dara* was lost. Many of our deck passenger ships had nested lifeboats, that is one stored above another using the same davits for lowering. It gave the vessels the required lifeboat capacity to comply with the Board of Trade rules, but we were never certain that we could launch the lower boats quickly enough in an emergency. In practices in Bombay, we got it down to 20 minutes and we just had to hope that would be sufficient. If we could not get the lower boats launched in time we decided the best we could do was throw off the gripes, the wires that held the boats to the deck, and hope they would float clear when the ship sank.

On *Dwarka* we had the second bomb on 19 June 1961. It went off just as we were leaving Muscat. Fortunately it was on deck at no. 1 deck hatch and most of its blast went upwards, although one female passenger who had been nearby needed treatment for burns. We returned to Muscat immediately to be close to assistance should there be another bomb on board and started a truck-to-keel search for anything suspicious. Nothing being found we sailed on up the Gulf the next morning, much more alert. Bombs became a fact of life for the company's ships for a while after that but as we had become much better at searching baggage and dealing with their effect we never had another

Dara. I led a charmed life for the next three years as when I left a ship she had a bomb subsequently or I would join one after it had just suffered a bomb but none occurred on the ships I was posted to. I was surprised more people did not follow me around!

Diving had become a consuming interest, but I had difficulty finding places where my air cylinders could be refilled. Then I discovered that the Royal Marines Special Boat Section had a diving air compressor at HMS *Jufair*, the Royal Navy's Bahrain base. I went round to see whether they could fill my cylinders and they were very helpful. This led to meeting the Royal Marine who was running intelligence for the Gulf. From him I learned that there was a threat building up against Kuwait from Iraq. Britain had a treaty with Kuwait and would have to go to their support if an invasion materialised. He asked me to keep my eyes open for any signs as we went up the river to Basra.

In June 1961, the threat suddenly appeared real and Britain mobilised forces in what became known as Operation Vantage. Three aircraft carriers plus other ships and 5,000 troops arrived in the northern Gulf within a week. The navy's helicopters could barely fly in the thin summer air and for the troops on the ground the temperatures must have been a misery. We first realised the extent of the build-up as we headed north from Bahrain for Kuwait during a sand storm. I picked up a smudge on the radar which should have been an island we used as a fix, but it was thirty miles too soon. I called Jack Hamilton, the captain, and we went through the dead reckoning. It did not add up. He told me to get the crew to lower the gangway to the water's edge and go and take a sight of the sun with my sextant to obtain a position line as a check. The point of this was that by being nearer the surface of the sea the horizon was much closer and visible. From the higher bridge the horizon was hidden by the sand haze. Our dead reckoning tied in with the sight. We checked the soundings and motored on, watching everything carefully. Eventually the puzzle was solved when the huge grey shape of the aircraft carrier HMS *Victorious* loomed up through the haze. The relief on our bridge was palpable!

Knowing that I canoed in the Shatt al-Arab I was asked by HMS *Jufair* to take a look at the Iraqi navy, which had just received some new fast patrol boats (FPB) from Russia. I usually canoed up the line of some 200 dhows awaiting the date harvest that was due shortly. Occasionally I accepted an invitation from the nakhodas, the skippers, to go aboard and drink the very strong sweet coffee so beloved by Arabs. This was my cover and having reached the top end of the dhow trot moorings next to the road bridge, I swung back to the western shore, which took me past the Iraqi navy base. The FPBs were moored with some pre-war Vickers patrol boats and looked smart and well-armed, although they never seemed to move. However, in the dry heat of the northern Gulf summer their planking had shrunk as they had been built with soft wood in Russia. I found I could easily put my thumb in the gaps between the planks. I was holding onto the side, having a close look, when I became aware of a noise above me. I looked up and found myself at the wrong end of a rifle. Fortunately, my camera was hidden and after quick greetings in Arabic I took huge breaths to indicate that canoeing had been hard work. This satisfied the guard, who waited a few minutes and then waved me away as I paddled back to where *Dwarka* was berthed. I had seen what I needed.

The threatened invasion never took place. A dhow full of

cement was sunk in the approach channel to the Kuwait port in the hope of blocking it and bottling up some of our frigates, but it sank to one side and the approach remained open. From the monkey island above the bridge we saw no sign of military activity beyond the date palms that grew alongside the Shatt-al-Arab. The palms only extended about half a mile and beyond lay an empty desert. Speedy reaction by the British government had averted the crisis but sadly the lesson had been forgotten 32 years later.

There was seldom any trouble with the deck passengers, although on one occasion a deputation of Indians came to the bridge and complained that Arabs were molesting their women-folk. I told them I would deal with it when I came off watch an hour later and was surprised that they remained just below the bridge until my watch was finished. I thought they would have been better off returning to protect their women. The problem was easily resolved and with the assistance of the gunner, I moved the slightly drunken Arabs to a different part of the ship.

It was not always so easy. On another occasion we were loading stores in Dubai and the captain was keen to get away. Some Arabs were blocking the direct passage for the saloon crew between the side port and the store rooms and I asked them to move. They refused, so I put my hand in the small of their leader's back and said, 'Come on, we want to get you to your destination.' He immediately pushed me roughly backwards and I retaliated. Right behind him was a trunk and he went backwards over it onto the deck. He leaped up and aimed a blow at my face. Where his punch went I have no idea, it did not strike me but mine landed squarely on his nose which exploded with blood. I immediately backed against a bulkhead so he and his friends could not get behind me with their knives but I needn't have bothered. They ran away.

I thought my plans to get married when I went home for flying leave at the end of the year were in jeopardy when we had to sail early from Bombay in November to collect the passengers from our sister *Daressa*, which had been involved in a collision with the American vessel *President Arthur* in the entrance to Karachi harbour. The damage was to her bow so she returned to Bombay for repairs and we took over her voyage, but it only cost us a few days and my plans were safe. That voyage Indian customs had rummaged the ship and discovered over 1,000 tolas of gold hidden away, worth close to £400,000 at today's prices, no doubt to be collected while we were still in port when the smugglers thought customs might be more relaxed. Gold smuggling was a common occurrence and customs told me they thought they might have found about 5 per cent of what had come into port on the ship.

The last bit of excitement that year came as we approached Bombay in December and were ordered by the Indian navy to keep 50 miles clear of the coast. It took a day before we learned the reason – India was invading the Portuguese territories of Goa, Daman and Diu and wanted freedom of action. This could have presented difficulties because on most BI ships the deck crew were Indian and Hindu, the engine crew, normally from the north-west of Pakistan, were Muslims and the catering crew were Goanese Christians. The Goanese were naturally worried for their families, but we had no trouble with any of our mixed crews on board any of our ships. In due course, we saw some of the results of this unequal fight when the pre-war Portuguese frigate *Alfonso de Albuquerque* was towed to a buoy in Bombay harbour, a large shell hole just below her bridge.

It had been an interesting year. There had been more excitement than was normal in the merchant navy but we had found ourselves in a hot spot of international activity. But now, with over a year's watch keeping sea time, I was eligible to sit for the next step in the qualification ladder, the Board of Trade Mate's Certificate. In between all the excitement, I had studied hard and thought I could cut the actual time I would need to refresh before the examination. I wanted to get home to get married to Sue and so took advantage of the one month flying leave we were allowed in the middle of our two-and-a-half-year contracts, By combining this with the two months' study leave at John Cass College, this gave me three months at home upon agreeing to cancel my existing contract and sign a new two-and-a-half-year one once I passed the exam. I flew home in a Comet aircraft from Bombay at the end of 1961.

4

Sara and Suhaili

Sue and I were married at Little St Mary's Church in Cambridge in January 1962 and went on honeymoon to Kitzbühel, where we attempted to learn to ski. On our return I started studying and six weeks later passed the examination for the Board of Trade Mate's Certificate. We had already decided to move to Bombay, so we spent time buying the things that were difficult to obtain there and packing them, with our wedding presents, in a large crate for shipment. We had a few weeks to spare so spent some time with Aileen and Kerr in Scotland before I flew out to Bahrain and joined *Dwarka*'s sister ship, the *Dumra*. Sue followed three weeks later, by which time I had sourced a small flat on Naoroji Gamadia Road in Breach Candy.

India is overrun by pi dogs, scruffy, disease-ridden, non-descript animals that the authorities were unable or unwilling to control. They ranged everywhere in Bombay, and had to be avoided since they were usually rabies carriers. On our second night together, we went out for dinner and as we were walking from the taxi to the restaurant one of these creatures ran up and bit Sue on the back of her leg. It was off before I could catch it, since the hospital would have tested it, but I got close enough to see that it had been chewing its own back. Dinner was forgotten. I grabbed another taxi and we charged back to the ship and up to see the doctor. A tetanus jab was essential, advice on rabies needed too. 'Yes, Third,' said the Parsee doctor, 'Of course I will give your wife the tetanus but it will cost you two bottles of gin.'

I was thunderstruck. This was the ship's doctor, a company employee like myself, whose medical chest was supplied for him and, apart from anything else, a shipmate. There was no time to argue, however. I raced back to my cabin, found a barely touched bottle of gin, borrowed another from the second and paid up. I was livid but there was no reaction to my complaint. The treatment was not nice. It called for large injections into the stomach over a period of time, but Sue took it stoically and fortunately there were no adverse developments. It was fortunate that the *Dumra* was due her annual dry-docking and survey so we were in port for five weeks, enabling me to be around while the treatment was taking place and giving us time to move into our first home and settle in.

Time has a habit of righting those sort of wrongs, though, as a couple of voyages later the same doctor was caught smuggling gold by the Indian customs and as duty officer I had to sign the report that would lead to his prosecution. He came to my cabin and begged on his knees that I would not comply and as I did I reminded him, 'Remember my wife's injection, doctor?' He was heavily fined, he ought to have been jailed but probably bribed his way out of it. Fortunately he was far from typical of our locally recruited doctors, Parsees to a man, and I did not sail with him again.

As with everyone else, we had a bearer to do the shopping

and cleaning, it was not recommended for white women to walk around the markets on their own. My standing went sky-high when my efforts to try to create arak from Basra dates blew a gin bottle in half and covered the kitchen with debris. There was prohibition in most of India; only New Delhi where the politicians worked was exempt so illicit stills were quite common. Indeed, the saintly finance minister, Moraji Desai, had the roof of his garage blown off by his chauffeur's attempts. There was country liquor, known as 'daru' or 'gunpowder', which was dangerous as the first product from the distillation process was not removed. It was possible to buy a pint of it for a rupee if you were feeling brave as it had the reputation of blinding people. Fortunately we had better stuff on the ships and customs did not mind us smuggling the odd bottle ashore to our flat.

It cannot have been easy for Sue to be suddenly abandoned in a strange country but she coped remarkably well, assisted by getting to know some of the other 50 wives of BI officers who were based in the city. Still, I was glad to get back after that first voyage away and find she was sorting her life out and settling into this new environment. When in Bombay we swam at the Breach Candy swimming club just down the road or went sailing from the Royal Bombay Yacht Club in their Seabird class yachts, which we were allowed to take out. There cannot have been any other shipping company where so many families were gathered in the same foreign place and this provided mutual support when husbands were away. We also took time off when we could when my ship was in port and hired a car to explore a bit of the nearby country, getting as far as Pune one weekend. On 10 July, Sue turned 21 and we celebrated with the other officers from the ship in the Venice restaurant. It ended up with the assistant purser laid out on a food trolley with a table-cloth draped over him being wheeled into the foyer. It caused consternation when this supposedly dead body suddenly sat up!

By that time I was back to the same run, Bombay to Basra, every four weeks. We still had the threat of bombs, but the huge effort made by Britain to contain the terrorists in Oman was beginning to pay off, plus our ship's security officers had got better control. Although bombs still continued to be planted they were not so large and were more dangerous to the terrorists than anyone else as on occasions they scored a number of own goals. I was back to my spear fishing and underwater photography and taught Sue how to use the scuba gear, which she picked up quickly having always been a good swimmer.

Then, in September, Sue announced she was pregnant. We had planned to have a family, although perhaps not this soon, but a child is the ultimate expression of the union of a marriage so we were both happy with the event. The timing was good, though, as the baby was scheduled to be born during our next annual dry-dock and refit and I would be around to help. In March 1963, we went to see *Hamlet* by the visiting Bristol Old Vic and the next afternoon I sailed again. I have always blamed Shakespeare for the fact that five hours after I sailed our child was born. I knew nothing about this until two days later when I received a telegram just saying: 'Sue. A girl. Both well.' from the wife of a fellow officer. This was a good month earlier than expected so I assumed we had got our dates wrong and it was not until we reached Dubai a week later that the third engineer dropped round with a letter from his wife in Bombay to confirm my child was indeed a girl and she'd been born in an emergency Caesarean section.

After that the voyage dragged on. I was desperate to get back to Bombay and see if Sue was all right and meet my new daughter. These days, of course, one would have been sent back immediately but employers were not so generous then. When we eventually berthed back in Bombay there was Sue but no baby, being so small she was still in hospital. The chief officer understood my impatience and I was quickly relieved from duty and we took a taxi to Breach Candy hospital. There in a cot was a perfectly formed but tiny little baby, only 5lb 4oz, but she was ours. We took her home and Sue decided she would be Sara. Had she been a boy I think he would have been called James, as James Bond was the rage at the time!

Life changed after that. Sara had difficulty feeding which meant that we were up a lot getting food into her and we watched her weight closely. Slowly it began to increase, much to our relief, and Sue fed her as much as she could, worried that any disease might suddenly cause her to shed weight. Then we went through that delightful time of recognition and seeing her character emerge as Sara progressed from sitting up to crawling and then her first uneasy steps. After that we had to watch where curiosity led her to wander. Swimming was introduced early on and I used to take this little scrap, lugs tucked between the fingers of one hand, put her in a life ring and let her splash around in Breach Candy's pool. Everything would be fine until she splashed water into her own face and that's when the eyebrows came together.

Staff changed from time to time as people's contracts ran out and replacements arrived. Peter Jordan and I had been friends on the *Chindwara* together. I was delighted when he joined as extra third as he soon became as interested in diving as me. But his arrival was to lead to a huge and unimagined change in my life. I was taking over the watch from him at midnight as we sailed towards Karachi along the Makran coast and he was concerned about a vague echo on the radar. We both looked hard and eventually a lantern flickered close to starboard. We were close enough to pick out a dhow heading east. We chatted about the trade as it slipped astern and then Peter went off watch. A few days later we discussed it again, and then again, and slowly the idea formed of buying a dhow and sailing it home to England.

The only person I knew of who had real experience in dhows was Alan Villiers, who had written a fascinating account of a voyage to east Africa on a dhow entitled *Sons of Sinbad* and so I wrote to him and asked advice. About three weeks later I received a three-page response basically saying that there would be no market for such a vessel if we sailed it back to the UK and we would be better off finding a yacht. It was a kind and thoughtful gesture to an unknown merchant navy officer. We took the advice but Bombay did not have any ocean-going yachts. The largest boat we could find there was a Dragon belonging to one of the Tata family and built in the 1930s. But we had become fixated upon the idea and we started looking for boatyards and boats in Asia, particularly Hong Kong. We found a suitable design, wrote home for the plans, but when the plans arrived they were of a different boat entirely. We needed to be ready to sail with the north-east monsoon which comes in late in the year so we had 15 months to build a boat. To avoid wasting further time we decided that the plans that had been sent to us showed a good-looking seaworthy hull, in some ways not dissimilar to the lifeboats we carried on our ships but finer, so we decided to go ahead with what we had. Prices were sought from a number of locations, Karachi and Hong Kong in particular. Soon we were joined by another third officer, Mike Ledingham, so our team was now three.

Walking back through the docks from the ship one day looking fruitlessly for a taxi in the pouring monsoon rain, I came across Mody Hard, opposite Cross Island, an old battery built by the Victorians to protect the harbour. This was one of the places where local work boats were built and repaired. I walked in and wandered around. I asked a couple of people working on boats who ran the place and it became clear that the Bombay Port Trust did but various businesses used it. I found out the name of one of them, Colaba Workshops, and then made contact with the owner, a Brit who had remained behind after independence. We met and I showed him our plans, explained that we had 15 months to build our boat and eventually got a price that was attractive. After talking to Pete and Mike, we accepted the quote.

Work was slow to start because the gate to the yard in the docks closed at 6 p.m. and the police would not allow the lorry with the large teak log that was to form the keel to travel until after 6 p.m. The teak came from the Central Provinces of India and was of good quality. Twenty rupees solved the problem as it persuaded the customs officer to remain at the gate until the lorry arrived. Boatbuilding skills were available, but not for yacht-building. However, the project was entrusted to the last man to have built a yacht in Bombay, the *Tata Dragon*, and he knew his business. The skills of the workmen varied: an elderly chippy, slow but sure, and a young man who rushed jobs with less than satisfactory results being the two extremes. The tools were rudimentary. There were no planes but they knew how to use an adze. Holes were drilled with an old-fashioned bow, whose string was taken around the bit and as it moved backwards and forwards the bit drilled into the wood. The keel, some 22 feet long and measuring 1½ feet by 10 inches, took shape and then the stem and stern post were shaped and fitted. To check that the surfaces were smooth, a red mix was applied to the surface of one piece and if it showed bare patches on the other piece the adze gently smoothed the surface.

The boat was to be carvel-built, that means the edges of the teak hull planks would butt against each other. The method of construction in India differed from European practice in that dummy frames were set up and the 1¼-inch teak planks steamed to let them bend and put onto these frames. To prevent water getting in between the planks, a groove was cut in each edge and rope, soaked in tar, was placed in the groove. In due course we discovered this sort of worked. When all the planks were in place the proper frames were steamed and installed, being bolted through two to each strake. Equipment for the boat was not readily available in India and as Peter Jordan had returned home on leave he returned by sea and BI generously shipped out to us a lot of the items we would require like a 32 horsepower BMC Captain Diesel engine, winches and WC.

In the meantime my promotion to second officer had eventually arrived and I shifted to the *Santhia*. It had taken a long time as the company promoted on seniority. Fortunately I remained on the Persian Gulf run and this made me the senior watch-keeper and the navigator of the ship on a route I knew well. My watch was now the four-to-eight, morning and evening, as traditionally the most experienced watch-keeper did the twilight watches when it was possible to take sights of the stars and get a proper fix of the vessel's position. However, my first issue was to try and remember how to operate a gyrocompass, which the S Class had but the Ds did not. Another duty was responsibility for the mail which came in bags and was stowed in a special locker. This led to a problem I had had some warning about.

Gold smuggling was a major industry between the Persian Gulf and the Indian subcontinent. Jewellery was very popular in India so there was always a market for good-quality precious metals, but they had to be paid for and India had very stringent foreign exchange regulations in place. So other means of purchasing gold had to be found, such as narcotics, which then had to be taken back to the Gulf. The bulk probably went in dhows but there were always attempts to use our ships, one being utilising the mail. We could not open the bags as they were sealed, but on one occasion I was asked to take a couple of additional mail bags.

A year previously the Indian second officer on my ship had suddenly left for a different run and, since we got on well, I asked him why. He carefully closed the door and explained that he had been asked to take a few extra mail bags, probably containing narcotics. Rather than become involved he had decided to move to another ship as, although his wife's father was head of the Indian railway police, the drug gangs were not the sort of people to tangle with. Now I had been approached in a similar fashion and with a wife and baby in Bombay there was no way I wanted to let them get their hooks into me. I played dumb and demanded the waybills. They explained at length that there would not be any, to which I responded each time that it was against company regulations to take mail without a relevant waybill and I could not possibly break those regulations. They kept trying for a couple of months and then thankfully gave me up as a bad job, but I was extra careful with the bag count thereafter in case they tried to slip one in.

Santhia was a larger version of the Ds and I knew, or knew of, the other deck officers so settled in quickly. Discussions elicited the information that we could just about raise a rugby sevens side if we included the sparks and the Australian cadet. Both agreed and we challenged Karachi RFC on our next visit. The ground was mud, awash at high water and since we only had gym shoes we slipped all over the place and lost. On our next visit to Bombay we bought proper boots and beat them over the next five games. Then we took on Bombay Gymkhana Club, normally out of bounds except to senior officers. They scored first and converted but then our third officer, George Beatty, ex-North Wales Schoolboys XV player, got the ball and no one could catch him. Sadly, and rather unusually for the time, I failed to convert and we lost 5–3. They went on to win the subcontinent's sevens championship that year so we did not do too badly for a scratch team.

The chief officer was a delightful Pole who had remained in Britain after the war, but he developed high blood pressure and had to go to hospital. I thus found myself, with six months' experience as second, becoming the temporary chief officer. I knew the job, well, most of it. What I had not experienced before was a death on-board and it was now my role to organise a burial at sea. I called for the gunner, who acted as a general supervisor on-board as we did not carry guns (except a pistol in the ship's safe if we could remember the code for it). He arranged for a canvas shroud to be sewn, which was weighted with sand as the traditional fire bars were not available. We slowed the ship, put a Pakistani flag over the shroud and lowered it carefully into the water on a hatchboard over the stern, the captain and I saluting. As we turned away the shroud floated into view! This was not meant to happen at all. I subsequently learned that it is necessary to put slits in the shroud to allow air to escape. The captain turned green and walked rapidly to his cabin. After watching the shroud sink eventually I reported to him in his cabin to find he was having a whisky at 1000, which was very unusual. He gave me a bollocking and then asked how many times had I performed a burial before and when I told him it was my first he just said, 'Christ, Robin! Have a whisky.' After turning the ship around in Karachi, which was unusual, a relief chief officer, David Colley, arrived and I handed over to him. He had been the cadet instruction officer on the *Chindwara* so we knew each other and got on well.

Back at Mody Hard our yacht started to grow but my plans for sailing home with wife and baby were creating discord in our married life. Sue was not at all keen on the idea, frightened that in case of illness we could be a long way from assistance, especially with Sara being so young. I was committed to the boat. Every penny we had was invested in it and I could not back out. The friction intensified and eventually Sue and Sara returned home in late 1964 after I had signed off my last ship in order to focus on the boat. Before she flew home we did a trip to southern India by car, visiting the game reserves at Periya Lake, Cochin, Ootacamund in the Nilgiri Hills, an old hill station which felt like Sydenham had been transplanted to

India. On to Mysore, where left is right and right is left, which causes confusion with driving instructions, and then Madurai to see the magnificent temple.

Peter, Mike and I started to work non-stop on the boat hoping to have her ready for the north-east monsoon at the end of the year. We moved out of the flat as money was short and stayed out at Bandra, taking the train each morning into the city. We were the subject of curiosity by the Indians who were unused to sahibs travelling on the local trains, often so crowded that people hung onto the outside, but that was the least of our worries. Meals were reduced to porridge for breakfast, bananas for lunch and a curry in a nearby restaurant in the evenings, the total cost of which was five shillings (25p) a day each, but rupees went a long way. Occasionally we treated ourselves, for example when the London Symphony Orchestra came out and we attended one of their concerts.

Our evenings were spent working on plans and, for a while, studying how to make a boat balance under its sails. This latter interest came about when our sails arrived from Cranfield's, and we found that although they were made according to the sail plan, the sail plan did not fit the hull plan. The issue was that the hull showed the positions for a gaff rig whereas we had chosen the Bermuda rig. Books were ordered and we settled down to work out the problem. It all depended on how far forward we wanted the sails' centre of effort to be compared to the centre for the hull's lateral resistance below the water. It was a vital decision that would affect the boat's handling and we decided to calculate it to keep the same lead as shown on the plans. A corn-flakes box contributed its cardboard and we drew the outline of the hull on it and then cut around the line. Next we suspended the cut-out on a knife until it was balanced fore and aft and that gave us the centre for lateral resistance. Calculating the centre of effort was simply plane geometry. Armed with this information we moved the positions of the masts to accommodate the sails. Fortunately, the hole through the deck for the mainmast had not yet been cut through the 3-inch-thick teak King Plank.

There were long discussions about what to call our boat but we eventually agreed on *Suhaili*, a star to the north-west which was where our destination, London, was. It had a resonance in Hindi too, a very similar word, *suheli*, meaning a female friend which seemed appropriate.

Work was very slow. Abdul, the foreman, a very large man who had been a professional wrestler, was forever apologising that the men had not been allocated to our boat but sent off on some other job. Withholding payments did not seem to work. Eventually, the hull and the basics of the interior were complete, the engine installed but not connected to its shaft, which would wait until the boat was in the water as boats can change shape once launched. Then we started painting. Teak is a difficult wood as it has its own oil which repels paint, so we applied a boundary layer of a special varnish and built up the surface from that. At last we were ready to launch. Champagne was not the normal christening liquid in India, and so to break the coconut over the bow we invited the wife of the Kuwaiti consul Munira to perform the honours. The ceremony took place on 19 December 1964 and our boat slid into the brown waters of Bombay harbour. We moored just off the Mody Hard and moved aboard. Two loyal friends, Mike and June Walsh, came down again later and we enjoyed watching the sunset with our red ensign fluttering.

She leaked for a while so it was just as well we were aboard to pump her regularly. During the following days the workmen were ferried out in a plywood dinghy we had made to get on with finishing work, while some of them worked on the two masts being made from Kashmiri pine.

All three of us were scuba divers and we had our own air compressor, so we dived from time to time around the harbour. Indian customs learned of this and asked whether we would look for some smuggled gold they thought was dumped in the harbour. We were taken out to where they said the gold was meant to lie and plunged in. It was quite impossible to see anything beyond two feet but we did the best we could in the mud on the bottom by feel but it was never going to work unless we had precise bearings for the site. We spent four days searching around lines laid between buoys but found nothing but empty beer cans.

Despite this disappointment customs next asked whether we would be prepared to go 60 miles down the coast to Janjira, where they had recently apprehended an Arab dhow and seen them throw a rope into the water with bundles attached. They assumed that the bundles contained gold. The Indian navy had done the interception so I went aboard the warship to find out the bearings they had taken. It was quite clear that they had not taken any accurate bearings and had only a vague idea of the location. The search area therefore would be large, far too large for us to have any chance of finding the gold unless we could cover a large area speedily.

We came up with a possible solution: a large rake, 14 feet long with 2½-foot prongs every 18 inches which could be towed along the bottom, indicated by the chart to be mud. Our idea was to have two divers holding onto the rake as it was towed across the area we were to investigate. Customs made the rake, we checked it, and then set off for Janjira in *Suhaili*, still awaiting her masts, accompanied by a customs launch named *Seahawk* which was to tow the rake and housed the customs officials accompanying us. This launch was a motorised dhow that had been confiscated for smuggling a few months earlier. There was no payment for the job but before leaving we negotiated a deal whereby customs supplied the food and we received 16.5 per cent of the value of anything we found.

Janjira then was a small fishing village at the end of a creek on the Indian Ocean. Around a headland lay a beautiful sandy bay dominated by a very large seventeenth-century fortress built on a rocky outcrop in the middle of the bay near Murud. We found a sheltered anchorage for the two boats behind the headland and I went ashore with the inspector in charge of the customs party to make contact with the collector, the senior officer in charge of the area. On the way we stopped at a small shack where the inspector demanded a glass of daru for himself and one for me. I knew the dangers of daru and so sipped cautiously while the inspector downed his in one. He turned and said I was not drinking very quickly and I told him it was the custom in my country to sip spirits, all the time watching to see what reaction he had to the liquor. He did not go blind so I drank mine down and we continued to our destination, eyes watering. The collector was friendly, asked after our plans and wished us luck.

With our air cylinders and spares fully charged the next day we went out to the search area and assembled the rake. It had bridles at each end so we could adjust its angle from both sides.

Another bridle connected to the tow rope. We dropped the rake into the water, some 30 feet deep, and Peter and I dived down. Visibility was reasonable, we could see each end of the rake, which was encouraging as we were hoping when we found the rope we would be able to see it caught in the prongs and signal the surface. Mike remained on *Seahawk* to supervise. It took three attempts to get the rake at the right angle and then we started to tow properly. The speed was far too great at two knots. Peter and I could hang on but our masks were ripped off our faces.

We surfaced and explained to the coxswain of *Seahawk* that he had to be less enthusiastic with the throttle and tried again. This time it was better. It had been a long day but now we were happy we had a system that would work if we were in the right area. We headed back to the anchorage, stopping on the way to allow customs to 'confiscate' some fish. *Seahawk* anchored near *Suhaili* and we got back on board and began recharging our cylinders. Within the hour customs called across that they had made a fish curry and invited us over to share it. We did not need to be persuaded so dived into the water and swam over for a proper curry.

The next day we intended to go back to the search area but we could not get the air compressor to work. We worked all day on it, but it stubbornly refused to start. Without being able to replenish our diving cylinders we could not carry on the search so it was agreed that *Seahawk* would return to Bombay with Peter and fix the problem and Mike and I would remain with *Suhaili*. *Seahawk* set off the next day and, with nothing else to do for a couple of days apart from sunbathe and swim, Mike and I decided to explore the Murud fort. It is an amazing structure with 40-foot masonry walls and rounded bastions. At one time it claimed to have more than 500 cannons including two enormous ones, still there, feared for their range in the days of gunpowder. The fort had been the base for the Siddi pirates who preyed on anyone's shipping and withstood attacks from the Portuguese, Dutch, Maharathi and British. It was never captured and walking round you could see why it had been so formidable.

The customs officer left behind came up to us later the next day and asked whether we would like to go hunting tigers. Well of course we said yes, this was something we had to see. There was a large area of jungle nearby which had been the hunting preserve of the Nawab of Janjira and we were told still contained tigers. We mustered in the evening and climbed into two Jeeps, hanging on as we drove down a corrugated earth road into the jungle. There were ten people in addition to us, including their acclaimed hunter who produced two rusty shotguns, one single barrel and one double. He took the double and gave me the single. Not only was I concerned at hunting a formidable beast with such weapons, which I felt might make any tiger we hit angry but probably not disable it, the state of the guns left much to be desired. I hoped they would not blow up when fired.

Still, off we went, shining searchlights into the jungle on each side of the Jeeps in the hope of picking up the animals' eyes. We had been driving for an hour, with enough chattering going on to send any self-respecting tiger slinking away, assuming it was frightened at all, when our hunter yelled for silence. Everyone shushed noisily. He dropped from our vehicle, and with a the-atrical crouch approached the jungle. Suddenly he raised his gun and fired and then charged into the jungle, followed by everyone else except the driver, Mike and myself. We certainly weren't going to go into the jungle if there was a wounded tiger there. After a five-minute search they returned, unscathed, to announce they had hit a deer but could not find it.

The hunter opened his gun to remove the spent shell but the extractor was not working. He took a knife from his pocket and began to bang the extractor, a fraction of an inch from the other live cartage. This was too much and I grabbed his gun from him and managed to extract the cartridge. I was now considered the safe custodian of the double-barrelled gun! We travelled on, the searchlight picked up two enormous eyes so I yelled to stop and aimed. From behind the eyes came an affronted 'moo'. I lowered the unfired gun feeling rather stupid. The total haul for the night was two rabbits which Mike and I cleaned and ate. Of tigers we saw nothing and we learned subsequently that none had been seen in the area for at least the past 30 years. Still, it was an interesting night.

When Peter returned we tried diving again but by this time the swell was coming into the bay and resulted in the rake stopping and then jerking forward suddenly. We could not search in those conditions so, after a couple of days hoping the swell would subside, we returned to Bombay. Whether there was any gold still there was anyone's guess. Whoever dropped it must have had contacts ashore who would not have hung around in waiting to recover it and passing it on. It was probably in the markets by the time we arrived on site.

The swell that had forced us to give up the dive was the signal that we had missed the north-east monsoon so on the return to Bombay we stepped the masts and wondered what to do for the next seven months. Peter and Mike decided that they did not want to hang around that long, and after some discussion I bought them out with a loan organised by my father. I, too, wanted to get back to England in the time now available so we laid the boat up at Mazagon dock where the BI marine superintendent had arranged for her to be hauled ashore and chocked off until I returned the next season. In the meantime I flew home at the end of March to see what my relationship was like with Sue, take my Master's Certificate as I now had the necessary sea time, and then spend five months with the navy on what was known as the P course, basically the sub lieutenants course without navigation as we were qualified navigators anyway.

5

FROM WHALE ISLAND TO
SHARKS AND DOLPHINS

I passed my Master's Certificate: Foreign Going in May 1965. This now qualified me to command a vessel but I knew it would be some years before my seniority got me a command with BI. Before going back to India I had some months to spare so I took the time to catch up on my long overdue induction into the Royal Navy.

The arrangements were that Royal Naval Reserve Officers should go through the normal sub lieutenants courses as quickly as possible after being accepted, but since I went out on Eastern service it was nearly four years before I was able to report. My Master's Certificate automatically promoted me to the rank of lieutenant. The quite generous uniform allowance enabled me to purchase two good sets of Number 5s. Every different uniform for sailors and officers was numbered, but this was the standard blue officer's tunic with brass buttons so beloved of film producers.

There were nine of us on the P61 course, all from different merchant companies. We did the rounds of training establishments, a divisional officers' course to explain how the men were looked after and to teach us some of the navy's customs, which are vastly different from those of the merchant navy. A car rally on foot in the New Forest took care of the need to strengthen our characters, apparently a perennial worry to the authorities. Then we were given a hard physical training workout by some instructors, who obviously relished having a go at officers, particularly our bunch with good upper body strength from our apprenticeships but not all that fit. Having brought on a good sweat they finished by producing boxing gloves and telling us, with a leer, that we would just have a little knockabout. The killick came towards me, he was about my height but looked meanly fit. 'Ever boxed before, Sir?'

'Not really,' I lied, because it was such a long time ago. We set to. He was quick and not bad but I found it coming back. The others all stopped to watch as we were still at it after ten minutes when he caught me hard and nicely on the side of the head. This was no longer a little knockabout and had become more serious. But he was getting overconfident. I swung a very lazy right and, as I hoped, he opened himself up parrying it. My left went in like a rapier and caught him hard on the chin. He went down beautifully. There was a shocked silence. He leaped up, shook his head, and then in a broad Liverpool accent asked if we should go on. I looked at him, hardly hurt, over the stun anyway, hardly puffing whereas I was blown. 'Thanks,' I said 'but I think we ought to call it a day as we have another class to go to.' I think if we had gone on he would have slaughtered me.

Course followed course. We learned about anti-submarine tactics and how to use the equipment at HMS *Vernon*, perhaps one of the nicest wardrooms, near the entrance to Portsmouth harbour, today Gunwharf Quay. Drill, including some thoroughly dangerous aerobics with a sword, was taught at Whale Island, known as HMS *Excellent*, the home of naval gunnery and that awesome creature the gunnery instructor. These gods, always straight and erect and immaculately turned out, ruled Whale Island. All courses, of whatever rank, marched double-time everywhere during working hours and if the sight of half a dozen lieutenant commanders being doubled across the four-acre parade ground by a petty officer puzzled outsiders, those of us under training soon learned to keep our eyes straight and not to notice.

Friday was their sabbath as this was the morning they held 'divisions'. This involved every course forming up on the parade ground or in the huge drill shed if seriously raining. We were brought to attention, inspected, one of us told to report to the parade training officer and before you had even saluted your ear-drums were collapsing on both sides by bawled criticism of the about-to-be-performed salute. You reported, that was wrong, so you had another salute to make. That one was, apparently and according to the decibel level, worse than the first which seemed to be taken as a personal insult by every instructor within yelling distance and at Whale Island that meant every instructor on the island. You marched, deafened, back to your group, wrong, yell, about-turned, wrong, about-turn again and stand your group at ease, about-turn, stand at ease yourself and then your own instructor told you where you had really got things wrong.

The captain arrived, more shouting, inspections and then the march past with a real marine band. I always rather enjoyed marching, but however good we thought we might be, it was never good enough and like most groups we were sent around again. It was all part of the great game. They gave you hell during training and you smiled and kept going. Just occasionally you rebelled, but it never paid off. I tried it once when we were being drilled by one of our number, an Australian with a rather poor power of command, which meant he had a squeaky voice.

We must have been 100 yards from him when he yelled an order which we could not hear. At the next indistinguishable order I felt we would be upsetting the GI if we did nothing so I gave one myself quietly and turned us away from the instructor. At the next yell we started to double away. We had gone about 15 paces when a roar sent us about-turning and back to the instructor. He halted us, looked at smirking faces, picked on me and sent me to double around the island with my rifle above my head. It was July, baking hot, and I was wearing a stiff collar and battledress. I returned some ten minutes later with a wet and soft collar and dripping battledress and reported. 'Won't be so keen to take charge in the squad again will we, Sir?' the instructor said happily. He had everything on his side but he could not be allowed to get away with this. 'Oh I don't know,' I said, in an annoying drawl, 'good training for the marathon, wouldn't you say?'

'Get back in the squad!' he shouted, smiling. Honours were slightly equal.

The Whale Island marathon was a great tradition. It took place every summer and everyone was encouraged to enter. The distance was twice around the island or about two miles. I thought we ought to enter an RNR team and the others responded. We were only ten days from the event but we went into serious training, encouraged by a mutual sense of representing the merchant navy and helped by a few snide remarks about our service from some of the regulars. Each evening I pounded round. Like sailing where there is nothing to beat time spent on the water, after an eight-year lapse in long-distance running I needed to get my muscles toned and my lungs working. We were getting better, indeed we began to pass some of the others in training, when the commander sent for me.

'Lieutenant Knox-Johnston, I understand you have entered an RNR team for the marathon?' I admitted the fact. 'How many in your course?'

'Nine, Sir.'

'How many in your team?'

'Seven, Sir.'

'Well, out of a wardroom of 220 I have three so I think it would be a good idea if you combined with them.' Oh no. This was an RNR team and his idle wardroom was his problem.

'Well you see, Sir, what keeps us going is the fact of being an RNR team so we'd rather stay independent.'

'Yes, but the wardroom has to have a team so I think it would be a good idea if you joined it.' I started to explain but was quickly interrupted and told that we were to join the wardroom. I fought hard for the right to have the team called Wardroom and RNR and got that as a small concession, but the title was soon noticeably dropped for just the Wardroom Team. Two of our number lost interest, the rest of us carried on training. Come the great day, the contestants lined up at one end of the parade ground and the commander fired a gun. I had got to the front and took off like a rabbit for the other end, an obvious choke point. I reached it first and then steadied my pace. Behind I could hear a faster pace coming which drew level. I tried to keep up but decided to let him wear himself out. He was the navy mile champion and he didn't wear out, he won.

Next came another better pace and I recognised a leading stoker I had been warned about. We had a similar pace and settled down alongside each other. After one lap we each tried to leave the other behind but failed, however I was weakening. 'Keep going, Sir, not far now,' he said between gulps of air. Bless him, I pounded on. We came to the finish shoulder to shoulder. 'Let's cross the line together, Sir,' he said. 'Go for it,' I puffed, 'otherwise someone else will catch us.' He put in a last spurt that I could not match and finished five paces ahead of me. He came over to congratulate me later as I lay, chest heaving, on the grass – what a sportsman. The Wardroom captain came in two behind me at fifth, but we had an RNR in 7th, 11th, 17th and 21st places so we felt we had upheld the honour of the merchant navy since it was the first time that the officers had won since the 1930s. Whale Island was fun provided you were prepared to work hard and had a sense of humour. When the long course, those regulars who were specialising as gunnery officers, was away our course was ordered to carry out the duties of the guard, a matter of much sword-waving and rifle-slapping and therefore dear to the establishment's heart. It was fortunate that the long course returned in the nick of time to save the navy's reputation. We did not get off that easily as the parade training officer decided to criticise us as if we had done the duty so he lined us up and bawled us out collectively and individually. When he came to my neighbour, while responding to the question as to what post he had held, a small drop of spit flew out onto the PTO's uniform. He paused, drew himself up to his full height and yelled, 'Don't spit over me. It is my right through position, age, debility and senility to spit over whom-soever I like, but you don't spit over me. Is that understood?'

He no longer had a line to address as we had collapsed into uncontrollable laughter.

After spending our days being introduced to the various types of gun and the new missile systems coming in we largely partied at night, joining a sub lieutenants course that had purchased a fire engine together to provide their own transport. The Portsmouth police were extremely forgiving. There were a number of times when they could have stopped us as we careered back from the Pomme D'Or night club in the early hours of Sunday morning, 40 of us hanging on, but they only did so once when the fire bell was rung and they made it clear that the good citizens of Portsmouth did not appreciate having their sleep disturbed.

Each summer Whale Island and Vernon, the homes of the rival disciplines of gunnery and anti-submarine warfare, visited each other's wardrooms for a dinner, followed by 'wardroom games'. Whale Island was short of its designated twelve guests that year and I accepted an offer to make up the numbers. The rig was 'mess jacket', which was appropriate for the first half of the evening but rugby kit would have been more sensible for the second. It started gently with a tug-of-war. Whale Island lost despite my efforts as anchor man to hold our place by taking turns around a radiator. The result was surprisingly predictable, the floor got very wet. High cockalorum can be dangerous as it calls for one team to brace themselves bent double as if for leapfrog in an extended line and then the other team leap onto this column and the winner is the team that supports the most of its opponents.

A new game was turning all the furniture upside down to form a tunnel. Each team started at opposite ends and the

winner was the first to get all its people through. The details of
how the teams get past each other are best glossed over. By this
time dress shirts were limp, some torn, everyone was flushed,
we had drunk wine earlier but now most of us were on beer.
The evening finished with rugby, I don't remember if there was
even a ball involved, but I can remember the padre blowing a
whistle to end a scrum and finding that the stickiness at my
left knee was caused by blood, that of Vernon's commander,
who was trapped beneath me. For young men this was a good
evening, plenty of hard physical work to sweat out the drink and
few of us felt any after-effects the next day. Gieves benefited as
well from the resulting repairs to uniforms.

The mysteries of encryption were included with the basics of
tactical manoeuvring or fleetwork at HMS *Mercury*, another
country house in Hampshire where our group distinguished
itself by managing to drive a contractor's dump truck onto the
wardroom patio late one night. It was discovered the next day
and no one could make it fit back through the gate so how we
did it we never worked out. In any case, we all had headaches
and few of us remembered we had even done it until we were
hauled in by the duty officer and given a rocket. A week at
Yeovilton, urged on by the offer of a flight in a Sea Vixen (the
navy's front line fighter at the time) which never materialised,
was followed by time at Portland and at HMS *Dolphin* to learn
about anti-submarine tactics and convoy operations.

The instruction officer earned our wrath by telling us that
the reason why the navy planned ten knot convoys was because
that was the average speed of a merchant ship in the British fleet.
This was significant because the chances of a submarine being

able to get into position to attack were greatly reduced if the convoy was faster. When challenged about this speed he told us he knew more about the speed of merchant ships than we did, despite the fact that we pointed out the slowest ship from which our group had come did 15 knots. This ignorance was to show up again and again during my time as a reservist and it was small wonder that there were mixed feelings in the merchant navy about the Royal Navy. Part of the objective of the RNR was to create a cadre of trained officers who understood the navy, but the navy failed completely to reciprocate by sending its young officers as a matter of course to learn a little about one of the major justifications for their existence, the protection of the merchant ships that kept our island supplied. It was not just that they knew little of the capabilities of merchant ships, they knew little of the training of the average merchant navy officer.

Our final course of the five months was at HMS *Phoenix*, again at Portsmouth, a fortnight of firefighting, instruction in atomic and biological warfare, or rather how to try and protect ourselves against its effects, damage control and stability. This was where we were subjected to CS gas to show us the effectiveness of gas regulators, and, in our cases, given a totally unnecessary lecture on stability because we knew a great deal more about it than the instructor. Our course was coming towards its end and two of us were competing to see who came out after with the most marks and I just pipped one of the others by obtaining a first-class pass. The reward was to find my Mini dumped in the middle of the parade ground at Whale Island just before our final divisions with its tyres let down. I pushed it out of sight, pumped up the tyres and went to class as usual. The culprits were clear and over lunch, having packed, I spent some time in the car park. I was in no hurry to leave when we were dismissed, but as I took the London road I passed the first casualty, fruitlessly looking under his bonnet for the reason why his engine had suddenly stopped. I sounded my horn, waved and drove on. All five were soon passed, all had pulled in with unexplained mechanical problems. I have no idea how long it took them to find the piece of chewed lavatory paper stuck into the connection between the ignition coil and distributor that had dried out as the engine warmed up and so created a barrier to the passage of electricity to their spark plugs, but longer than it had taken me to pump up my tyres!

During our training we had been asked whether we would be prepared to volunteer to spend one of our further training periods of either five or eight months on the coastal minesweepers that were being used to patrol the rivers during what was referred to as the Borneo confrontation. Indonesia had tried to take over Borneo and Britain had honoured its treaty and was fighting them off. It was quite a vicious war, mainly in the jungle and at its height involved some 60,000 British servicemen from all three services. I initially expressed interest but a sudden outbreak of war between India and Pakistan, during which the latter were said to have bombed Bombay, forced me to change my plans. *Suhaili* was my sole asset, and the bank's loan for half of her was my principal liability. When Lloyds withdrew their insurance cover as Mazagon dock in Bombay was an obvious target, I had no option but to get back and get her away from the war zone as speedily as possible.

With Peter and Mike gone I needed crew. As usual, plenty of people offered to join me but when it came to committing few could actually make it. So I persuaded my younger brother Chris, who was working at Lloyds, to join me and Heinz Fingerhut-Holland, a radio officer with whom I had sailed in BI made it three. We gathered in Bombay in November and were put up by the Sarstedt family, whose nephew Peter was to become a pop star soon afterwards. The Indo–Pakistan war was over but armed police still guarded the docks; however, we were soon accepted as part of the scenery. We launched *Suhaili*, finished rigging her and stored up for our first ocean crossing. Chris was elected chief steward, but was given a lot of assistance by June Walsh and family who drove him around to find what was required.

The route we had chosen was designed to include some of the places that had become familiar over the previous five years so we sailed for Muscat on 18 December 1965. It was a bit of a diversion but turned out to be a good decision. The Walshes came out with us into Bombay harbour and we dropped them off at Ballard Pier. After swinging the compass to make sure we knew its errors we headed out into the Arabian Sea. The wind was light but *Suhaili* was pitching a lot, which we could manage, but alarmingly she began to take in a lot of water.

We found we were bailing more and more. It seemed to be coming in around the mast heel and it did not take long to discover why. There were no frames that hold the keel to the side frames, known as floors, from just behind the mast all the way to the bow. The wind increased and so did the water ingress to the point where we were bailing constantly, relieving each other with the bucket every half an hour. It was back-breaking work that continued for 30 hours until the waves subsided. We collapsed into our bunks to be awakened some hours later by water sloshing around almost level with our bunks. We bailed her out again and cautiously set some sail. Water was still coming in and we obviously could not go on like this, so when the seas calmed down we dropped the sails, got out the caulking cotton, a screwdriver and a hammer and went overside to try and plug the gap that was opening and closing between the strakes of the hull.

'There's a large grey fish circling!' yelled Chris as I surfaced for air between hammering caulking cotton into the leaking seam. I looked in the direction he indicated and there it was, its sinuous motion quite distinctive. 'What is it?' asked Chris. 'Shark,' I answered and went back to caulking with Heinz swimming guard behind me with a spear gun. It was only seven feet long and we needed to stop the leak. But pretty soon it was joined by four friends and the time had come to get out. The caulking was rough and unfinished but had reduced the leaking to manageable proportions and we resumed our course. We were at sea for Christmas and Chris made a special lunch, *poule Suhaili*, cold Danish ham, petits pois and *pommes de terre* followed by Christmas pudding and then brandy and cigarettes. We lay back for an hour to digest the meal, allowing *Suhaili* to sail herself and then it was back to bailing.

We made a good landfall south of Muscat and it took a day to tack our way north so on the last day of 1965 we sailed into Muscat harbour. We could have got there sooner but the shaft on the fuel pump had broken so we had no engine. Halfway down the harbour there were the remains of an old Portuguese battery and just beyond a small shallow bay, the home to the Omani navy which, at that time, consisted of a single motorised dhow. We anchored just off a Pakistani fishing boat that had been arrested for poaching, inflated our dinghy and went ashore to report to Teddy Hunter, the Grey Mackenzie agent. There were no port officials available as it was a Friday. The rules were that we were not allowed to stay ashore after 6 p.m. as there was a curfew dating back to a mass escape of prisoners from one of the two forts dominating the harbour. So we went back to *Suhaili* and started to plan what to do about the floors. We learned we had timed our arrival well as the previous day there had been a public execution of a murderer which we were happy to have missed.

The repairs took time. First we made some templates and then, with the help of the agent, went into Mutrah and found a workshop which could create the floors from mild steel. They took a few days to manufacture but once we had them they did not take long to fit. Our next problem was to caulk the seams now the hull strakes were firmly held. This meant drying out and there were no haul-out facilities available so we adapted the system that had been used to launch *Suhaili* in Bombay. Two large logs were heaved beneath the keel and two more placed on deck above them and then we connected the top and bottom logs by means of a Spanish windlass at each end to hold them tightly together.

Just after high water we hauled *Suhaili* onto the beach until the lower logs grounded and then waited for the tide to go out. It should have worked, but the only logs we could find were palms and as the tide descended the full nine-ton weight of *Suhaili* crushed the lower ones and without support she heeled over onto her side. I still have a vision of Heinz desperately trying to hold her upright and me telling him to get out of the way in case he became trapped. The logs used in India had been hardwood. There was nothing we could do until the tide came back in; fortunately *Suhaili* began to lift before too much water came over her side and flooded her.

We looked around for an alternative method of drying out, noticed an old and rusting lighter lying aground nearby and the next day floated alongside. We took a halyard to the other side of the barge to heel *Suhaili* slightly in towards the hulk. Caulking now progressed at each low tide and was soon completed with the help of a working party from the BI vessel *Pundua*, which included the captain and chief engineer, chief officer and second engineer, who kindly offered us showers and dinner each day while they were in port

The problem with the fuel pump was not something easily fixed, but Dad sent out a new shaft for it. The convenient arrival of the Tribal Class frigate HMS *Gurkha* provided skilled artisans and a workshop and a chief engine room artificer (ERA) soon had the new shaft installed and the pump refitted. We were properly mobile again. We spent a couple of days diving in the bay I knew so well and, of course, painted 'SUHAILI' on the rocks on the southern side of the harbour entrance as was the custom and then, after a final dinner with the consul and agent, we sailed on 25 January 1966. The work we had carried out in Muscat seemed to be effective as even when we pressed *Suhaili* she took on little water through the hull.

Our next objective was Salala, the capital, where Stan Baxendale, one of the ex-Palestinian policemen who had been recruited as BI security officers, was now based. This was not usual yacht-cruising territory and there were no reports to read, but we had the admiralty pilot which was more than sufficient. The wind was mainly southerly at the outset and we tacked our way south, rounding Ras al Hadd on the second day where we should have turned south-westerly but the wind swung round from that direction so we tacked offshore again. Eventually we picked up a light north-easterly as we sailed passed Masirah Island which gradually increased and we achieved our best run of the voyage so far, 134 miles, on 31 January. On the way one evening we were suddenly surrounded by a huge school of dolphins heading south leaping out of the water. They reappeared an hour later heading in the opposite direction. Attempts to get a photo of a dolphin completely airborne were not successful. We debated whether they were heading for some huge international dolphin conference because I have never seen so many in one place before or since.

Along this coast somewhere lived the notorious Janeba tribesmen. Their solution to handling injured sailors had been to treat them by branding the wounds with red-hot irons. While this was seen as torture by the sailors, it was in fact the tribe's standard practice for dealing with injuries. Not certain whether the practice still continued we kept a good offing from the coast. Although we saw fishermen the only danger came from a tanker that came almost disastrously close and, from what we could see, had no one on the bridge or if there was the last thing they expected to see would have been a small yacht. The violent rolling caused by its wash broke most of our china cups and plates. We tidied up the mess and added crockery to our next shopping list, deciding that plastic might be a better choice in future.

We arrived off Salala the next day. There was no harbour then, just a beach, so we anchored off in a moderate swell. Stan had been expecting us and watched us arrive. Knowing we did not have a dinghy he sent out a surf boat to take us ashore. It was an interesting craft, sewn together with rope and did not look very secure, but as we rode through the surf and onto the beach we could see why the boat was so elastic as it took the crash onto the beach without damage. Stan took us straight to the air base in a Land Rover whose floor was covered with sandbags to provide some protection against mines. A mini war was being waged against the rebels and the British were supporting the sultan so were a target, just as we had been on the Gulf run ships.

Our plans to sail on the evening of 3 February were thwarted by the chain bobstay breaking. I left it until the following morning to fix, diving in to fit a new shackle at its lower end. Then, with the anchor weighed, we were on our way heading south down the Indian Ocean to Mombasa. So far *Suhaili* had shown that she could be balanced to hold a course if we lashed her helm and played with the sheet tensions. So she would sail herself, just as Joshua Slocum had managed with *Spray*. But a lookout was essential as we were passing through 'tanker alley', the route from the Suez Canal to the Persian Gulf.

After two days of annoying south-westerly winds the wind backed round to the east and we set the spinnaker for the first time. It was a disaster but we eventually got it under control and relished the additional speed it gave us. The only land we saw during this voyage was the island of Socotra, which came in sight to the west on the 8th, a tempting attraction that we declined, partly due to a lack of wind and because a stop would delay us. When the wind was light we took the opportunity to swim around the boat which is a good way of washing in a small boat as there is always a limit to the amount of fresh water available and we needed that for drinking and cooking. So far the wind had been variable, but 200 miles south of Socotra we picked up the north-east monsoon and *Suhaili* showed us that with the right conditions she could easily average 5½ knots. This was faster than we had managed so far and I put it down to our improving skills. We were getting to know how to sail her better and Chris and Heinz rarely called me now for advice when they were on watch.

Balancing a boat so she will hold a course depends upon a number of factors, not least the shape of the hull and the sail arrangement. With a ketch like *Suhaili* hauling in the mainsail or the mizzen tends to push the bow into the wind, so the tiller needs to be held 'to weather' to compensate for this. Easing the sheets on the sails reduces the amount of weather helm needed and so, with minor adjustments, a balance is finally achieved on the desired course. Changes in the wind strength will cause this balance to alter, so the boat cannot be left entirely to herself and must still be tended. But we developed a technique so that adjustments to the helm were seldom needed. Obviously the less rudder required the better, as when put over it not only alters the course but also provides resistance and acts as a brake.

As dawn was breaking 16 days after departing Salala I began to sense that familiar earthy smell of Africa. I awakened Chris to come into the cockpit so he could have his first, unforgettable experience of the continent. We sat companionably in the cockpit as the day lightened and we sailed slowly through the reef and then motored into Kilindini harbour, mooring initially on the MV *Melika*. After contact with the agents, Messrs Smith Mackenzie, who came out with some mail, we were directed to the anchorage off the Mombasa Yacht Club which proved a very friendly host.

Our stay included a rally with the yacht club up to Mtwapa creek and a free haul-out on the local slipway. Here I was assisted by Bertie, now seamanship instructor on *Chindwara*'s sister cadetship, the *Chantala*, who came over with some cadets to give me a hand. It was good to get *Suhaili*'s hull cleaned off and re-antifouled ready for the next part of our voyage, and while there Bertie did a thorough survey of the rigging, I think more than anything to check whether I was still splicing wire the way he had taught me.

The next part of our voyage took us through one of the most beautiful and underdeveloped coastal zones in the world. The east African coast of Kenya and Tanzania from Mombasa down to Mtwara has five ports, but in between it is coral and white beaches with occasional fishing villages. There are islands offshore, particularly south of Dar es Salaam, which had never been possible to visit in large merchant vessels. The waters are clear and there was very little tourism so the coast was largely as it had been for centuries. The Arabs had been trading here for more than a thousand years and only recently expelled from Zanzibar in a vicious massacre two years previously that did not gain much world attention at the time. Following independence from Britain in 1963, it joined Tanganyika shortly after the revolution to create Tanzania. Zanzibar has such a romantic reputation that we decided we had call in to see what reception we would get from the new government. But we were warned to avoid Pemba Island, famous for its cloves, just to its north as we sailed south as it was rumoured to have a lot of Chinese soldiers stationed there who would shoot at us if we came close.

Pemba was passed without trouble but our arrival in Zanzibar was made unnecessarily exciting because the engine refused to start as we worked our way into the dhow anchorage. We dropped anchor to avoid drifting ashore and then a friendly launch towed us to a safer spot. We only spent one day wandering around the Arab-style buildings and narrow streets. We found the town quiet with a notable absence of the Arab and Indian populations who had provided so much activity when I had come this way before. I felt an uneasy post-revolution feeling to the place and we sailed the next day. This was my 27th birthday and a sharp rain squall sped us on our way towards Dar es Salaam, the principal port of the country. It is one of those 'retort' type ports, with a narrow entrance through the reefs into a wide bay. We anchored off the customs jetty late that evening. We spent four days in Dar as I went down with a high temperature and pulse and the kindly BI agent took me into his house to recover. This is where we were joined by an American, Rob, who asked us to take him to Durban and meant we could reduce our time on watch from four to three hours.

Rather than go out to sea from Dar es Salaam, we decided to coast south via the Mafia channel which was fascinating. It lies between the Rufiji Delta, where the German cruiser *Konigsberg* had been sunk in 1916, and Mafia Island. The channel is quite shallow and with plenty of coral heads so we took to having someone sitting on the spreaders wearing Polaroid sun glasses to act as lookout and call out obstacles. Thus prepared we could thread our way through the coral at a cautious speed. This was not a place for safe night sailing so the first night we anchored on the west side of Niororo Island, a favourite place for the British warships blockading the *Konigsberg* in February 1915 and then we worked our way down the channel itself – coral watch in place.

For our next night's anchorage we chose the island of Songa Songa where, having arrived earlier than expected, we went ashore. We were soon picked up by some local villagers who took us to see their headman. To welcome us he hospitably sent a young man up a coconut tree to send down fresh coconuts for us to drink. A rather lovely place with just one brick building covered in adverts for politicians and laxatives as far as we could see, which was clearly not used to the sudden arrival of rather dishevelled Europeans. I would have liked to stay a bit longer and learn more about these friendly people but when we returned to the boat and thought we would sleep ashore on the beach, we discovered the sand flies. These soon drove us back on-board and we raised anchor early next morning to continue our journey.

Next we made a brief stop at Mikindani, another retort harbour that used to be the centre of trade for the coast until Mtwara was developed. An attractive old Arab town with a decaying Portuguese fort from where slaves had been exported to Arabia, this was where Dr Livingstone had started his last trek into the middle of Africa. Mtwara was our next destination, just a few miles to the south and after threading our way back out of the channel we rounded the corner to the new retort port, built for the ill-fated Tanganyika groundnut scheme for which modern facilities had been built large enough to take ocean-going ships. We had called there during my time on the *Chindwara* but I don't remember groundnuts being part of the cargo we took. *Suhaili* was the only boat there so we had the quay to ourselves and were able to refill our fuel and water tanks. We also dived along the pier, picking up quite a bit of BI crockery and avoiding some enormous clams. The next day was spent relaxing in a bar nearby run by a retired guardsman and looking at the grandiose plans that had been prepared for the expansion of trade that never came. It would have been nice to have explored further, but we needed to get to the Cape before winter so the following day we set course for Beira in Portuguese East Africa, now known as Mozambique, where a vicious colonial war was continuing.

Our progress was slow. Calms were interspersed with violent squalls, but at least some of these produced rain which was very welcome as the water tanks in the bilges had become contaminated. The fishing was good though and we caught a large dorado which provided some excellent eating. But between the squalls we motored quietly, enjoying the warmth of the sun. Eight days into our trip we became aware of the British blockade of Rhodesia when a Sea Vixen from HMS *Eagle* flew low over us and gave us a fast roll. From then on we must have been on their schedule as they flew over us every day.

Our stop in Beira was short. The river Pungwe is fast flowing and there is a large tidal range so at low water we were stuck in mud in the small boat harbour near the ore terminal. There were no facilities for small boats like ours so after a day we moved on. It took us four days to get to our next port, Lourenço Marques, today renamed Maputo, as we were beginning to pick up the Mozambique current, pushing us southwards. The sailing was better, although on the way our American was fooling about and fell overside. Once he surfaced he panicked at the thought of sharks. I went in to get him while Chris and Heinz brought *Suhaili* into the wind. He may have been right as we caught a small shark on our trolling line as we sailed into Delagoa bay.

The port was busy and a large passenger vessel was disembarking some very young-looking Portuguese soldiers destined for the fighting against FRELIMO, the revolutionary group seeking independence. Portuguese wine, bread and cheese was taken aboard and then we were off down the coast to Durban, a short five-day trip. We entered the harbour and were directed to the Royal Natal Yacht Club jetty where we berthed. Customs and immigration were quick and friendly, the customs officer even giving us two packets of cigarettes when he discovered we had been driven to trying to smoke tea leaves wrapped in lavatory paper for the last two days!

The east African coast, largely undeveloped between the ports, had proved a wonderful cruising ground and remains high on my list of places to revisit. We saw no other yachts after leaving Dar es Salaam until we arrived in Durban. There were occasional dhows and sometimes small fishing boats, but the main traffic was further out to sea. I would have liked to have spent much longer exploring, anchoring where we liked and snorkelling where my fancy took me, but we were aware of winter coming on and the dangers of taking our little boat round the Cape of Good Hope in that season.

6

DURBAN AND HOME

For the first few days in Durban we relaxed, overwhelmed by the vast number of new people we met in the friendly Point Yacht Club. From fellow yachtsmen we gleaned all we could about the weather situation ahead. The local advice was strongly against continuing this late in the season. The Cape of Good Hope was originally called the Cape of Storms before Portugal's King João II, showing an early grasp of public relations, decreed it should have its present name so his captains would not be discouraged. I had seen it a number of times before – albeit from the deck of a 7,500 ton cargo ship – and was aware it could be the subject of ferocious weather, causing ships to disappear since westerners first rounded it in the fifteenth century, so it was not to be taken lightly.

The members of the Point Yacht Club were not in the least impressed with the voyage we had already achieved down the African coast, despite Mombasa Yacht Club advising great caution about it; the east African coast was a doddle, we were now informed, it was the Cape that was really dangerous. To emphasise the point we were regaled with numerous stories of the sufferings of yachts who risked a winter passage. Perhaps

we should have pressed on anyway but we had yet to appreciate the 'local waters rule', which states that every yacht club is
convinced it is based adjacent to the most dangerous waters in
the world. At this stage, we also did not comprehend that local
sailors had not always sailed beyond their own limited region, so
the well-meant warnings were often based upon hearsay rather
than experience.

It was now May, nearly mid-winter in the southern hemisphere. If we waited for the next season it would involve staying
in Durban until at least October and was only viable if we found
a profitable use for the five intervening months. But there was
another good reason for staying: we were out of money and
needed funds to buy food for the remainder of the voyage. The
Yacht Club was a likely place to put out feelers for employment
and a number of unhelpful suggestions were made, including
the selling of *Encyclopaedia Britannica*s to the impoverished railway shunters. This task was reserved for less-able whites and
involved little more than hanging onto a train and swinging an
arm or lamp at night to signal to the driver that the track was
clear ahead, altering the points and connecting up wagons. It
was a wicked con because most of them were Afrikaans speakers
and their English was not very good.

We also learned that Colonel Mike Hoare was recruiting
mercenaries for the Congo but no one, least of all myself,
believed that a sergeant in the Combined Cadet Force qualified
as having the military experience he was looking for. Within a
week I came across something far more suitable and accepted an
offer to work for the manager of a stevedoring company where
palletisation was being introduced to speed cargo handling, the
major activity within the shipping industry at the time. I took

the job, Heinz went back to sea as a sparks on a deep-sea bulk carrier owned by the South African company Safmarine and Chris quickly landed on his feet obtaining work in an insurance office where his experience in London was of value.

Rob presented a problem almost immediately. He discovered that, as owner of the yacht which brought him into the country, I was responsible for him and therefore he demanded I paid for a ticket home to the USA, without which he would have to remain in *Suhaili*'s crew, since he claimed he was penniless. This was contrary to our arrangement, but stupidly I had no evidence of this agreement nor had I taken a deposit to cover his repatriation costs, should it prove necessary. We simply had no money for an airfare and told him so, but he responded that this was my problem. His living with us became uncomfortable, as he stopped contributing towards food costs but expected to be fed and, legally, he did remain my responsibility. It was an impasse and we could not just chuck him off. A week passed until, while passing Chris on deck, he lost his footing and fell overside. We hauled him out and he stripped off and laid his clothes and the contents of his pockets out to dry. Among the latter was a wallet and I was amazed to see him lay nearly $1,000 in notes out in the sun. Chris and I scooped it up and Chris went off and bought a ticket to the USA in Rob's name with his money while he was still protesting. Problem solved. He should have realised that you don't muck around with brothers!

The Durban docks are the largest in southern Africa and Grindrod Gersigny, my new employers, operated from Maiden wharf with their fleet, African Coasters. They traded to all South African ports plus Mauritius, but the hub of the service was Durban where we loaded anything up to six ships at once.

This was a job I knew well and found the technical side easy. The hours were long. Labour allocation started at 5.30 a.m. when the Zulu dockers were assigned to ships for the first shift of the day. Each ship had a white stevedore, under the control of the supervisor, Kurt Visser, a large, hard-working Boer. Work began at 6 a.m. and continued with short breaks until mid-afternoon, when another shift came on duty. My boss, Captain Almond, who had recently emigrated from Port Sunlight on the Mersey, was interested in experimenting with any new technology that could speed cargo handling and it was intellectually rewarding to throw ideas about in the evening and then go to practise them the next day.

One of my best innovations concerned a valuable cargo, newsprint, which was vulnerable to bad handling. I came up with a form of pincers, rather like scissors, with rubber pads on the hard points to lift the rolls of newsprint. As the weight was taken on the slings, the pincers tightened on the roll of paper so we could lift it without damaging it or fear of it falling. It worked, and so we made another and tried two at a time. That worked as well and we ended up lifting four at a time. This was a huge improvement and saved a lot of time and damage, but stowing the rolls in the holds took just as long as before as it was still done manually. So we tried placing fork lift trucks in the holds, with rubber pads on their claws and that speeded things up. It was so successful that we were turning ships with a large newsprint cargo around in two days instead of six. This endeared us to Grindrod, but made enemies of the ships' crews who wanted more time at home.

I soon realised that there was a fundamental difference between British and Boer stevedores. The British would agree to your face with an instruction and then not do it. The Boer would tell you why he disagreed, but if you insisted he would do what you asked once he realised that, if you were wrong, you would accept responsibility and not try to pin the blame on him. It took time to gain this confidence, but after two or three cock-ups that were my fault, and I said so, we started to develop a good working relationship.

I was learning a great deal about cargo handling, very much a part of a merchant navy man's life, but this was the shore side of the operation. I was also enjoying the freedom to look at our methods and try faster alternatives, but I could never have contemplated stevedoring as a long-term career. In any case, I missed the sea. So when an advertisement for a relief master for a company called Durban Lines was brought to my attention, I told Captain Almond and applied. While I had no command experience, I was qualified and perhaps my application was not harmed by the fact that the ultimate owners of Durban Lines, King, Sons, Dunn & Company, were the BI and P&O agents for the port. They owned one vessel, the 950-ton MV *Congella*, built in Sweden ten years earlier and typical of small cargo ships built for a master who was also the owner. The current captain was due for long leave to his home in Wales and they needed someone for three months, which suited my programme admirably.

I joined in Durban with the captain still on board for one voyage to Lourenço Marques to pick up the ropes. The captain's accommodation was substantial for such a small vessel, a large day cabin, guest cabin, bedroom and bathroom which stretched right across the main deck beneath the bridge. The crew consisted of fifteen in total: captain, mate and second mate, plus three engineers, all white, and nine Zulu crew. There were two holds and the usual run was from Durban to Lourenço Marques or Beira with manufactured goods. The ship was operated on very old-fashioned lines by the owners. I was told to open a bank account and given 2,000 rand, the equivalent of £1,000, as an advance to manage the ship. At the end of each month, I produced a portage bill showing all expenses incurred, from paying the crew to purchase of food and spares, and the company then reimbursed me. My pay was at the rate of 4,000 rand per annum, slightly more than I would have earned with BI and the tax rate was very low.

This portage bill was the only fly in the ointment as far as I was concerned and took a disproportionate amount of time. Keeping track of the money, calculating the crew's wages, tax and other deductions presented no problems, but getting the account to balance was almost always a mathematical nightmare. It defied logic that each column and line added up to the same figure, but when the totals were compared they nevertheless differed. In frustration at the end of the first month, after countless attempts to get a balance I went to the owners' accountant with the accounts and gave him the seven cents difference that was evading me!

The run itself was everything I could have hoped for. I had been to the ports before, which were interesting places in their own right, both very African but with European influences. Lourenço Marques had a strong Portuguese flavour, more so than Beira although they lacked many of the developments we take for granted in Europe. But therein lay the charm, it gave them a pioneering feel. Having a command is why every young man goes to sea and the responsibility of running a ship was something I had long trained for and welcomed.

The *Congella* had a single screw but was easy to manoeuvre and there was sufficient horsepower from the diesel engine to allow her to cruise at ten knots. The company ruled that we should always stay at least five miles off the coast, sensible when you could see the previous ship of the name beached just north of Cape Bazaruto in Mozambique, but highly inefficient when heading north since this put us right into the Agulhas current running southwards down the African coast to the Cape at a rate of up to five knots. After two voyages they allowed my request to go closer in, especially when passing points such as Cape Natal where the current came inshore, so I could avoid the adverse current.

There was an added bonus as we discovered that the fish seemed to congregate off these points. If we had time in hand when we closed the land, the chief engineer would man the engines and I the bridge and we would slow to five knots, quite fast enough for fishing, while the entire crew trolled for barracuda with lines over the stern. They came in all sizes, four to six feet being average, although we once hooked a nine-footer which broke the line as we hauled it onboard. Our Zulu cook made a special fish dish by putting a little oil in a pan then adding the cuts of fish as steaks, plus onions, tomatoes, peppers and a little curry powder, all of which was allowed to stew quietly. The result was delicious and a treat for everyone while saving the company money on provisions.

After the second voyage, I received a surprise summons to a small, dingy office off the main street to explain why I was using the ship's radio without an operator's licence. My interrogators were large, beefy men with thick Dutch accents and a confident authority, not the sort of people to argue with. Fortunately,

I had already passed the exam in Durban before taking over command and the paperwork had recently arrived. I never did discover who they were, how they had found out, why it bothered them or what their powers were, but they knew a lot about my background and I was thankful I did not interest them again.

On voyages to Lourenço Marques we hugged the coast but when going to Beira we had to go offshore, taking a direct line from Cape Natal to Cape Bazaruto. This was one of the rare occasions when sextants were used to calculate our whereabouts. On merchant ships, although all deck officers are qualified navigators, the second officer is the navigator. It is his job to see that the charts are in order and the courses laid off in accordance with the captain's wishes. I wandered up to the bridge one afternoon and discovered the second, a Greek man, fiddling with the parallel rulers. He was redrawing a position line on the chart, saying he was adjusting its position which is always a suspicious sign. I glanced at his working sheet and quickly realised that the position was hopelessly out of place, in fact, when I plotted it, it went through the middle of Zululand! He refused to admit he was wrong, so I took a sight and plotted it roughly where I thought we were. He had proved competent enough when we were coasting and he could fix the position by bearings and the radar but I realised that in future I would have to watch him when we went offshore. There was no point in reporting his failings to the chairman as he was the chairman's spy aboard, a situation I found distasteful, as I realised that although I was the master he had more influence with the chairman than I did.

My seventh voyage proved that this number is not necessarily lucky. We loaded for Beira, a mixed cargo which included about 200 drums of lubricating oil carried on deck and consigned for the Rhodesian railways. Although the United Nations had imposed sanctions against the Smith regime, as far as I was able to discover these lubricants were allowed as the railway provided the only connection with the outside world, apart from through South Africa. Our departure was delayed when the engine room phoned the bridge, just after we dropped the pilot and were making our way through the approach channel, to say we must stop the engine as it had lost oil pressure.

On either side of us were the stone breakwaters of the entrance channel. If we stopped here we would be blown onto them in a couple of minutes and wrecked long before a tug could assist us. Letting go the anchor immediately was not an option either as by the time we had released enough cable to check the vessel we would have swung round and the stern would be on the breakwater. I told the engine room to keep the engine running at all costs until I could get into open water. The chief engineer protested of course, it was his job to point out that the engine could overheat and then seize up, thus putting the ship out of action for months. But the alternative was to lose the ship completely and in a pretty public place. Over the radio I advised port control of the situation as we chugged slowly out of the channel and then anchored as soon as we were clear. Once we had brought up I left the bridge to the mate and went down to the engine room to inspect the problem. The chief and his second were standing by the door, looking shamefaced. They had located the cause of the issue – they had forgotten to close the valve on the lubricating oil filling pipe after topping up the sump and with the valve open no pressure could build. There was nothing further to say. We got underway and headed north.

I did not think much about our deck cargo as the manifest was clear, but when we got close to Beira we became suspicious. We checked the cargo by removing one of the bungs and the pungent aroma of spirit assailed us. It said lubricating oil on the drums and on the cargo manifest with which we had been provided, but those lubricants turned out to be aviation spirit with a very different and dangerous flashpoint. We realised that it was a deliberate deception to avoid UN sanctions and one that could have caused us a lot of trouble. Both the mate and I were British subjects and, although the vessel was South African registered, this was a breach of the sanctions. It was not just that we, the crew, would be in trouble if the ship was stopped by the Royal Navy blockade, the cargo was itself hazardous and a very serious fire risk about which we had been given no warning.

We were approached by a Royal Navy frigate as we made our way towards Beira and if we had been stopped arrest and prosecution would almost certainly have followed. As it was, the Tribal class frigate just challenged us, we responded in all innocence and they turned away. But the situation could have got more worrying because, as the frigate turned away, we had heard the drone of engines and a Neptune bomber from the Portuguese air force swung over our two ships. Within minutes a Sea Vixen fighter from HMS *Ark Royal* arrived above the Neptune and began to circle. Things could have got out of hand with all this ironmongery about and we could have found ourselves in the middle of an international incident. The Neptune remained for a few more minutes until we crossed the three-mile limit into Portuguese waters and then headed towards the shore and the Sea Vixen roared seawards. Whether the Portuguese were aware of what we were carrying I never found out.

We offloaded the drums with relief, loaded a return cargo and headed back to Durban, again being investigated on the way but not stopped. On our return I asked to see the chairman and put it to him that he should not have sent us with that cargo and we needed to know what we were carrying from a safety perspective. He denied all knowledge initially, but then told me I was being paid to do a job and to obey orders. I told him that it was criminal to send us to sea with a false manifest and especially with a hazardous cargo and I would not sail the ship if this happened again. He went white with anger, but it was a stand-off. I did not want to lose the job and he had no one at the moment to replace me, although he would obviously start looking for someone now. The good news was that the next voyage to Beira was with safe cargoes.

I solved the chairman's problem of getting rid of me in a manner I would rather have avoided. The summer of 1966 was a good one for English football, I was in Lourenço Marques when England beat Portugal in the World Cup and only the fact that I was having a drink with the chief of police made it wise for me to stay ashore. He was accompanied by his unarmed combat instructor, a wizened but tough-looking customer who had beaten Willie Toweel as a professional boxer. I felt safe from physical violence in such company, despite the Portuguese claim that England had cheated, but they could not protect me against a far greater risk: the onset of an illness which was potentially life-threatening.

I had no idea what was wrong with me, all I knew was that on the next voyage I began to feel very tired and off-colour. My reaction, foolishly, was to assume I was unfit and indulge in a spate of exercise. By the time the ship reached Lourenço Marques my skin was waxy and urine a bright yellow and it did not take a genius to realise that something was wrong. I saw the port doctor who, having examined me, said in an interrogatory tone, '*Hepetite*?' Misunderstanding him, I explained that I was not eating and had no appetite! We could have gone on like this all day, but the doctor reached for a book and pointed to the word – hepatitis or jaundice. It meant little to me. I had never come across it before, except during cursory readings of the *Ship Captain's Medical Guide*, but the doctor impressed on me that it could prove fatal. I had always enjoyed rude health, never broken any bones, kept myself fit, but now I was faced with an internal menace. It was a scary experience.

I returned to the ship, told the mate the problem, and went to bed to rest and contemplate this new strange vision of mortality. I asked the agent to inform the owners of my illness and we returned to Durban. Of course this played right into the owners' hands and they quickly found someone with a Master's Certificate to accompany me for the next voyage, 'Just in case your illness deteriorates' as the chairman put it. So I was not surprised when, at the end of the voyage and when I had passed on the ropes, they told me I was not required anymore and they were ending the contract. If nothing else their prompt action avoided the responsibility and potential costs of putting me into hospital. I signed off the *Congella* with regret. Whatever the behaviour of her owners, the crew, with the exception of the second mate, were good friends and I enjoyed having a ship to drive.

The doctor who treated me in Durban, Hamish Campbell, was a character in local sailing circles. He was descended from the 1820 settlers, a British government attempt to increase the proportion of Britons in the Cape colony and provide a barrier of European farmers against the Xhosa tribe moving down from the north-east. A gynaecologist by training, he had two standard cures for illness: 'If you can see it, iodine, if you can't, take gin.' In my case, he banned alcohol and then forgot this instruction the same evening in the club bar when he offered me a drink! His advice was no alcohol for at least six months and to take a rest. The former was not difficult, the latter impossible. I had to work to live and there was no National Health Service. I went to see Captain Almond with whom I had kept in touch and he immediately offered me the job of joint supervisor with Kurt Visser back at Grindrod. The company was expanding, extra shifts were being organised and it was becoming too much for one person.

My restart at Grindrod was not without incident now I was in a more senior position. I liked and respected Kurt, he was very straight and good at his job and inevitably I leaned on his experience for the first weeks. Others in the company did not fully appreciate what was happening and saw my arrival as a threat to Kurt's job. One in particular, a huge Boer called Burger, did not believe that in the long term we would both be needed. Visser was his friend, I was an interloping '*roinek*' or 'redneck', as they called the British, and he did not see why his friend should be pushed out of work because of me.

He did not buy my explanation that there were going to be two supervisors in future. His tactics were typically direct. He picked on me one evening in the office the way he knew best by starting a fight. It appeared good humoured, he was smiling, but his eyes weren't. This was serious, as he was much larger and stronger than me. We grappled and he picked me up as if I weighed nothing and flung me across the room. What he had not counted on was an apprenticeship spent scrapping, plus quick reactions. As he threw me I flicked my arms up around his head so the whole force jerked hard on his neck and hurt. This caused him to lose balance so we stumbled across the room and finished up against the wall. It was a stand-off. He would undoubtedly win if we continued but he was aware that I would fight, so it stopped. It took another two weeks before he realised that I was telling the truth and, as so often happens when two men have faced up to each other, the atmosphere cleared and we became good friends. These were good, direct people, but I had learned one important lesson from my time with Durban Lines so it did not take me long to discover who was the company spy reporting directly to the director, a sad reflection on the lack of trust shown by management.

For the next three months, days started at 5 a.m. and finished at six some evenings, 9.30 p.m. the others, six days a week plus a half day on Sunday. The pay was not as good as it was at sea but I was earning enough to have work done to *Suhaili*, and put aside money for provisions to get us home. Chris and I were still living aboard although she was hauled out by this time, lying alongside the dry dock. When I was back early we worked on the boat until darkness fell or the police made their evening patrol, a white sergeant and black constable. Despite invitations, endorsed by his sergeant, the constable would never come aboard for coffee but insisted on sitting beneath the boat to drink it alone. He wasn't missing much as the inside of the boat was a real mess with bits and pieces laid about everywhere.

The policemen were a friendly pair and we learned much about the state of law and order during these evening chats, and also a little Afrikaans. They called in as usual the night President Verwoerd was assassinated, as all police leave was cancelled in the expectation of trouble, but the only crime in Durban that night was one robbery quickly solved.

When we could we also took time out. I discovered that the music master from Berkhamsted, Ron Charles, was now head of music for the broadcaster SABC in Natal, although to be honest my interest was more in his daughter, Jennifer, now working as Ian Player's secretary at Hluhluwe Game Reserve – a beautiful place where she told me that rhinos were meant to be short-sighted. I was never entirely convinced.

Once we had finished the work ashore we put *Suhaili* back in the water and returned to the yacht club. Durban's international community of world cruisers had increased and now numbered nine boats. The numbers were augmented by two South African returnees, the Cullen brothers in *Sandefjord*, an original Colin Archer design, and Bruce Dalling in his *Virtue* from Hong Kong, who was later on to come second in a disputed Observer Single-Handed Transatlantic Race and remained a friend until his untimely death. With local wine costing 12s. 6d. a gallon (62.5p in today's terms) parties were inexpensive and frequent, although the jetty was usually very quiet for most of the following day.

John Pragnall, the secretary of the Point Yacht Club, had introduced Chris to some producers, telling them he was an experienced actor, and he ended up obtaining some work and adverts to do for radio. I first realised what was going on when I picked up the local radio station while sailing back on the

Congella to hear a voice describing an escape from disaster in a programme called 'Death Touched my Shoulder', broadcast weekly. Later I heard the same familiar voice doing a Silvikrin shampoo advertisement. I realised that it was my little brother!

Our departure for Cape Town was delayed almost two months by an accident as we were returning to the mooring from a sail one evening. A squall hit and over we went, right in front of another yacht motoring out. There was neither time nor space between the moorings to luff up, the masts hit and our bowsprit broke, bringing down our mainmast. Luckily, no one was hurt and we gathered up the pieces, motored back to the mooring and took stock of the situation. We needed a new mast. Fortunately, we were covered by insurance so we asked for quotes from three yards for a replacement, picked the middle one and waited for it to be constructed.

The period without a mainmast coincided with the arrival of *Rehu Moana*, sailed by David Lewis and his family including two very small daughters, Vicky and Suzi. He arrived in the harbour at night and went aground on a sandbank just off the yacht club. On seeing his predicament the next morning we started to cast off to go out to tow him clear, but were told not to bother. This was a job for locals who knew the ropes and off they set in a totally unsuitable ski boat. We continued to work on *Suhaili* but after a while, since nothing came into sight, I climbed the mizzen mast to see over the breakwater and there was *Rehu Moana* in the same position while the ski boat was hull down with its crew swimming round it. They had taken the tow, revved up to get power but had girded, or swung round broadside onto the yacht, and capsized. Towing is best done with controlled power from a large propeller, not engines designed to achieve efficiency at high speeds. We started the engine, motored out, threw *Rehu Moana* a line and took the weight. She came off the bank without difficulty and we brought her alongside the jetty to join the swelling number of visiting yachts. David later described his arrival in *Children of Three Oceans* and referred to his rescuer as a motor launch. Well, we were not able to sail, so I suppose he was right!

Our new mast was ready eventually. It was made of spruce and hollow, a beneficial saving on weight that we could afford as *Suhaili* was far too tender with the old Kashmir pine mast, which had made her heel over too easily. This tenderness had saved us from damage thus far as *Suhaili* had heeled very quickly when a squall hit so nothing had broken, but it meant we could not push to windward so hard. The new lighter mast improved our performance. Although promised in three weeks it took five but was worth waiting for. We painted it white, stepped it, took it for a trial and declared ourselves satisfied and ready to sail. Chris, still in his role as chief steward, went to the market and we stocked up ready for the next leg to Cape Town

I said goodbye to everyone at Grindrod with some regret. They had become good friends and I would miss them. I had enjoyed the job but the hours took their toll and I was not coming up with any new ideas. Murray Grindrod offered me the job of assistant manager if I wanted to return, but I was not sure. I had seen the Zulu stevedores in their quarters. Under apartheid rules they needed a permit to come and work in Durban from their native Zululand. The barracks were located behind the docks and I only visited them once to collect a man who had been knifed and take him to hospital. The incident occurred late one evening as our Zulu stevedores were entertaining themselves dancing with wooden spears and shields to their powerful rhythms, and the hair had risen on the back of my neck. I suddenly appreciated what British soldiers had to face at the battles of Isandlwana and Rorke's Drift. These were fine men, full of pride in their nation and heritage. I had seen them treated as second-class citizens with that pride considered a liability, not something to be respected, and I did not like it. South Africa is a beautiful country and the standard of living was high for most white people and a few black people but I was never comfortable with apartheid.

Heinz rejoined us in November. The day before we sailed as I was obtaining port clearance an apologetic port official arrived and handed me a note. Inside was a statement from King, Sons, Dunn & Company saying that I owed 45 rands for the wages of the person they put aboard the *Congella* for instruction when I went down with jaundice. I had not seen the invoice before, nor had I ever been told to expect it. I phoned the office but could not reach the chairman and everyone else there was evasive. The official, while appearing embarrassed, was adamant that I could not leave port unless the bill was paid. The chairman had influence in the town, I had none, so I had no choice but to pay up as we wanted to sail. In any case there was no time to fight it in court, nor was I confident it would achieve anything. To slip out without paying was not an option, as whatever the rights and wrongs of the case, the authorities would pursue us and we intended to call into other South African ports.

It was a petty and mean action and I felt angry and frustrated but there was nothing to be done about it. Mr Big had leaned on someone he considered Mr Little, abusing his position. There was restitution of a sort later when I got home and was asked by the BI directors how I got on with the agents and I mentioned this incident. King, Sons, Dunn & Company lost the whole P&O and BI business for Durban a short time later as they had booked banned cargo for Beira for the *Kampala*. It was a sad finale to what had otherwise been a most enjoyable stay in Durban. However, one person's meanness, for just a few pounds that probably meant nothing to him, could not destroy the happy memories we had of the friends we made and kindness we received.

We eventually sailed from Durban on 30 November 1966. We had a strong north-easter for the start of the voyage and the boat's motion, along with the fried lamb chops for breakfast the next morning, meant that seasickness had its toll on half the crew. The voyage around the Cape of Good Hope to Cape Town took ten days, stopping off at East London for half a day to drop off a South African yachtsman who had joined us from Durban. Land was nearly always in sight and, despite its reputation for south-westerly gales, we rounded Cape Agulhas, the southernmost point of Africa, under spinnaker in a light easterly. We came into Cape Town with a real 'buster' though, blowing a good gale force 8 in the Duncan docks in the harbour and had to anchor clear of the Yacht harbour until it eased.

Although I had visited Cape Town many times, this was the first occasion I was in charge of my own vessel and could decide how long to stay. Our hosts were the Royal Cape Yacht Club, tucked away in a small boat basin at the top end of the docks. The club has a deserved reputation for hospitality, which we appreciated. We relaxed for a few days, climbed Table Mountain and damaged a bar door one evening when I met five ex-naval gunnery officers and we put our collective recollections of gun drill to a test with one of the ceremonial guns outside the front door of the club, which demonstrated how much we had forgotten. Much to my embarrassment the mark on the bar door was still there twenty years later and always pointed out to me with delight by the barman whenever I revisited. The club secretary, luckily another ex-Royal Navy man, just muttered something about people forgetting this was not Whale Island and said no more. Nevertheless, I thought it a good idea to sail before I fell among thieves again. Also Christmas was coming, our second away from home, and we all felt it was time to press on.

There was no need to sail non-stop from Cape Town to London. The usual stopping places on the voyage back to England – the whole length of the south and north Atlantic oceans – were St. Helena and the Ascension Islands but, being homesick and wanting to make what was, at the time, a long voyage, we decided to sail to London non-stop, a distance of roughly 6,850 nautical miles. Friendly doubts raised by concerned club members that such a distance and time at sea was not sensible as food and water would not stay usable, could be countered by Francis Chichester's current voyage around the world. He had just sailed non-stop from England to Australia in *Gypsy Moth IV*, a considerable achievement that was giving me ideas as we approached the end of our African adventures.

We carefully calculated the food requirements for a passage averaging three knots and decided to allow for 110 days to provide a sensible reserve. This meant we needed to carry sufficient food for a thousand individual meals. Chris and I worked out menus to produce the total requirement of tins and fresh food, which was then broken down to give variety. The simple method, which I still use, was to create menus for a week, trying to provide variety with the nourishment needed when involved in heavy physical work, and then multiply that by the number of weeks we thought the voyage would take. Then we added a few treats.

Heavily laden with food, fuel and spare water, *Suhaili* laboured out from Cape Town on Christmas Eve. Now well seasoned, the three of us settled quickly into our usual routines of four hours on and eight hours off watch, as we picked up the south-east trade winds and began a fast run towards the equator. The average of 136 miles each day, or 5.5 knots, was fast for *Suhaili* and although it was hard on our arms, we loved the swooping sensation as she accelerated and surfed when positioned correctly.

With the prospect of more than three months at sea ahead, Heinz and I decided to shave our heads for no particular reason other than we had never done it before and we wanted to test the theory that if shaving encouraged growth on the face, cutting hair from the head might ward off baldness. My father retained a good head of hair but my grandfather went bald at an early age and I was uncertain which of these genes dominated in me. The result of the experiment was that we suffered sunburn almost immediately, coupled with the discomfort of a bristly pate.

We enjoyed the south-east trade winds and the resulting very satisfactory speeds which gave us daily distances in excess of 120 miles. When the wind eased after eleven glorious days of fast sailing we found other things for amusement, such as diving off the bowsprit and catching the stern or our safety rope trailed astern as they passed. Heinz missed the rope on one occasion and Chris luffed up immediately to get him back. It was a sign of how much he had learned since joining in Bombay with no experience as I did not need to tell him what to do any longer.

In the middle of the ocean we picked up glass fishing floats attached to nets, which must have drifted from Angola since they were clearly Portuguese in origin. We dived into the sea with spear guns after dorado whenever they appeared as they are great eating and also tried methods to cook flying fish so the bones were removed and the heavy fishy smell could be reduced. We came to the conclusion that the only way to reduce their intense fishiness is by covering the flesh with large dollops of tomato sauce. There were plenty of them about as they are attracted to light and frightened by the dark shape of the hull. Their panic is manifested in a startled eruption of fish from the sea and a long glide, as they cannot actually fly in the bird sense, to avoid the supposed predator. They can rise two metres or more above the surface as an agonised yell from Chris proved one night when one flew into his face. His revenge came at breakfast the next morning when he cooked and ate his attacker. Flying fish were not the only visitors. Small squid were to be found on deck most mornings and we threw them back into the sea, leaving it to the sea water coming onto the decks to remove the black inky stain they left as a calling card.

In the warm, balmy conditions of the trade winds we rarely needed to wear more than swimming trunks and those off duty could lounge on deck or read in the light but cool cabin. Before departure someone gave us a copy of *Puckoon* by Spike Milligan and you could tell when it was being read by the inevitable laughter coming up through the hatch. Progress was good, the log recorded 2,000 miles on 9 January. Ascension Island was in sight on 13 January but we resisted the temptation to call in. We crossed the equator on 19 January and later that day the wind shifted from the south-east to the north-east, indicating we were into the northern hemisphere wind circulation system. The log book for 21 January 1967 describes a typical afternoon:

School of dorado dolphins swam with us. Speared three of ten pounds before shark appeared. Speared shark but harpoon broke off. Started engine but governor jammed unable to rev up.

Now into the north-east trades, almost northerly to start with, we were discovering the sharp squalls that are familiar to sailors in the Intertropical Convergence Zone, or better known as the doldrums. It was a hard slog, the leeward deck underwater a lot of the time as we pushed north or as close as we could get to north. But slowly the wind veered and *Suhaili* showed her beautiful balance. This allowed us to spend a total of sixteen days playing canasta down below in the cabin to avoid the sun with the helm lashed and only occasional adjustments to the sails. It seemed to take ages, occasionally motoring but mainly drifting slowly, but one factor assured us we were making progress: as our latitude became more northerly it gradually became necessary to don more clothing as we bashed, close-hauled, towards the north and the European winter.

As the wind slowly veered our speed increased, but not by much. Although we were only making some 60 miles a day progress was faster than we had anticipated even though we were being pushed westward. These were the horse latitudes, an area of the southern north Atlantic which becomes dominated by a high pressure system, known as the Azores high, and the winds can be flukey. Sargasso weed was now all around us and fishing up clumps to look for small animals like shrimps and crabs living in the weed became an amusing distraction. Christopher Columbus had problems with this weed as his seamen were convinced that it would become thicker as they progressed westward and eventually completely entangle the ship, leaving them to run out of food and die.

By mid-February we were approaching the Azores, much earlier in the season than was really desirable. We had not seen much shipping, but a Russian cargo ship came over and with three blasts of its foghorn gave us a nice salute. If this seems surprising it should be remembered that in those days there were not as many yachts sailing around oceans. Winter gales frequently lash the Azores and one storm which came through nearly finished the whole adventure prematurely. It hit us hard and we hove-to, the helm lashed amidships and all sail stowed. This was one of the recommended methods of dealing with storms conditions at the time. We were thrown about by the occasional larger wave which threw us over onto our beams ends but provided the hatch was closed we stayed dry, if a bit bruised. *Suhaili* was reasonably comfortable like this. She lurched but she was not being bashed about so it seemed safe.

A sudden horrendous banging from the stern brought everyone on deck to discover the rudder throwing itself from side to side in a manner designed to smash it to pieces in a very short time. The tiller had broken. We lashed its remains back to the rudder head, held in place by numerous lines and while receiving frequent cold douches down our necks as the waves broke over us. The repair held, the boat became quiet again, and the rudder was safe. But we weren't. The sky had been overcast for a few days, which had not allowed me to get a sight with the sextant, so I was uncertain of our position. The dead reckoning indicated we were somewhere north of San Miguel in the Azores archipelago and the wind was pushing us southwards. Heinz managed to obtain a radio direction bearing which confirmed this and alerted us to another problem – the batteries were now dangerously low.

We tried to start the engine but there was insufficient power left in the batteries. So not only were we drifting towards a lee shore in a storm, we had no engine so we could not try to bash our way clear under power. The generator was in pieces as usual but in any case I doubted it could run for long as it had to be set up on deck to remove its exhaust fumes and the waves coming inboard would swamp the dynamos. We started to reassemble it so we could take advantage of any change in our circumstances. If the situation became desperate we would just have to run it in the cabin and evacuate the accommodation for a while since we did not have an exhaust pipe long enough to reach the deck.

We kept watches but I had difficulty sleeping between my tricks as I was worried about our predicament and would have preferred to be doing something positive. When I climbed onto the deck the next morning and looked south there was a hardening of the horizon, which indicated the presence of land. The wind was showing no signs of easing but now we had a lee shore in sight and the time had come to break clear into open water. We set a small amount of the mizzen to hold the bow into the wind and then hoisted the staysail to provide some forward power. We began to move forward but at first I could not tell whether we were making on the land. As time went by and no end to the land was visible, it was obvious that we weren't heading towards safety, if anything we were still making leeway towards the danger. The choice was either to hoist a fully reefed mainsail in the hope of giving extra impetus, or to run the now-assembled generator. We went for the mainsail.

Suhaili responded like a horse to spurs and crashed forward. We headed up about two points but she was pounding terribly and I tried not to think about those floors we put in at Muscat. But the risk was worth it as we could see that we were making progress on the land now, at a guess less than seven miles away. And then the wind headed us. But what might have been a disaster in some circumstances was an enormous bonus, as it made the other tack a fair one. There was no point in attempting to tack in those waves, so we wore round onto the starboard tack and hardened in the sheets. The course was now north-west and towards the safety of open ocean at last.

The greatest advantage of living in a country like Great Britain, beset by a series of depressions from the Atlantic ocean, is that the wind never stays strong or weak, or even from the same direction for long. Usually sooner rather than later it all changes. This keeps sailors alert and creates opportunities to use the change in the wind direction to take the best course for your destination. So it was in our case. Almost as a reward, the wind lightened shortly afterwards as it veered round through east to south and then south-west.

With the wind behind us and no water coming aboard we put the generator on deck, recharged the batteries and set a course for the English Channel. We could almost smell home now and after nearly eighteen months away I wanted to see my little daughter, so every additional day at sea became a frustration.

The wind stayed astern and we tore up the Channel, past Land's End, The Lizard, Start Point, the Isle of Wight and eventually, on 8 March, the day after Sara's fourth birthday, rounded the White Cliffs of Dover at the South Foreland, sailed through the downs off Sandwich and Ramsgate and into the Thames estuary. We radioed our ETA in advance and family came to meet us at Gravesend where we cleared inwards with the Customs. The next day we motored upriver and achieved a childhood ambition of having the great arms of Tower Bridge raised for us to pass through. A day later we took *Suhaili* to Limehouse Basin, but finding the charges rather high, I accepted an offer of a mud berth at Benfleet, next to Canvey Island and took her there with the help of members of the Benfleet Yacht Club, which became the first yacht club I ever joined.

The whole voyage, despite all the problems that we had encountered, which tend to be forgotten with time, now seemed like a wonderful experience. I had relished the almost gypsy-like freedom and independence which having one's own boat gave – being able to choose a destination, how to get to it and how long to stay if a place took one's fancy. I also knew that in a professional sense I was now a very competent small-boat handler, skills which could always prove useful in my career.

It was not a conscious decision at the time, but I had also satisfied myself that a really long voyage was possible with *Suhaili*. She had shown that she was a good sea boat. We had also learned that it was possible to carry sufficient food for almost a year for a single person and had learned what food would keep and for roughly how long. But you cannot maintain a sybaritic lotus-eater's existence for long, practicalities like earning money to pay for your chosen way of life interfere. So the time had come, at least temporarily, to rejoin the real world. Heinz went back to sea with Marconi, Chris returned to Lloyds and I reported to the BI offices at One Aldgate to discover what my immediate future was to be.

7

THE GREY FUNNEL LINE

The first surprise awaiting me when I reported to the British India office in Aldgate was that promotion had speeded up in my absence and I was now on the chief officer list after barely two years as a second officer. Being mate of a ship gave one real responsibility: handling the crew, keeping the ship smart and effective, deciding where cargo would best be stowed both for its own protection and to keep the ship trimmed safely – I relished the thought.

My expectation was to be deployed to one of the older cargo ships, but with the sureness that bureaucrats exhibit when they do not really know the detail of their subject, I was informed that I lacked cargo experience. My time as a stevedore in Durban apparently did not count, despite the fact that I had been loading up to six ships at once, so I received an appointment as first officer to one of the two crack east African liners, the *Kenya*, which was not the end of the world. A spell on a home-based ship was probably due anyway. She and her slightly newer sister, *Uganda*, were beautiful ships of 14,430 gross tons, 539 feet long with a beam of 71 feet, capable of a service speed of 16.5 knots, although *Uganda* achieved more than 19 knots on trials. They were built specifically for the well-established UK to east

Africa service in the early 1950s to replace five older vessels and designed to carry 250 passengers in two classes, as well as 415,000 cubic feet of cargo space in five holds.

The officers were accommodated on the boat deck, one down from the bridge and above the promenade deck, which was given up entirely to public rooms, including a lounge, library, drawing room, two bars, a dance hall and a swimming pool. The ships made four round voyages a year from the Royal Docks in London, calling at the by now familiar ports of Mombasa, Tanga, Zanzibar, Dar es Salaam and usually turning round at Beira. They were designed to use the Suez Canal on both outward and return voyages. Since the *Kenya* was not due to arrive home for another two weeks, I was sent to Glasgow to undertake a radar simulator course which, as the only students were myself and a Canadian salvage expert, proved very good value. An unexpected danger attached to this course was that the only train north from London was filled with noisy and exuberant supporters of a victorious Scottish football team, who had just beaten the English world champions, and I appeared to be the only person aboard with an English accent. I went for a beer, asked in my best Scottish accent for 'two beers, pal,' to be rewarded by the steward handing over two cases!

Efforts to repair my marriage to Sue came to naught. There's a flaw in the legal system in that any solicitor has to consider his client's best interests and, since any move towards reconciliation could be interpreted as a weakness or damage their case, no real effort is made to patch things up. Sara was not fought over. We obviously agreed she would stay with Sue as my career made it impossible to provide a home for her, and we agreed that I could see her whenever I was back. A sailor's life means that you sadly

I was born in 1939 in Putney, west London, but because of the war we soon left.

We moved up north to Heswall, Cheshire.

With my younger brothers Mike, Chris and Richard, in about 1950 after we moved to Beckenham in Kent.

In my first canoe, Selsey 1953.

As a raw recruit (second right) in Plymouth, 1956, when I was lucky enough to join the battleship HMS *Vanguard*.

The MV Cadetship *Chindwara*, owned by the British India Steam Navigation Company, and my first merchant navy ship in 1957.

Cadet Knox-Johnston, 1957.

Our wedding day in January 1962. Sue and I cut the cake after we'd married in Little St Mary's Church in Cambridge.

Sailing in Bombay harbour later that year, after we moved out to India.

Sue and I (centre) with Warwick Harwood and Peter Jordan and their companions on a swimming trip in Bombay.

Suhaili, nearly planked up, but progress in building her was frustratingly slow.

Putting the finishing touches to *Suhaili*'s paintwork.

The christening ceremony on 19 December 1964 for *Suhaili*, named after a star to the north-west, which was where we were heading with her – back to London.

With my brother Chris and Heinz Fingerhut-Holland, a radio officer I knew from BI, in Kilindini harbour, as we sailed *Suhaili* back to England, having left India in December 1965.

The 950-ton MV *Congella*, the cargo ship I captained in South Africa which, unknown to me, was used to deliver oil to sanctions-hit Rhodesia.

Chris setting the jib on *Suhaili*.

Saying farewell to my parents as I prepared to set sail around the world on *Suhaili*, in June 1968. (Bill Rowntree)

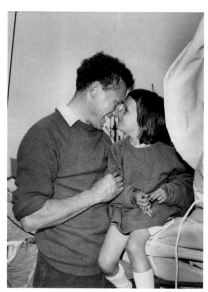

My daughter Sara was only five at the time, so she didn't really understand what was going on when I said goodbye to her in London, a few days earlier. (Bill Rowntree)

Leaving dry land for the last time in a long while, Falmouth 14 June 1968. (Bill Rowntree)

A self-portrait while sailing in the Southern Ocean during the *Sunday Times* Golden Globe Race.

I'd been sunbathing naked on deck when a plane flew overhead, hence the towel wrapped round my waist.

A makeshift water-gathering device while sailing in the Roaring Forties.

A flotilla of small craft came out to greet me as I returned to Falmouth.

22 April 1969 – first step ashore after 312 days at sea.

Suhaili had weathered everything the oceans could throw at her.

miss so much of your children growing up and the fascinating development of their characters. When I was home I saw her as often as possible and she came to stay at the Rookery, my parents' home in Downe, and where I stayed when ashore. I am not certain that all the influences there were beneficial, though. On one occasion when my ninety-year-old grandmother, the formidable Granny Cree, was staying, she was corrupted for life.

Granny Cree was an inveterate jumbler and auction attender. A village fete could not be passed if she thought there might be a jumble stall and she bought items on impulse rather than considered thought. She rarely made offerings to jumble sales, so her garage was an Aladdin's cave of rubbish. On this occasion my mother was preparing for the Downe village fete, hence Granny's visit as this was irresistible to her. Coming into the hall at the Rookery I found three bottoms in the air and three heads almost buried in a large trunk full of second-hand clothes – my grandmother, my mother and my daughter. I remonstrated with Granny immediately, 'Look here, Granny, your weakness for jumble is notorious, you corrupted your daughter years ago, but I don't see why you should corrupt mine.'

'It's too late,' she replied triumphantly, pointing to a grinning four-year-old Sara with dresses in each hand. I am afraid this disease, once it takes a hold, cannot be cured. Many years later, Sara found the end of an interesting-looking garment at a jumble sale and was tugging enthusiastically, believing she had competition from someone else, only to discover that she was trying to remove the skirt being worn by the stallholder!

I joined the *Kenya* in the Royal Albert Docks at the beginning of June 1967. Already the signs of reducing trade in London were noticeable. There were a dozen or more empty berths in the huge Royal Docks, something unthinkable ten years before. Air travel was becoming more accessible and the future of passenger transport by sea was beginning to suffer too, although we still sailed close to our full complement. The writing was on the wall, however. *Kenya* sailed until 1970 when the service came to an end after nearly 100 years and she was scrapped. The newer *Uganda* was converted to school cruising when the east African trade no longer proved economically viable. She was still going strong 12 years later when, at the age of thirty, she was hurriedly converted into a hospital ship for the Falklands War.

As first officer I was the senior watch-keeper and cargo officer, thus freeing the chief officer to handle the routine running of the ship such as the crew and maintenance. The chief officer was Alastair Methven, ex-second on the *Chindwara* when I was a cadet, so someone I knew. There was a second officer, Chris Blake, who I was to get to know later in our careers when he became one of the best-qualified square-rig sailors, and two good third officers. The chief and first officers had tables in the saloon at which we were expected to host passengers, an added duty which could be extremely pleasant. Now, as we were discharging there were no passengers and the captain and chief officer were on leave, which gave a wonderful opportunity to learn my way around. Among the tasks left for me to deal with was cleaning and cement washing two water tanks. I ordered the gangs through the office and arranged for the Chinese fitter in our crew to remove the tank tops so they could be accessed, as we did in India. In the evening as I was sitting reading in my cabin the door flew open without a knock. 'You want everyone out, Mr Mate?' said the figure of the shop steward in the entrance.

'What on earth are you talking about?' I asked.

'Your man has taken the tank lids off.'

'That's right,' I responded, 'they are down to be cleaned.'

'Removing tank lids is a boilermaker's job. I can have the ship blacked for this.'

The awful truth was that he could. I had not dealt with Britain's Neanderthal union rules, having been away for seven years on Eastern service where things were very different. It was necessary to apologise, of course, to pander to his ego. I ordered the fitter to replace the lids and then we waited six hours while a boilermaker plus a mate made their casual way to remove the lids again. None of the dozen boilermakers on duty around the ship's boilers, where they were not actually needed but just had to be there on standby as per union rules, was allowed to do this job. This meant the cleaning gangs had barely started work in the tanks when their time was up, so very little was achieved. I was sympathetically bollocked the next day. The deputy super-intendent, Barney Leeson, knew I was out of touch with the UK's working practices but I felt angry and frustrated by the plain stupidity of it all. The shipping industry needed resources for investment in the forthcoming container revolution if it was to survive and these sorts of activities wasted the money that would keep British seamen in work.

I believe that union practices like these destroyed the London docks in the Upper Thames. What shipping company would have work done on their ships in London when it could be done much faster and just as efficiently in Holland or Germany? Another factor in their demise was that containerisation was coming and it needed different facilities. The old warehouses were not suitable when cargo came in steel boxes needing clear space and different cranes. But to twist the knife even further, the London dockers went on strike, led by Jack Dash, just as the Dutch created Europort, a huge complex which had the space and created the facilities for containers. By the time the London dockers finished their strike, the business had moved abroad. Only Tilbury held out on the Thames as it managed to adapt to deal with containers.

We completed discharge and moved across the dock to the loading berth, taking on a mixed cargo of manufactured and luxury goods. One of the valuable cargoes we took aboard was spirits, gin, whisky and others. It was an expensive product and the insurance companies insisted that there was an officer watching the loading. These insurance people had no idea of the various abilities of London dockers. The pallets of boxes of spirits came aboard to be stowed in lockers which could be locked so it could not be broached. The point they missed was that the cargo was broached before we finished loading. The stevedores used to take a box, say of Gordon's Gin, and the drop it on its corner. The result was that all the bottles inside the case broke, and then the dockers could strain it through the remains of the box into their enamel mugs and enjoy the spirit. The problem we had was that if interrupted, the dockers would drop as many of the cases as they felt like and we had to explain this damage when we reached the discharge port.

The solution seemed simple, I went to the foreman of the gang and said 'one'. He looked at me and said, 'All right, Mr Mate, but we don't want to be watched.' I put the newest cadet on duty to satisfy the insurers, because he was too new to understand, and we loaded. The fact that the dockers were less than sober as they finished their shift was not my problem.

What mattered is that when we discharged in Mombasa the agents could not believe I had only one case broken instead of the usual hundreds. The foreman had been as good as his word.

Traditionally we sailed on a Thursday afternoon. The passengers came aboard that morning and settled in before we towed out into the river Thames. The voyage then began down the river through the English Channel, the Bay of Biscay and around the Iberian peninsula to the Mediterranean. On this voyage we were due to sail our normal route through the Suez Canal but were aware of rumblings in the Middle East. We had been met as we approached Port Said by Egyptian missile boats making a show, but their station-keeping was abysmal. As we made our transit through the canal, we could see the military build-up by the Egyptians. We counted more than two hundred Egyptian tanks waiting for our convoy to pass so they could cross over to the Sinai side of the canal. The Egyptian canal pilot boasted in a sickening manner of the Israeli girls he would be given after they destroyed that country. And with Iraq, Jordan and Syria all making equally warlike noises, the Israeli future looked bleak.

I had rifles in a locker for the British Army in Aden and it took time to get there. But eventually we offloaded them and sailed for Mombasa. Shortly after we left Aden war erupted in the Middle East as the Arab nations attacked Israel. Despite the odds against them, the Israelis threw back all attacks. In a remarkable campaign Israel destroyed armies on three sides and captured large slices of Arab territory, including land on the western side of the Suez Canal. People did not seem to understand that you may have the latest Russian equipment, but you have to know how to use it. Training and understanding your equipment had

proved more effective than huge quantities of sophistication –
what the Israelis had they knew how to use. While we were
interested spectators to these events, the main effect as far as
we were concerned was that our homeward journey would be
longer than anticipated. The Suez Canal was closed again for
the second time in my career, which meant we would have to
return home via the Cape of Good Hope, a much longer voyage.

During the summer of 1967 Francis Chichester completed
what was, up until then, perhaps the most remarkable yachting
voyage this century. He sailed around the world, alone, with just
one month-long rest and refit in Australia. As a feat of determination it was remarkable, made all the more so by his age. At
65 he was completing a voyage that most much younger people
would never have contemplated. We watched his arrival and
knighting at Greenwich on television in the engineers' mess.
Until now I had been readjusting to merchant navy routine
quite well, but the sight of his yacht and listening to accounts
of his voyage was thoroughly unsettling.

I had been considering entering the Observer Single-Handed
Transatlantic Race in 1968 but now I knew this would never
satisfy me. There was only one real voyage to do – a non-stop
single-handed circumnavigation and I knew I must attempt it
or spend the rest of my life regretting the obvious opportunity I
had to go for it. The idea blossomed so I asked Colin Mudie to
design me a simple boat and went to BI and asked them whether
they would support my plans, The boat was simple, a 56-foot
hull with two Dragon-size masts. I asked Proctor's for a price
for the masts, but when BI asked them they obviously thought
that a shipping company could afford a lot more and their quote

was ridiculously high. As a result BI naturally assumed I did not know what I was talking about and withdrew their support. It was a hard blow but I was not in a position to contradict it. Colin Mudie and I knew it was an absurd quote but how do you disprove it?

I was called into the BI office at One Aldgate and told the bad news. So what was I going to do now? I was determined to try to achieve what I considered to be the last great sailing challenge. If BI would not support me I would go somehow. I owned a boat which I knew and had proved herself a tough and good sea boat. She might not be fast but I thought she was tough enough to get round, although no one knew for certain what strains would be put on a boat and sailor in a voyage twice as long as anything attempted before without support. Not unreasonably, I was told that BI could not go on allowing me time off to go sailing, so if I did this I would not have a job if and when I got back. My mind was made up and I was going.

As far as I was concerned the only unknowns were how *Suhaili* might fare in the huge waves generated in the Southern Ocean and what food, equipment and spares would be advisable. Sir Francis Chichester had commented that wild horses would not drag him back into the Southern Ocean. It was not encouraging, but as someone once said, 'To do what other men have done is to live in the shadows of others.' However daunting this all sounded I was going to make the attempt. I knew that without sponsorship my limited financial reserves could not stretch to luxuries and I had to plan carefully enough to ensure I did take all the basic essentials that might be required on a non-stop voyage that I estimated could take ten months. To the inevitable loneliness I did not give a thought. There is always plenty to do on a boat at sea and that would keep me busy enough.

After two voyages on *Kenya* I received a shifting chit on arrival at Tilbury in September to join the *Chindwara* as cadet instruction officer. Since I was marking time prior to entering the Royal Navy for a spell of sea service, it was a relief appointment for a month, replacing the usual CIO while he took leave. When he duly returned in October I was sent to Genoa to relieve the chief officer on the homeward-bound *Waroonga*, one of two fast cargo ships built subsequent to the N Class.

On vessels with fewer than 100 crew members, there was no requirement to carry a properly qualified doctor, which was one of the reasons why all merchant navy deck officers had to hold a valid St John Ambulance First Aid Certificate. In the event of a serious injury we would normally radio for advice, but most of the work was of a mundane sort and, in particular, with many Indian crew taking an almost morbid interest in such matters, the usual request was for laxatives.

I faced a queue for the usual cure when I opened the surgery each morning After a while I became fed up with the constant demand for Epsom salts or a particularly evil thick dark brew known as Black Draft and decided to sort this out once and for all. One afternoon in the surgery I heated two pints of Black Draft and then added Epsom salts until the solution was so concentrated that the crystals would dissolve no more. The new, improved mixture was issued the next morning with dramatic and almost instantaneous results. Wan but contented-looking Indian seamen were to be seen hanging around within easy reach of the heads by the afternoon and my stock rose to unimagined heights. Unfortunately, the work rate fell commensurably and the new brew had to be withdrawn from the market!

The *Waroonga* was a 23 knot ship, but we normally steamed at just over 18 knots. She and her sister were employed on a P&O charter for the UK to Australia run, so after discharging in London and Rotterdam, we went via the Irish Sea to Liverpool to load. We had an inexperienced third officer on the bridge who the captain and I were keeping an eye on, and after breakfast, as I was preparing to go round the decks with the *serang*, I was called urgently to the bridge. The third had lost us. There was no land in sight in any direction and soundings (the depth of water beneath the ship) put us about the middle of Cardigan Bay.

We started to calculate the dead reckoning from the last position at 0800, but with difficulty as the third had made two course alterations and not logged them properly. We were scanning the horizon through binoculars looking for anything that might indicate where we were when an expletive came from the captain. Following the direction he was looking, I saw the cause of his concern, a seagull standing on the water! Was this a sand bar or an isolated rock? We quickly checked the soundings again, but this was all right. Carefully watching the echo sounder, we pressed on towards the bird which flew off as we approached. As we passed its position we saw that the seagull had been perched on a piece of barely floating hardboard, but it nearly gave us grey hairs.

We were due to load in two weeks but once again the unions were hell bent on self-destruction and the anticipated two weeks lengthened into four due to strike action. The whole attitude was depressing at that time. While inspecting a locker where special cargoes were stowed, I noticed a crate which was clearly

marked, 'Woomera – Scientific Instruments – This Side Up' and
it had been placed upside down. I drew the foreman's attention
to it and then jumped quickly as another crate was pushed down
from above and landed where I had been standing. Furious, I
found the stevedore and told him if that gang ever did anything
like that again I'd shut them in a locker and throw away the key.
Later the stevedore came up and said the men wanted to apologise; apparently, as I was wearing a boiler suit they did not realise
I was the mate – as if that made any difference to their attempts
at murder or mutilation. We eventually completed loading and
I signed off *Waroonga* in December, having handed her back to
her regular chief officer and joined the warship HMS *Duncan*
in Portsmouth at the beginning of 1968.

HMS *Duncan* was an anti-submarine frigate of the twelve-strong
Blackwood Class. They were tiny, just 1,180 tons, and designed
for mass production should an emergency arise and the UK have
to keep the sea lanes open to ensure supplies of food, fuel and
other necessities to allow our island nation to survive. Small
they might be, but they packed a sophisticated anti-submarine
punch with a powerful sonar for seeking out submarines by use
of sound waves linked to two three-barrelled mortars, which
could each throw a bomb containing 325 pounds of amatol
more than 600 yards. The rest of the armament was puny, two
Bofors guns and rifles somewhere I was told. With a total complement of just 140, there were only eight officers, augmented
by up to four midshipmen. I was immediately put on watch
with the navigator to learn the navy routines and to find my
way around the ship. The navigator, John Leach, was a delightful companion. An excellent navigator, his explanations of the

navy's procedures were clear and informative so that within two weeks the captain put me on watch alone and in two more gave me a Naval Watch-keeping Certificate

I soon began to feel a proper member of *Duncan*'s crew. In part this was due to a very pleasant group in the wardroom, but also because of the captain's attitude. Lieutenant Commander Peter Pinkster was in his mid-thirties and awaiting promotion. He knew the job, expected perfect results and could be quick but amusing in his reactions when things were not working properly. A long-winded technical explanation as to why we had lost contact with a submarine led to, 'Ted, results, not facts', a useful expression which I committed to memory for future reference. After I had been on board for three weeks, he appointed me his communications officer, responsible for a division of twelve under a petty officer who handled all the signal traffic and the electronic warfare equipment. It was perhaps fortunate that Petty Officer Downey was good at his job because I was not much help, except as a buffer between the captain and the department.

On my first day in the new job I came off watch at noon, had lunch and turned in for the afternoon as I was due on watch again at 2000 hours. In the halfway house between sleep and wakefulness I vaguely heard a pipe for someone, but this happened constantly. The third time it was repeated I woke up, it was for the comms 'O' to go to the ops room. I suddenly realised that this was me. Hastily putting on clothes, I rushed up top and reported to the captain.

'Why can't I get a message through to the Admiralty in London?' he asked. I hadn't a clue but I looked him in the eye and said, 'Ducting, Sir.' We looked at each other, I could see he was puzzled, but I maintained a confident front so he just said, 'Well, fix it.' I went back to the wireless office to find the PO and the killick, a leading seaman, his number two, waiting apprehensively.

'What's the problem, Sir?' was their question and I explained. 'Which radio station are you trying?' I asked, to be told Portishead, not very far away. 'Well, try Halifax as the radio wave is bouncing over Portishead,' I told the PO, referring to an alternative Canadian radio station. We got through almost immediately, which improved my standing enormously as they were now unsure as to how much or little I didn't know. 'But what is ducting?' asked the PO. 'I haven't got time to explain it at this moment,' I told him.

In the middle of my time aboard George Greenfield, my literary agent, with whom I had shared my plans to sail around the world non-stop alone, contacted me and asked me to go to a meeting with the *Sunday Mirror* in London. He had handled Chichester's book and contacted the *Sunday Times* about sponsoring me. They had not responded so he asked the *Sunday Mirror*, who showed immediate interest. George put a sensible deal to them, so much in advance and the rest to be paid in instalments as I passed obvious landmarks like the Cape of Good Hope, Australia, the Horn and return home. It seemed a good deal to the *Sunday Mirror*, as the initial cost was not high and they would not mind paying more if the voyage proceeded and became a better story. They signed up and George did similar deals with the publisher Cassell, and in the USA with *True* magazine and Morrow, which gave me enough money to pay for my preparations and buy the food and stores I needed. My other efforts to gain sponsorship only achieved a £5 voucher from Cadbury's and a more useful 120 cans of lager from Tennent's. Requests for a camera from the BBC and ITV were refused. Confident that I now had the resources, I got down to serious planning.

Most of *Duncan*'s time was spent in the company of the seven other frigates exercising with submarines. We made up the Londonderry Squadron, one of a number in those days when the navy had more than 70 destroyers and frigates. We communicated with submarines by a rudimentary underwater telephone, which sounded as if the person speaking the other end was gargling, so we normally used hand grenades to signal a submarine when it was safe to surface or that we were starting a new exercise. We kept a few in a box on the bridge and the first time I used one I carefully removed the pin, held the handle in until it was over the ship's side and then let go. Seven seconds later there was a muffled bang from near the stern. Fifteen seconds later the sub lieutenant erupted onto the bridge to ask what was happening. He had been in the ship's office when the grenade went off the other side of the hull about two feet from him! I threw them well away from the ship after that!

The captain kept on to me to spend a week with the Royal Air Force, flying in a Shackleton Maritime Reconnaissance aircraft out of Northern Ireland to acquire knowledge of another aspect of submarine hunting, but I was reluctant. I was enjoying myself on *Duncan*, getting into the job, and did not relish an interruption. Every day, it seemed, I felt more confident and hopefully was a better officer as a result. He persevered and I continued to object. Then he produced his master stroke: 'Well, if you won't go up in an aircraft, you'll have to go to a submarine and see what it's like from their perspective.'

This sounded really interesting, so I agreed and reported aboard HMS *Oracle* at Faslane one Sunday evening shortly afterwards. She was quite new and a conventional submarine, which meant her propulsion was diesel electric, not nuclear – we only had two of the latter at that time. The accommodation was incredibly cramped, everyone lived and slept surrounded by vital machinery of some sort or other, and the wardroom was tiny, six officers lived in a space eight feet by ten. The next day we went to sea in thick fog. I was allowed on the bridge while the captain took the opportunity of the perfect conditions in which to practise blind pilotage!

Once out into the Firth of Clyde the klaxons sounded, the diesels stopped and the electric motors were engaged. Drawing power from the vast bank of batteries that filled much of the boat beneath the living and working space, we dived. Those in the conning tower climbed down the ladder into the control room as the boat submerged. It was eerily quiet in the control room and there was no sensation at all. The long cigar tube tilted very slightly and the only indication we were diving was the movement of the needle on the depth gauge. Lieutenant Commander John Coward wasted no opportunity to practise his craft and mock attacks were made on anything afloat which came near.

I watched from a corner of the control room, eyes quickly accustomed to the red lights, totally fascinated, as a well-trained team went through its paces. The submariners have always prided themselves on being the real professionals in the navy and everyone in the crew, officers and men, must be able to locate any valve in the boat (always called a boat never a ship). The fact that even at 100 feet, the pressure of water on the hull is over

6,000 pounds per square foot (even the tiniest leak would send water into the tube like a powerful hose) does concentrate the mind. Apart from the captain and myself, all the other officers were Australian and the captain took a delight in calculating attack angles in his head while the others did it with a computer. He was much faster and usually right, which explains why he ended up as an admiral.

We snorked that afternoon. This was a system whereby we remained underwater with just a tube sticking out above the surface through which air was sucked to allow the diesel engines to charge the batteries. The only problem was that if a wave covered the open end of the tube a valve closed immediately to keep the sea out and air was sucked from inside the submarine instead. This lowered the pressure which would suddenly rise again the moment the tube was uncovered and caused everyone's ears to pop. There was no sensation of day or night in the tube, but when it was night outside, if we were not exercising we usually dived to a safe depth and lurked around at slow speed on the electric motors listening to various vessels passing nearby or overhead on our hydrophones. Although we had sonar, which sends out a sound wave and waits for it to return if it strikes another vessel, submarines prefer to listen and not give their position away.

The week went all too quickly, the highlight being when *Duncan* fired its anti-submarine mortars at a safe range. I watched the exercise through the search periscope. It was possible to hear the sound of the thud of the mortars firing through the water and see the bombs climb into the sky before tumbling down not far away. Not far enough away as far as I was concerned, as the whole boat shook to a succession of enormous crashes putting out the lights and showering everyone with small pieces of cork insulation from the inside of the hull. I had seen this on numerous war films but here it was for real. Later it was explained to me that these explosions had occurred at ten times the submarine killing range and I began to reconsider my earlier enthusiasm to transfer to submarines. It had been a fascinating experience to see what the 'enemy' got up to, how he manoeuvred to mislead our sonar and get within torpedo range, and they gained my profound respect, but I was not sorry to rejoin the surface fleet.

We spent the whole time training in one way or another and a great deal of an officer's life was spent ensuring that the men in his division were progressing their careers, doing necessary courses on time, taking exams and coming up for promotion when due. This was new to me as this did not happen with merchant navy ratings who, like the officers, were responsible for their own advancement. Training the midshipmen was very similar to training cadets though, except all the midshipmen attended the merchant navy equivalent of pre-sea school at Dartmouth.

There was a good and a bad side to this. On the one hand they acquired theoretical knowledge, but at the same time Dartmouth appeared to fill some of their heads with fanciful ideas as to their status. One of ours was on watch with me on a particularly unpleasant day in the Firth of Clyde when it was blowing a gale and the lookouts on the bridge wings were frequently covered by spray. We picked up an echo on the radar and I mentioned conversationally to the middy that it would be informative to discover how long it was before the lookouts saw the target so we could tell what his range of visibility was. I went back to check the target's progress on the radar and was vaguely aware of the outside door opening, some shouting and, as I returned, the middy slammed the door. I asked him what he was doing and he told me he had been giving the lookout a rocket for not seeing the target earlier as it was now just visible as a fishing boat.

'Ever been a lookout in these conditions?' I asked him. He replied in the negative, as he did to my query as to whether he had foul-weather gear on the bridge. I told him to fetch his foul-weather clothing and, when he returned, to put it on. Then I told him to relieve the lookout he had bollocked. He just stared at me. 'I don't have to . . .' he started, but I interrupted, emphasising the two bands on my arm. 'Go and relieve the lookout,' I told him, not in the mood for argument. A puzzled lookout reported that he had been relieved by the middy so I sent him away for 20 minutes to have a cup of kye, a heavy chocolate drink that is very warming. As the lookout disappeared, the captain appeared from the screened–off chart table behind me. 'How long are you going to leave the middy out there, Robin?' he said. I told him it would be about 20 minutes. 'Right ho,' he responded. 'I'll be in my cabin if you need me.' This was exactly how I would have treated a merchant navy cadet, although in the merchant navy a spell as lookout was a normal part of the training.

Characters emerge when you cram sharp, fit young men into a small and frequently isolated metal box, and the navy was an all-male environment in those days. Our ship's butcher was Able Seaman Booth. He was a good advertisement for his catering profession, being large with a rubicund face. We met from time to time when doing the rum ration, measuring out the tots into copper jugs mess by mess and mixing all but the chief petty officer's ration with two parts water to ensure it would not keep and could not be stored.

One grey day in February in the Firth of Clyde we were part of an exercise group of eight frigates providing a screen for a fleet tanker and trying to pin down one of the two submarines that were attempting to get into a firing position. The night before we had been invited aboard the submarine, *Rorqual*, and her captain had accused us of being unaggressive. Our captain was livid at the slur and when we returned to *Duncan* ordered us to go flat out at any periscope sighted the next day. As luck would have it I had the 8 to 12 watch, known as the 'forenoon' in the navy, and we were on the western side of the screen. Off Lamlash I saw a periscope, grabbed the intercom and ordered, 'Periscope. Green 50. Hard a starboard. Full Ahead, tally-ho.'

Unfortunately, I picked the wrong intercom, so the whole ship heard the call. It was also unfortunate that no one had informed me that 'Full Ahead' was an emergency order in the Royal Navy. *Duncan* heeled over under the full rudder and accelerated. I was oblivious to the heel as my whole attention was on the attack periscope, making sure we steadied and steering straight at it as it came ahead. Then the submarine's search periscope popped up, indicating that someone down below wanted to check what was happening, then both disappeared and swirls appeared where they had been. We thundered through these swirls at 25 knots and then I swung the ship back onto course. The intercom went: 'Bridge – captain.'

'Bridge, Sir,' I answered. Just one word came back, a very satisfied 'Yes.' Later we learned that we probably missed knocking our sonar dome off our hull, which extended beneath our keel, by perhaps three feet. Well, they should have dived more quickly. We were training for war after all and how dare they say we weren't aggressive!

I had just settled the ship back onto the zig-zag course again when Booth's face appeared at the top of the vertical metal ladder which lead to the bridge. He was one of those who, if deprived of the reproductive adjective, would have instantly become a strong silent type. 'Excuse me, Sir, but what the f***ing hell is going on?'

'Ah, morning, Booth,' I responded. 'What's the matter?'

'Morning, Sir,' he said. 'I was down in the f***ing freezer getting the f***ing meat for lunch when the f***ing ship suddenly went over on her f***ing side and the f***ing meat knocked me flat, Sir. Can't you give any warning?'

'Sorry about that, Booth,' I replied, 'but we are training for war and we have to go for the periscopes when we see them,' I told him.

'Oh, well, Sir, f*** the f***ing war, if you can't give any f***ing warning, have you got a spare pair of f***ing binoculars, as I might as well f***ing help you?'

I was convulsed inside but this was not the moment to add insult to his feeling of injury. I waited for him to calm down and then said that as we were coming out of the run he had about 20 minutes before we started a new serial so he would be quite safe for the time being. With honour satisfied, he returned to the freezer and the sailors got their lunch.

Booth had a strong personality, but it did not stop him feeling that his reputation needed a regular polish. We had been carrying out live firings with the anti-submarine mortars and were hanging around waiting for the stunned and dead fish to surface. Navy ships have an allowance of so much money per man per day and we could buy what we liked within that allowance, normally at special rates from naval stores. Thus, fresh fish caught with the mortars was a bonus on two counts. It gave us a very tasty meal and we also saved money on the catering account.

After we had fired the anti-submarine mortars both the ship's boats were manned and lowered and the remainder of the crew were ranged along the deck with grapnels, buckets, anything in fact, which might haul up a fish. Attention became focused on a very large cod floating slowly past which no one seemed able to catch. As it came level with the stern there was a big splash and the cry of 'Man overboard!' I ordered the engines to be stopped and put the helm hard over to swing the stern away from the casualty who, in the meantime, grabbed the cod and was swimming back to the ship.

The captain appeared at my shoulder, took a look and said he would be in his cabin if required. What he was really saying was that he was leaving me to deal with the matter of the offence of jumping overside without permission. Willing hands hauled the sailor back on board. I could not identify the culprit initially because the fish was tucked into his shirt head first and the tail was in the way of his face, but I recognised the figure. Picking up the tannoy, I called, 'Able Seaman Booth, bridge, at the double.' Booth appeared a minute or so later, face wreathed in smiles, the hero of the moment. The smile had to go, so I laid into him verbally until he looked worried at the potential of the charges and then I dismissed him. Discipline was unthreatened.

The captain of a ship has considerable powers, similar to those of a magistrate ashore, but in the navy these are backed by the necessity to maintain military as well as civil discipline.

Personally I hated putting someone on a charge, not because it wasn't necessary from time to time, but because I always stumbled over the wording of the charges. The ultimate sanction was cells, which only the captain could order, and this meant handing over one of the crew to the Regulating Branch, the navy's police, who, if they were convicted, escorted the culprit to the detention quarters at Portsmouth to serve the sentence.

As duty officer I had to read out a charge on one occasion. It was usually done on deck in front of the duty watch and always included some of the articles of war, most of which ended with '... and such punishment is death.' It was a winter afternoon and we lay alongside the jetty at Faslane with the brooding hills hiding the sun to the west. I read the articles and our seaman was led away and conducted to the detention quarters. It impressed me then, but what was far more impressive was our sailor when he returned four weeks later. His eyes were bright, he stood erect and his upper body had expanded noticeably. I don't know what they did to him, but he looked incredibly fit. The tragedy was that he had matrimonial problems but had not told us about it, so he tried to sort it himself instead of asking for help – which would have been willingly given.

I finished my time aboard *Duncan* at the end of April in order to prepare *Suhaili* for what had now become the *Sunday Times* Golden Globe Race around the world. The paper had turned me down after one of their reporters had come to visit me in Surrey commercial docks where I was working on preparations during a free weekend. He asked whether I was going to beat Chichester. Having no idea of PR, I answered truthfully that I did not know. That answer, he decided, indicated a lack of determination and he went back to the paper and advised they should back a fellow Australian, 'Tahiti' Bill Howell, a well-known single-hander. The *Sunday Times*, having learned of three other people preparing for the same challenge decided, probably rightly for them, that they did not want to support an individual but would organise a race instead. As the newspaper knew my plans, I was incorporated into their race without being asked.

Duncan was refitting in Portsmouth and I brought *Suhaili* down from London and put her on Alec Rose's mooring at Whale Island, as he was away at the time making his solo circumnavigation, which he completed successfully with two stops. There was still much to do so I asked for volunteers in daily orders to give a hand and received responses from four of the crew. There was only one problem: three of them had been deprived of shore leave for various misdemeanours. However, Mark Kemmis-Betty, the first lieutenant, let them go but made me responsible for their behaviour. They were a great bunch and we used to drive round in my Mini, borrow a dinghy, row out to the mooring, work for three hours, go to a pub for a drink and return by 2200 hours.

One day when I was officer of the day they asked if they could go without me. I willingly agreed and only later realised they would not have the dinghy. I need not have worried – they 'borrowed' someone else's! Sadly one of my volunteers was about to be dismissed from the service because he was constantly in trouble, but he was as good as gold when working on *Suhaili*. His problem was a low threshold of boredom, something I could sympathise with, but he was excellent when kept busy and the navy lost a potentially very good hand as a result.

While I was aboard our captain reached the end of his time with the ship. We were still in dry dock in Portsmouth so we could not row him ashore in the traditional manner. So the first lieutenant was desperately keen to find a special way for the captain to depart the ship and came up with a novel plan. He decided the only way to be different was by sending the captain ashore in a dockyard rubbish bucket, suitably cleaned, painted and decorated with bunting. For two days a small team worked to prepare the bucket and a crane driver was organised to lift the bucket off from the bridge and deposit it ashore.

Mark Kemmis-Betty went around with a pleased, self-satisfied smile on his face as the appointed time approached and it was all too irresistible. I went ashore and parted with £2. The bosun's pipes wailed, the officers stood to attention saluting as the bucket slowly rose from the deck carrying the captain in his civvies. It swung slowly away from the ship towards the side of the dock and then, halfway across, stopped. Everyone looked at Mark. Was this part of the master plan? He looked nonplussed, so everyone turned to the crane driver, who shrugged his shoulders and said it must be a power cut. 'I suppose you turds organised this,' the captain yelled from his lofty, if precarious position. I don't like lying, so I just nodded my head behind my salute. It was well worth the £2.

The navy had been a very enjoyable experience and being on List 1 of the Royal Naval Reserves provided the best of both worlds. The navy was a wonderful hobby for me and although it could not affect a merchant navy officer's career it had been fascinating to learn how another branch of the maritime world operated and know that if my country became involved in a war I would be on something that could fight back. But now I was off to make a voyage of a very different character.

8

ROUND THE WORLD

It was the beginning of May 1968 and having left HMS *Duncan* I was now unemployed. My plan was to sail, if I was ready, by 1 June, so my entire focus was on preparing *Suhaili* for a voyage that no yacht had ever tried. The *Sunday Times* had told me that they planned to start the race at the end of October, but that was not good for me. *Suhaili*'s speed, which I now knew was roughly four knots on an oceanic voyage – averaging out the zones where we could make good speed with those where the wind was light or non-existent like the doldrums, meant that in order to round Cape Horn in its midsummer I had to sail much earlier. I had to be practical if I wanted to survive and that meant avoiding the worst of the weather that the Southern Ocean could throw at a boat. If I waited until the *Sunday Times* date, I would be approaching the Horn in autumn or early winter in the southern hemisphere, when the frequency of gales made it a decidedly dangerous prospect.

Apparently I was not alone in seeing it this way. Both John Ridgway and Chay Blyth, who as serving paratroopers had rowed the Atlantic the previous year, had found support and were included in the newspaper's plans. They had small boats

162

like mine and they made it clear they intended to sail in June as well. Faced with three of their advertised entrants departing before their chosen date, the newspaper changed the rules. They now announced that an entrant could start at any time between 1 June and 31 October from any British Islands port and there would be two prizes to allow for the different departure times. The Golden Globe trophy would go to the first to complete the voyage and £5,000 (about £80,000 today) would go the person who made the fastest voyage, assuming that more than one finished.

I was now working flat out preparing for the voyage. I moved *Suhaili* to Portsmouth when I went into the navy. As a result, I lost my local volunteers so was doing everything myself, except when with the navy's help I took *Suhaili* over to Souter's Yard in Cowes for a haul out and to fit the shoe for the self-steering gear that was going to be essential. Once I left *Duncan* I took *Suhaili* back to London to the Surrey commercial docks, which was only handling a few timber vessels by this time so there was plenty of space for a small yacht.

Creating a suitable self-steering system presented some problems. Although Lt. Col. Blondie Hasler, of *Cockleshell Heroes* fame, had developed a wind–actuated self-steering system, it could not work on *Suhaili* as her mizzen boom prevented the fitting of a wind vane at the stern. But I had some luck with this. Through Ken Parker, editorial director at Cassell, who had now become an enthusiastic supporter of the project, I was introduced to Wing Commander Alan Merriman RAF, who came up with an alternative idea. Instead of a single wind vane at the stern we would fit two vanes, one on each side, and he worked out a simple system that enabled me to clutch in the windward vane which could then connect to a tiller at the stern. It was its simplicity that attracted me. But the steering rudder needed something to hold its foot, hence the need for a shoe extending from the keel.

While working on the boat on the slipway at Souter's Yard in Cowes one weekend, I was approached by a gentleman in a blazer and some yacht club tie who asked if I was the person planning to sail solo non-stop around the world. I admitted it. He then told me that the voyage could not be done and in any case I would not be able to do it! I looked at him. Had he ever faced me in a boxing ring he might have thought differently about saying that. Instead, I said that I hoped he had never been a school teacher. He appeared affronted and asked why. I responded that he would have been the sort of teacher to discourage his pupils, and to clear off – or words to that effect. I never saw him again. The world is full of that type: they don't have the guts to do anything themselves and so they sneer at people taking risks because the doers in life make them feel even more inadequate. A poem by Shel Silverstein, entitled 'The Mustn'ts' summarises this rather well.

One of my concerns was how to deal with a dismasting. With poor communications, and even those would be lost if the mast broke as the aerial was the backstay, there would be no means of calling for assistance and I would just have to work out how to set sail on something or other to get to land. Once the contracts were signed and I had the money, I ordered a new aluminium mizzen mast to replace the heavy Kashmir pine one built in India. I heaved it about a bit before stepping it and although it was quite heavy I thought I could manhandle it if necessary to replace the mainmast in an emergency. If I lost both masts, well then I would have to sort something out with the two small spinnaker poles.

Research into what I could expect in the 'Watery Himalayas' of the Southern Ocean was hard to come by. There was very little recent information about sailing in that area, normally avoided by small yachts. Miles and Beryl Smeeton, with John Guzzwell, had been pitchpoled in their 46-foot-long ketch *Tzu Hang*, the boat's stern being lifted up and thrown over the bow, which sounded terrifying. Chichester's book had only just come out and he had described the Southern Ocean waves as not being measured in feet and yards but in levels of fear, which was not encouraging. There are two types of wave: the swell which is left over from previous strong winds, and the sea waves that are created by the current wind. They usually have different wave lengths, but when their peaks coincide they are certainly huge, rising up to as much as 30 metres in storms.

There was no agreement on what would prove the ideal boat for the voyage, nor what was the best rig. The variety of types of boats and rigs starting what had become The *Sunday Times* Golden Globe Race showed this uncertainty. Ridgway, Loïck Fougeron, Bernard Moitessier and I had fairly typical cruising yachts. Chay Blyth had a bilge keeler. Bill King had an interesting-looking boat with a junk rig, built especially. Alex Carozzo had the largest boat at 60 feet and therefore was expected to be the fastest. Crowhurst and Tetley sailed in trimarans, considered by many to be totally unsuited to the expected conditions. I had what I had. She was not fast but she was strong and seaworthy and I would just have to work out how best to help her through the roaring forties when I got there. Of the nine of us who started, Moitessier and I had the most experience of our boats and he knew his boat could get through the Southern Ocean. It was larger than *Suhaili* but only by six feet, which gave me confidence.

I eventually got *Suhaili* as ready as I could. All the food, tinned in those days before freeze-dried food, had been coded with white paint, their labels removed and then given a coat of varnish. Paper labels soon fall off and can block a bilge pump. I also wanted to be able to select what I wanted not guess what was inside a tin, hence the coding. Tins rust quickly in a salty environment and the varnish provided some protection. Eggs had been coated in grease to slow down their deterioration and fresh food, onions, potatoes and the like, were stowed aboard.

I hoped I had thought of everything I might need to keep the boat going in the event of damage and to keep her properly maintained during a voyage that might be as long as 300 days, far longer than anything tried before at that point. My merchant navy time and the voyage back from India had given me more experience than most in what might be required but to be safe I took aboard enough supplies for an extra 30 days. Thus prepared, I sailed down to Falmouth with Ken Parker and my *Sunday Mirror* team of Bruce Maxwell and photographer Bill Rowntree. I chose Falmouth because it was in the far west of the country and therefore when I sailed I would be avoiding most of the heavy shipping traffic in the English Channel.

One of the last jobs before I sailed was to apply a final coat of antifouling paint to the hull to prevent weeds growing and slowing the boat down. I put *Suhaili* alongside in Mylor and worked away. While I was waiting for the tide to come back in, a crowd of spectators arrived on the quay, accompanied by what I can only call an

'Expert'. He was dressed for the part – yachting cap, submariner's sweater, reefer jacket, sailing trousers and boots. He looked down from the quay and asked where I was going. I answered that I was heading for Australia. 'What, in this?' he asked. Now any sailor will understand that you might insult a man's wife and get away with it, but never insult his boat. Somewhat crossly I answered yes. 'Who is going with you?' was his next question. I told him no one. 'What are you going to do at nights then?' he asked, and I told him that I had this self-steering system. 'Does it work?' he asked. I answered honestly that I had not tried it out yet. His audience were now looking down on me with a mixture of pity and contempt. Before he walked away he had some last words of wisdom to demonstrate that I was obviously taking on far more than I was capable of achieving: 'It won't work and you be careful around Land's End.'

By 14 June I was ready to go at last. Apart from Bruce, Ken and Bill, my parents had come down with my brother Michael to see me away. I had said goodbye to Sara some weeks before in London, but at the age of five I don't think she appreciated what I was about to take on, and it was best she didn't. The drawn look on my mother's face was hard for me. There had been so much written about the dangers that she was worried she might not see me again. Dad was probably as worried, but he hid it. He knew I was determined to sail and would back me all the way as usual. At the time I had another worry as well, which I kept to myself. I realised that the jaundice I had contracted in South Africa had returned. All the yellow signs were there, but if I reported it I would be hospitalised. There was no time for that if I was to sail on time.

*

The race has already been fully covered in a number of books, including mine, *A World of my Own*. Suffice to say, in those pre-satellite days, communications were far from easy. We used single-sideband radios with limited power and there was no weather information, no Global Positioning System so navigation was by use of a sextant and having accurate time. There were no means of tracking a boat, so once we sailed no one really knew where we were until if and when we reported in. It also meant that if we got into difficulties there was no one we could contact for assistance; we were on our own and dependent upon our own efforts.

After my departure I sailed easily, trying to allow my body to get over the jaundice, so my progress was slow. This was misinterpreted to mean that I was nervous or my boat was very slow. In fact, apart from feeling tired easily, I was perfectly happy. The worry about feeling lonely did not materialise. Each Thursday I contacted Baldock where the long-range radio station was based for my radio link with Bruce Maxwell. One of my first questions was to find out where had the razor blades been stored. I got my answer the next week: they were in Ken Parker's bathroom. He had forgotten to put them on-board so I was fated to grow a beard. For added interest, Bruce and I started to play chess each week when we contacted each other. Whoever's turn it was sent across their next move. This was quite interesting until Bruce was sent to cover the rising in Prague against communism and it was his turn to move. He went to the British Embassy and asked them to send his move and they flatly refused. They told him that the Russians would never believe it was a chess move and would think it was some new code!

Suhaili soon indicated that she was not going to make life easy by developing a leak that allowed 200 gallons of water a day into the hull. The leak was along the garboard strake again, the same problem I had experienced two years before in the Indian Ocean, and I knew that there was no way it would be safe to enter the Southern Ocean if it was not fixed. Pulling into port to haul-out was not an option as that would have meant disqualification, so the problem would have to be resolved at sea. There was only one way to do it and that was to dive and try and caulk the seam. But that might only open the seam more.

Searching around inside the boat I found a long sheet of copper, left over from installing the earth plate for the radio. I cut it into two-inch-wide strips and then put holes along the top and bottom an inch apart. I made up a slightly narrower length of canvas with caulking cotton sewn into its middle. Then I awaited a calm day in the doldrums. Putting a box of copper tacks on the deck and hanging a hammer by a line, I went overside with the canvas and tacked it over the seam. Once that was in place, I took the copper strip down and tacked it over the canvas. The job took all day as I could only get one tack hammered in before coming up for air. I was delayed by an hour when disturbed by a shark that swam around and would not go away. Not wishing to suffer a sudden attack, I climbed on deck, got out my rifle, threw some lavatory paper into the sea and waited. Sure enough the shark came up to investigate the paper and as its head broke the surface I shot it. I waited half an hour to make sure none of its friends appeared and then went nervously back into the water to work. The next day I repeated the job on the other side. The results were satisfactory and the water coming in dropped to 20 gallons a day, which was manageable.

Once across the equator and into the south-east trade winds, I made the mistake of turning south-east too early, which ran me into headwinds and lost time but eventually, on 6 September, I crossed the latitude of 40 degrees south into the roaring forties of the Southern Ocean. It is a cold, merciless, miserable place ravaged by a frequent succession of low pressure systems that bring gales and storms, building up some of the largest waves on the planet, frequently exceeding 30 metres. In itself a wave is not particularly dangerous. It slopes up from its trough to its peak. But when the wave begins to break and the peak becomes vertical a small boat can be in a perilous situation. The wave can, and probably will, break over the boat, or rush it forwards down its slope so the steering ceases to be effective and the boat will yaw sideways to the pushing wave and then be rolled. This would almost certainly remove the masts. These were the conditions I had to survive for the next five months.

During the first ten days south of the 40th parallel of latitude, we were hit by six gales. *Suhaili* held up well and the self-steering, after the first rudder broke and I had to dive in to fit the spare, was working, so I was getting rest when I could and was asleep when a cross wave came in and threw *Suhaili* onto her side. Everything stowed the other side of the boat fell onto me as we went right over – jam, oatmeal, curry powder, flour, the mess was indescribable. I could tidy that up later though, but what was the state on deck? In the dark I found my torch and went up top convinced the masts must have gone and heaved a sigh of relief when I saw they were still standing.

It was some time before I realised that there was some other serious damage, such as the port steering vane which had been pushed over so hard it had been cut by the mizzen shroud.

Until I fixed it, I would have to stay on the starboard tack or hand steer. There was nothing I could do to rig the spare in those winds so I went below, made a mug of coffee, and started tidying up the mess. I soon became aware of another problem as water dripped into the cabin. It was coming from around the join of the cabin with the deck so the cabin top must have been shifted by the force of the wave and was allowing water in. I spent another day putting additional bolts in the covering board, which held the cabin top to the deck, as without the cabin *Suhaili* would be an open boat and I did not like to think of trying to sail her onward when a single wave could have swamped her and sent us to the bottom. It did not stop the ingress of water but I felt safer. That dripping water eventually got into the radio and shorted out the transmitter.

Only later, when I went to make another mug of coffee, did I appreciate that something had happened to the water tanks, as the water coming out of the galley tap was brown and filthy. Taking up the sole in the cabin I checked the tanks and discovered that one of the connecting pipes had broken free and all my fresh water was contaminated by the water in the bilges. I had a spare five-gallon container, which would last a few days, but now I had to find a way to collect fresh water or head for the nearest port. The obvious source was rain. From then on, for the next eight months, whenever it was raining I topped up the main boom, which had a channel cut in its top, so that the rainwater running down the sail would fall into this channel, would run forwards and could be collected at the gooseneck in a bucket.

It would be dishonest to say that I did not wonder whether *Suhaili* would be able to survive the next five months in the

Southern Ocean if what had happened in the first couple of weeks was a sample of what could be expected. But the damage so far was repaired, the boat was still seaworthy, I had plenty of food and I was gathering water, so there was no reason to pull out. Before I lost the radio, I had learned that I was in the lead and that Ridgway and Blyth had withdrawn. No one else was near so there seemed everything to go for and I reflected that if this voyage was easy someone else would have completed it by now. Plus, if I did decide to pull out because I was having a bad day, I would be throwing away the effort I had made all those days so far to get where I was.

It was during a later storm, a really nasty one with the sea white with spindrift so that if you looked to windward the spray blinded you for almost a minute, that I eventually worked out how to get *Suhaili* to lie comfortably and safely to the waves. Up until then I had just taken down the sails and left her to wallow in the big seas, as I had done off the Azores the previous year, but on this occasion with a cross sea, which means waves coming from different directions, she yawed a lot and waves were hitting her so hard from the side it sounded as if someone was swinging an anvil against the hull. She could not take that sort of punishment for long, so I decided to try the old lifeboat method of streaming the sea anchor.

Then I thought of the 720-foot coil of two-inch polypropylene I had bought with my last funds before sailing. I took it on deck, made one end fast to the king post in the bow and then led the other end around the stern and back to the king post before paying out all the 650 feet of slack. With this drag *Suhaili*'s stern swung round immediately into the waves and with the little storm jib set it held her that way. It worked brilliantly and from then on whenever the storms became bad that was my tactic. Thereafter, having streamed this warp as a bight there was little more I could do until the wind eased so I used to go below and get a good sleep, relying on the changing motion of the boat to awaken me so I could go on deck, put up more sail and then slowly haul in the warp to keep pressing on eastwards.

It was seven weeks before I reached the Melbourne pilot vessel on 7 November and asked them to report me as safe and going on despite the fact that the self-steering had now been broken beyond repair and I would have to sail the rest of the voyage, halfway round the world, by steering myself or balancing the sails if I was to finish successfully. It was while chatting to a seaman aboard the pilot vessel that I rediscovered the local waters rule. He questioned where I was heading and I told him towards New Zealand. 'What, across the Tasman Sea?' he asked, then added, 'You be careful crossing the Tasman as it's very dangerous.' He was not in the least impressed by the fact that I had sailed solo all the way from Britain – his local waters were the ones to watch.

Off New Zealand I ran into another real storm and was swept past Bluff at the bottom of the South Island through Foveaux Strait. Listening on the radio receiver I realised there were aircraft out looking for me in the appalling weather conditions so I headed up for Dunedin, the next port to leeward, just to report that all was well. By the time I got near Dunedin I was very tired after 72 hours on the go, not daring to fall asleep with land so close, and in getting into the entrance of the harbour I went aground and there I was stuck until the tide rose and I could sail away.

In the meantime, Bruce Maxwell had learned where I was

and came out in a fishing boat to see me. He had some mail for me but told me the rules had changed so he had to open my letters and read out the contents as, under these new rules, passing them over would have counted as outside assistance! Learning that I had grounded briefly the *Sunday Times* phoned Cliff Pearson at the *Sunday Mirror* and said they were going to disqualify me for using my anchor. Cliff pointed out that they had allowed Carozzo to remain moored at Cowes on a buoy for two weeks after the official start date and while their 400,000 readers might understand their actions, the *Mirror*'s four million wouldn't. That's the last we heard of disqualification and also the last anyone heard of me for four and a half months.

I pressed on into the southern Pacific. Bruce had brought me up-to-date with everyone's progress. I was in the lead and my nearest competitor was Moitessier, who was more than four weeks behind me. Halfway around the world he had closed the gap by nearly a month after a fast run down the Atlantic, but he had slowed in the Southern Ocean. After a slow start in the Atlantic, I was now sailing faster so there was everything to go for. I tuned in the radio receiver daily to try and get news and a time signal to check my chronometer and in December I picked up a radio station which told me about Apollo 8 going around the moon. Now that really was doing something for human progress. For the first time we had left our planet and voyaged to our nearest satellite, an amazing achievement. Compared with that my voyage was nothing and I was out just enjoying myself – part of the time, anyway.

In one very bad storm I looked astern and saw a huge wave, at least 30 metres high, stretching from horizon to horizon and racing towards me. There was no time to go below and I knew if I stayed on the deck I would be washed away. Even Alastair Maclean's heroes could not have withstood the force of one of those waves sweeping across the deck. I climbed quickly up the rigging and the wave broke over us, hiding the whole boat, so there was me and two masts and no land in sight for 1,500 miles in any direction. *Suhaili*, hidden for what seemed like eternity, shook herself and popped back up after the wave had passed, but the main hatch had been knocked open by the force of the wave and a couple of tons of water poured below. The next three hours were spent busy with a bucket bailing the water out!

We sailed passed Cape Horn on 17 January 1969. Of course I would have liked to have told people I was at the great Cape, and have someone take the classic photo, but with no radio that was not a possibility and in any case I went round in a calm. I did try calling the lighthouse with my signalling lamp but got no reply. Only after I got home did I learn that Moitessier rounded on 5 February, so I was 19 days ahead at that point Could he have caught me? It's the question everyone asks. It might have been close but he had slowed, taking 108 days between the Cape of Good Hope and Cape Horn whereas I took 130, so on that basis I would have won by a few days. But it is meaningless to speculate as we cannot tell what different weather we might have had.

I made a fast run once I got around Cape Horn and was into the south-east trade winds about the time Moitessier passed the Horn, reaching the equator on 7 March. At the time I was suffering from what I thought was acute indigestion, but it lasted three days and was extremely painful, leaving me doubled up for a couple of days. I looked up my symptoms and was frightened to discover it looked like appendicitis. During this time a ship passed close by, the first I had seen for ages, so I called it with the Aldis lamp, then lit a flare and finally launched a distress rocket, but it sailed blindly past. Their officer of the watch must have been asleep. Eventually the pain passed, which convinced me it must have been food poisoning. I got on with battling through the headwinds of the north-east trade winds. It was only 18 months later, when I had the same pains again and was rushed into hospital to have my appendix removed, did we discover that I had had a burst appendix before but somehow had managed to recover. Every day since has been a bonus.

On Easter Saturday, 5 April 1969, I was crossing one of the main shipping lanes from the Americas to the Mediterranean, not far from the Azores Islands. I spent much of the day with the Aldis lamp trying to get a ship to respond and report my position to Lloyds so people would know I was still alive. It was not until mid-evening that the 18th ship responded, the British-registered *Mobil Acme*. I repeated my request and he acknowledged at 1920 hours and asked for my estimated time of arrival in Falmouth. After four and a half months, I felt I had at last got a message through. The next morning, I tuned into the BBC news but there was no mention of the sighting. In fact, though, Lloyds had phoned my home at 2040 hours and my brother took the call to learn that I was alive and close to home. The Reverend David Roberts, the Mission to Seaman padre in Falmouth, who had given me a Bible before I sailed, was so excited that he began his sermon on Easter Sunday with 'Have you heard the news? Robin's been sighted. Most appropriate on the day of the resurrection.'

With nothing on the news I had listened to, I only learned

that I was leading on 12 April when a French cargo ship, the *Mungo* of Le Havre passed, and I called him up. He asked what I wanted and I said to please report me to Lloyds. He asked the name of my boat and after I told him he swung round, came back and gave us a wave. He told me I was reported missing and that Moitessier was in the Indian Ocean. Later that day another French ship came over and gave me three blasts on its foghorn so I knew the news was out at last, family and friends could stop worrying and all I had to do was finish to win the trophy.

The next nine days were a flurry of activity ashore as I sailed towards the Lizard, the southernmost point of Cornwall. I could hear Baldock radio station calling and tried to answer between fuses blowing on the transmitter, which I thought I had repaired by using the terminals on the bottom of the useless sidelights as solder. Three newspapers hired boats to come and find me and I was unaware of the shenanigans going on in Falmouth between them all. The rivalry between newspapers for the story on my return to Falmouth in April 1969 was intense. On the one hand, there was the *Sunday Times*, loftily lauding it as their race; the *Sunday Mirror*, which had supported me; and the *Sunday Express*, which was trying to scoop their two rivals.

Bill Rowntree of the *Sunday Mirror* recalled one episode: 'Cliff Pearson, our assistant editor, had established himself in the Green Lawns hotel, Falmouth, to mastermind our coverage of Robin's return. Before the start, Bruce and Robin had developed a secret code so that anyone listening in to their radio communications would remain in the dark. The *Sunday Times* were desperate for a sighting, but Cliff was not going to help them. That morning, with deadlines looming, there was a call over the hotel intercom during breakfast. "Urgent phone call for Mr Pearson, urgent phone call for Mr Pearson." Cliff picked up his papers and charts and went to the phone booth in the lobby, pursued by rival reporters. They watched as Cliff had a long, animated conversation.

'As he left the booth looking very preoccupied, a slip of paper fell to the floor. The moment he turned the corner out of sight, the *Sunday Times'* reporters grabbed the paper. On it was latitude and longitude reference numbers. Their reporter immediately drove to the RAF base at St Mawgan, where the photographer was waiting with a chartered twin-engine plane ready to fly out to sea. The pilot, photographer and reporter all leapt on board. "Just head south-west and I'll give you *Suhaili's* position as soon as we're in the air," said the reporter. A few minutes later he handed over Cliff's piece of paper, and the pilot got out the chart to do his calculations. Very soon after, and without a word, the pilot turned the plane around and headed back to base. "What's wrong?" asked the reporter. The pilot looked pitifully at him and said: "This is the latitude and longitude for Birmingham!"'

Aware that I had contractual arrangements with the *Sunday Mirror*, I wanted them to find me first. I discovered that *Suhaili's* rigging acted like an aerial and by swinging her around I could use her as a radio direction finder. This told me where the various newspapers' boats were, so I headed for where *Fathomer* was, the *Sunday Mirror* boat and eventually met up with them. From then on I was escorted the final few miles through a host of French fishing boats square-dancing on my route. Eventually, on 22 April 1969 I rounded the Lizard early in the morning and headed for Falmouth.

The *Sunday Mirror* and Cassell asked me what time I thought I would finish and I told them about 0900. There was an embarrassed silence. Then they asked me whether I could slow down please because the mayoress, who would be in the welcome party, had her hair appointment at 0900 and so would not be there to greet me. 'Come on,' I said, 'I have been at sea for 312 days and what I want is a pint of beer, a steak and a bath in that order.' But, after that length of time alone I was in a compliant mode. I did slow down, and then the wind changed round to a northerly which meant beating into the harbour, so I did not cross the finish line until that afternoon. When I eventually finished at 1525 customs clearance was quick. 'Where from?' asked the customs officer. 'Falmouth,' I responded, having called nowhere else during the whole voyage. Officially, because I had not stopped anywhere on the way my voyage did not count as a foreign voyage so I was not entitled to the duty-free whisky, brandy and cigarettes I had taken aboard before sailing, but the customs officers were lenient and there was no duty to pay on the remaining three bottles of spirits left from the 24 I had started with. I was given the usual Inward Clearance Certificate. We were officially home.

The *Sunday Times* Golden Globe Race has gone down in history because it was the last great sailing voyage we humans had yet to complete. Nine started, one died, one finished. There cannot be anything quite like it again. Just like once Everest was climbed the mystique of the impossible challenge was broken. I was fortunate that the concept came to me at the right point in my life where I was still looking for adventure, had the necessary skills and experience and was prepared to take the risks. Those of us who took on the challenge, Chay

Blyth, John Ridgway, Commander Bill King, Lt. Commander Nigel Tetley and Donald Crowhurst, plus myself, from Britain, Bernard Moitessier and Loïck Fougeron from France, and Alex Carozzo from Italy, all of us were responding to that great urge of trying to be the first at something.

The others' experiences show just what an unknown challenge it was. Carozzo fell sick when off Portugal and had to pull out. John Ridgway, whose boat had been damaged by a BBC boat as he departed, found it was leaking too much and as a result had retired in Brazil. Chay Blyth disqualified himself in Tristran de Cunha when he spent a night aboard a vessel anchored off that island, but even he would admit his boat was far from ideal. Fougeron and King pulled out and retired to Cape Town. Moitessier, probably the most experienced sailor, asked a fisherman off Tasmania where I was and, having learned that I had left New Zealand waters some two weeks earlier, announced 'It is finished' and did not bother to come back. Nigel Tetley nearly made it home and would have won the monetary prize if his boat had not broken up when he was only 1,000 miles from home. He had pushed his trimaran too hard towards the end trying to beat Donald Crowhurst, who apparently had suddenly reappeared after a long period of silence and, having announced his reappearance, appeared to be closing in. Tetley's was a remarkable voyage in a very simple trimaran, which still stands as a major achievement in multihull sailing.

In fact, Crowhurst had never left the Atlantic. He had sent radio signals indicating he was sailing around the world, but they were false. Francis Chichester was very suspicious of Crowhurst, who had earlier claimed a new world record for the distance covered in 24 hours by a single-handed sailor, a record then held by Chichester himself. The problem was that Crowhurst claimed he had done this in an area of light winds, which naturally aroused suspicion.

It ended in tragedy for both Crowhurst and Tetley. Crowhurst's own claims had created the problem. When he heard that Moitessier was out, I had finished and therefore won the Golden Globe trophy, and Tetley's boat had sunk, he realised that he was now going to be the person who would claim the financial prize for the fastest circumnavigation. This meant Crowhurst's logbooks would be double-checked and he knew they would not stand up to scrutiny. Until Tetley's boat broke up, Crowhurst was likely to finish third, a very creditable position, but as he had not won anything in third position there was no reason to check his logbooks. But with Tetley gone he would be second and vulnerable.

Faced with the huge problem of not being able to withdraw from the race without losing his house, plus the fact that he had invented his voyage, he eventually found the pressure too much and probably jumped overside. His boat was found floating unmanned after his last log entry. It was a very sad end to someone who should never have taken the race on. He was ill-prepared when he sailed on the last possible date allowed under the rules and had signed contracts that left him no easy way out. If he had just pulled into Cape Town on his outward passage, he would have completed a very commendable voyage. His house was at stake, but there might have been a way out of the contract.

Because I had been so focused on just getting there, I had no plans for the period after my arrival in Falmouth, so I was able to relax and enjoy being among fellow humans again and get used to holding conversations. The long time alone spoiled me in some ways, I had become used to allowing my thoughts to roam where I liked, pursuing an idea to a conclusion without the need to consider others' views or adjust to them. Those close to me who had seen me off said I was much more relaxed after I got home, perhaps because I had got something out of my system.

The days after my arrival in Falmouth went in a blur. It is not a large town, so when I walked about I was soon spotted and people stopped for a chat. I probably appeared much more sociable than I am, as after ten and a half months of being confined to a world 32 feet long and 11 wide, I found walking any distance soon caused my ankles to ache, so I stopped frequently to rest them. I had put on seven pounds in weight overall but most obviously in the upper body where my chest had expanded by two inches, as had my arms. My hands were hard and callused, more like the soles of someone who customarily walked barefoot. Perhaps most surprisingly, my eyes, which had been fairly normal hazel, were now much bluer, although this faded in time.

Privacy was difficult and I soon saw why Sir Francis Chichester and Sir Alec Rose were bustled away from the public soon after they arrived home. There were more than 40 journalists in town and in order to have a quiet afternoon tea with my parents the *Sunday Mirror* had to arrange for one of their cars to stop in a narrow lane to jam the pursuing cavalcade long enough for us to get away. A psychiatrist was brought in to talk to me and we chatted for an hour about nothing particularly significant, which became boring so I asked him whether it was true that 50 per cent of the world's human population looked like the female

nude pin-up poster the *Mirror* people had put up on the wall.
Not surprisingly his response, when asked what I was like, was
that he is 'distressingly normal'. I assumed the distressing bit was
because I was not going to prove a lucrative patient!

Suhaili was not forgotten. I checked her the morning after
our arrival once I was up and about – the welcome-home party
had gone on until six in the morning. The *Mirror* wanted her
in London as speedily as possible as they wished to put her on
display in Holborn Circus. Ken Parker was asked how long it
would take to get her there and responded it might be five days
or three weeks depending on the wind. 'Can't she be motored?'
they asked. 'No,' responded Ken, 'the engine is completely
ruined.' It was all solved by the *Mirror* ordering a new engine,
a piece of gross but wonderful extravagance as far as I was concerned, and the task of removing the old and fitting the new was
completed in four days. The party that sailed from Falmouth
that Saturday consisted of me, Ken Parker, Bruce Maxwell, Bill
Rowntree and my brother Mike. I was glad to get away. People
were well-meaning and friendly, but I found the constant attention wearing and was becoming snappy as a result.

The trip round to London was perfect relaxation. Fishing
boats met en route came across and gave us fish or crabs, and one
very large one emptied the cockpit when it was discovered that
it was far from stunned. We left Falmouth with three cases of
beer and never had to re-stock as well wishers kept us supplied
as we sailed along the Devon and Dorset coasts, through the
Solent and on up to London.

At Cowes we stopped so I could meet the legendary Uffa Fox,
a delightful raconteur with a bright and mischievous twinkle in
his eye, who took a pleasure in being outrageous. I was told to

make sure I admired a painting he was finishing for Max Aitken of the Birth of Venus. I did so, it wasn't bad, but he stopped me mid-compliment by saying he had to redo part of it as he had based the bottom on a naked female-shaped bottle opener and, nudging me with a wink, he said we know that they weren't shaped that way!

There is a story that he once had a row with the Island Sailing Club whose new secretary pointed out that members were not allowed to bring their dogs into the bar. Uffa stormed out with his dog and the secretary waited for him to return, somewhat worried that he had offended the club's most famous member. He waited a week, a month, two months and was highly relieved when he came into the bar some three months later to find Uffa ensconced. However, dog was also present and feeling he could not back down, the secretary reminded Uffa that dogs were not allowed in the bar. The response was typical, Yes, but you allow members don't you, this dog is a member. And he was. In the intervening period Uffa had his dog proposed, seconded, put up for membership by Max Aitken and Johnny Coote and elected without anyone realising what they were up to!

Suhaili was hauled out on our arrival in London and taken through to Holborn Circus where she was put on display for a fortnight. I returned home, collected a new car as a present to myself, an MGC which was to give me enormous pleasure over the next 20 years, and then drove up to see Sara. Someone had tipped off the *Express* because when I got close to Grantchester I found myself being followed. Anticipating some such action, Bruce Maxwell and Bill Rowntree had given up their day off and come with me so that as Sue hurried Sara across to my car, the *Express* car pulled in but found itself boxed in by the two

Mirror cars. I drove away leaving him storyless and photoless, and Sara and I spent an undisturbed day punting on the Cam and seeing *The Sound of Music*. She had grown, of course, she was now six years old. She had watched my return on television and understood that Daddy had 'Hit the headlines' but was otherwise unimpressed, a chocolate sugar mouse was far more interesting!

My plans to relax once I got home were interrupted by Ken Parker of Cassell reminding me that I had a book to produce within sixty days, according to the contract, and that if I was not going to get on with it, he would like to get in a ghost writer. The thought of someone else writing mine and *Suhaili*'s story was unthinkable so I settled down to work, initially living in the Lansdowne Club where we employed a secretary to handle all the mail and answer the school projects that had been sent in but later I moved back to my parents' at Downe.

Ken came to check progress and I took him to the Queen's Head in Downe for lunch where we ran into Alan Civil, a friend, French horn player and brewer of a fairly lethal line in beer. When the pub closed we went back to Alan's house and started tasting his latest creation, accompanied by Mozart's Horn Concerto played on a plastic funnel, nine feet of garden hose and an expensive eight guinea mouthpiece. Returning home fifteen hours later, Ken slept the rest of the night and most of the next day before then departing with the manuscript so far, muttering about impossible work conditions.

Although I had started a book once before, suddenly faced with the need to produce 80,000 words seemed daunting. There was no time to be clever, the work would have to be my style and I settled to write the only way I could, Ken checking for bits missed or making suggestions as we went along. It was ready on time, just, and I followed it through its editing, printing, proofreading and final production like an expectant father. Seventy-two thousand hardback copies were printed and I spent two months with the Cassell representatives going round the country talking and signing. The largest number sold in one place in a single day was 740 at WH Smith's in Bromley, Kent. Only the Bible sold more that year in non-fiction. The paperback, which came out a year later, sold 120,000 copies in the UK.

A short trip to the United States in June to support *True* magazine, then a magazine about adventure which had carried my stories, was followed by a month in New York the following January, doing the various TV shows to help promote the book, giving me a chance to get to know that vibrant city. On one of these trips, I was meant to meet the President but he was called away. Instead I was taken to meet Senator Edward Kennedy for ten minutes. In fact, we happily discussed sailing for nearly an hour, just two weeks before the Chappaquidick incident.

But the high point as far as I was concerned was being a guest on the *Frost Show*. I followed Tony Bennett singing and resolutely refused Frost's invitation to sing a sea shanty on the grounds that one of the reasons I have to sail single-handed is because of my awful singing. The next guest was the actress Dyan Cannon who turned to me and breathlessly said she would love to do a voyage around the world. I responded politely by saying that she should come with me next time, but I could not guarantee we would make it. There was collective drawing-in of breath by the 600-strong audience. 'Make it' meant, as far as I was concerned, succeed in our sailing objective, in the United

States it had a very different meaning which was not then in use in England!

It was 13 years before another solo around-the-world race was organised, and I was involved as the race chairman for the BOC Challenge, the race that lead to the development of the Open 60 racing boats that now dominate solo around-the-world racing. But 50 years on in 2018 there is a new non-stop race, using boats of between 32 and 38 feet which must use the same equipment that was available to me. From the flash, high-tech racing machines that have developed in the Open 60 since 1969, which cost millions, we are seeing a return to what one might call real adventure sailing at prices that are affordable to the average sailor. Money isn't what matters, all that is required is the determination to go.

9

OCEAN SPIRIT

Once the book was written and published I had planned to return to sea. BI greeted me back as one of their own, they even gave me my salary for the time I was away. They intended to send me as first officer to the *Nevasa*, the company's largest ship, which had been converted from trooping to school cruises. While I appreciated the compliment, I would have been just as happy if they posted me to one of the Eastern service ships trading around the Indian Ocean where I felt more at home. The time alone had put me off crowds and the gentle pace of life taking cashew nuts from Tanzania to India had definite appeal.

The lands around the Indian Ocean were now almost a second home. I knew most of the ports and enjoyed the variety of cultures, sights and sounds – listening to muezzins calling the faithful to prayer in the Gulf, through the spicy, earthy smells of India and central Africa to the towering landmark of Table Mountain. BI had seemed a permanent fixture in that part of the world, immovable and everlasting, so a return to those waters would have been easy and reassuring. It was not to be, though. One of the directors took me out for dinner and quietly explained that, as a result of a McKinsey report, BI was soon to disappear along with all the other companies within the P&O Group. The huge, diverse fleet of ships was to be combined into one homogenous accounting unit. It sounded awful. What did I know of the tanker trade or the New Zealand coast and, conversely, what would others know of carrying deck passengers in the Persian Gulf? All the companies within the group had flourished thanks to their knowledge and awareness of their areas and trades, an understanding of local customs and needs that dictated when a cargo was required and what it should comprise. Without that expertise and experience those trades would wither.

With containerisation a coming fact of life and air travel slowly replacing the established liner runs, these dramatic changes were almost upon us as far as sea transport was concerned. We accepted that many of our trades would be containerised in time, but we thought we would continue to carry them along our own routes. Aside from a few exceptions, this was not to be. Within two years, only the *Uganda* and *Dwarka* carried the BI funnel, the lovely *Kenya* was scrapped and crews were spread among a rapidly reducing fleet of dry cargo ships. The change was huge for a large proportion of British seamen, most of whom had to leave the sea and search around for new careers. I was one of the lucky ones. I at least now had some funds to invest in a project if anything suitable came along; most of my contemporaries had nothing except hard-earned skills, no longer of use except abroad where the British seafarer was held in high regard. The stuffing seemed to go out of the industry, almost like an old man lacking the will and energy to make another adjustment. From holding the premier position in tonnage and numbers of ships in 1970, by 1995 British shipping was outside the top 30 on the international scale.

I did not remain idle for long. I met Leslie Williams at a lecture I gave in Poole, we had last seen each other at the Boat Show in 1968 and he went on to come fourth in the Observer Single-Handed Transatlantic Race. He proposed we should team up and build a racing-cum-charter boat based on a new Van de Stadt-designed 71-foot hull being moulded by Tyler's for Southern Ocean Shipyard. Since he had a track record of putting these projects together, I was tempted and after investigating further we went ahead. Our initial target was the Two-Handed Round Britain race, due to start in June 1970 and it was a mad rush from the start. The plug, a full-size model of the yacht from which a mould would be taken, was not started until the late autumn and inevitably ran behind. The mould was only begun in February 1970, three months before the race. Our core team moved down to Hoo in Kent to work on the hull as soon as it was laid up, putting in bulkheads, engine, plumbing and then spending an interesting weekend floating the deck, still attached to its mould and supported by oil drums, down the Medway from Tonbridge to Hoo.

The Royal Navy was not slow to realise that it had two lieutenants together in the race and I was called up so that something could be made of it for recruiting. There were minor objections to this from a civil servant, but Rear Admiral Godfrey Place VC, the admiral commanding the reserves, took the view that the reserves were his responsibility so he was not going to be told how he could run them. I had first encountered the rear admiral soon after I returned from my solo circumnavigation.

He was the navy's last serving VC, having been awarded that honour after making an attack on the German battleship *Tirpitz* in a midget submarine.

He invited me to join him on-board the *Discovery* on the Thames embankment, which I of course accepted. The lunch was interesting and during it he offered me an anti-submarine long course, a very great privilege that I often think I should have taken as the subject had great appeal. His staff captain looked vaguely familiar and he eyed me thoughtfully throughout the meal. Towards the end he suddenly said, 'The beard fooled me for a bit, but I remember you. You're the one who nearly broke my nose during the annual *Vernon/Excellent* Mess night.' I acknowledged that I had attended one such dinner, then I remembered him. He was the commander I had ended on top of in the scrum, but I did not want him to start remembering that evening too much, because I was responsible for flooding the hall of the wardroom . . .

Being on duty gave us a certain amount of support from the navy, but the real bonus was that I met Admiral Michael Le Fanu, the First Sea Lord. When we won, he had under the ability heading in my training book the comment 'Above the Average!' entered. Perhaps even more thoughtful was a box of chocolates that appeared on the table in the saloon with a short handwritten note in green ink: 'Well done, lads, signed Mike Le Fanu, the archetypal admiral.' One of the best-loved First Sea Lords, and you can see why.

My world was turned upside down in April when Dad died suddenly. He had not looked well for the past year but his enthusiasm was still present, enjoying my new project and planning routes, one of his favourite occupations, so perhaps we did not notice his increasing worries concerning the Irish linen business, of which he was a director, after the IRA burned down the factory in Belfast in 1969. He went suddenly overnight following a massive heart attack, I suppose it was some consolation that it was quick. He is buried at Downe Church, where he was a zealous church warden in his later years.

Fifty-nine years seemed too short an innings for a very good-natured man who, with my mother, made enormous sacrifices to provide us with happy childhoods and good educations to put us into careers. I am glad he at least had the pleasure of seeing me get around the world and his pride in that probably gave me more satisfaction than anything else. I was lucky that I had a project to concentrate on. Having spent my life at sea, with only occasional short breaks at home, I was used to long absences from family, present in memory more than reality, and I could look upon this as just another of these absences.

Work on the boat was now becoming frantic. Realising we were on a very tight schedule we concentrated on essentials and ignored any of the usual internal fit-out. When launched, as *Ocean Spirit*, she was an empty shell, albeit with a magnificent galley donated by Hygena, but with just one bunk fitted, since we had not read the rules properly and worked on the basis that as one person would have to be on deck only one of us could sleep at any time. The race organisers gave us a nine-hour penalty for this, which we felt was totally out of proportion to the crime but perhaps a feature of the certain amount of who-do-they-think-they-areism that greeted our arrival in Plymouth for the start. If anything the lack of a second berth was a hindrance not a benefit since in port one of us had to sleep on the bare deck, which was nothing like as restful.

To add to the frenzy, plans I had made with Peter Longmore to buy a site on the Hamble and build a marina started to gel. We had put together a syndicate of seven people, all prepared to put up the money to buy Bourner's boatyard just above the old *Mercury* training ship site at Badnam Creek, opposite Universal shipyard. There was a boatyard employing some 30 people building powerboats and 22 acres of land with outline planning permission for a marina. Negotiations were completed during the summer for the purchase of the lease for £120,000. Suddenly I not only had a boat to complete, I had a boatyard and marina project as well. Fortunately, Peter had worked at Halmatic and had some experience of running a boatyard, but he wanted to concentrate on sales so I was to take over the management of the yard when I finished the race.

I have never been in favour of tattoos. There had been a spate of tattooing aboard the *Chindwara* and the captain had told us that since we might become involved in a war any time, and therefore subject to capture, we should not have tattoos as they could mean we might be identified making escape, our duty, impossible. Thus, when the boatbuilders who put *Ocean Spirit* together came back from a run ashore in Dover sporting a tattoo each, I did not approve but it was their business. I believe their wives had something to say about it. Because of the shortage of time our only training and opportunity to get to know the boat was the trip down to Plymouth for the start of the race. We managed to get a rather hairy tow behind a minesweeper from Dover to Portsmouth which saved time and then, after bolting on the deck lead blocks we set out for Plymouth, the first real sail in our brand new ketch.

The Two-Handed Round Britain race was, like the Observer Single-Handed Transatlantic race and the Golden Globe, one of the great classics introduced by this country in what was a golden age of British domination of short-handed sailing. It was first run in 1966, with one of its purposes being to show that multi-hull yachts could not compete against mono-hulls in a very testing course. That theory went out the window when *Toria*, a Derek Kelsall-designed trimaran, won the race and to this day a mono-hull has only come home first once.

It is an incredibly testing event and requires the crews to call up all their mental and physical reserves. The execution proves too much for many and the race leaves retired competitors littered around the ports along the route. It is not just that the crew is limited to two people, the course, right the way around the British Isles with the exception of Rockall and the Channel Islands, gives a magnificent tour of the weather forecast areas around some of the most breathtaking shores anywhere in the world, particularly the west coasts of Ireland and Scotland. The navigation is not that difficult, although harder in those early days when it was dependent upon a sextant or radio direction beacons when no land was in sight, but since the shortest course was often close to the rocky shores, the crew had to stay alert and frequently short tack, to make fast progress. To allow for rest there are four compulsory stops – at Cork, Barra, Lerwick and Lowestoft – where the boats must remain for 48 hours. In theory this time is to be spent on repairs and rest, but in practice the hosts at each stop arrange a non-stop party and are deeply hurt if you do not show some willingness to join in.

Serious ocean racing is like chess with press-ups. The tactics are dictated by the weather and the navigator spends his time watching the forecasts to decide where the boat should be in the days to come so that it will enjoy the most favourable sailing conditions, while all the time striving to get to the destination as speedily as possible. All the various computations for wind changes must be taken into account and one simple error makes the difference between winning and losing. It is also physically demanding. Sail changes involve the speedy lifting onto the deck of the new sail in its bag, laying it out, dropping the old one, hauling up the new, sheeting in to get speed on and then folding the old one so that is ready when needed, before stowing it below decks. Often the foredeck crew will be washed by waves as they do this, which can tear the sail from their hands and delay the task. Stronger people do the job faster and those with stamina can do it for longer. You can train in a gym but I have always found the best build-up for an important race is to go sailing under a bit of pressure and of course we had not had time for that.

The general view among the followers of the race was that Les and I had bitten off more than we could chew. It was felt that a 71-foot ketch was far too much for just two to handle and we would be in trouble and calling for help in no time. The opposing view was that we were professionals and should not have been allowed to enter as it was against the spirit of the race. We were far too busy with last-minute preparations to be bothered with either view. We were professional seamen after all, although as we were not being paid we did not see how we could be professional yachtsmen, but took the remark as a compliment to our attitude.

*

The race was really hard work. We arrived in Cork in first position just over a day after leaving Plymouth following a scintillating reach at 11 knots all the way across from the Scilly Islands, but were too large to go upriver so had to anchor near the entrance. Sir Francis Chichester rowed over and invited me ashore for a quiet lunch and to show me his new yacht that was being built there. An offer by a journalist to pay for lunch in exchange for a story was politely declined and we spent an enjoyable couple of hours together. With this pleasant distraction and the inevitable maintenance, the 48 hours passed all too quickly but we were ready.

The next leg was much tougher and to add to our labours we had a hard beat around the south-west corner of Ireland. This was the first time we had had a serious beat to windward and we quickly discovered a major fault with the boat. We could only get her to make 4½ knots to windward, whereas her length would have suggested that nine was to be expected. There was something seriously wrong, so we contacted the designer and builder for advice. We also took in a lot of water and flooded the engine room. All new boats seem to have leaks that escape the notice of the yard and that is what a shakedown is for, and the race was our shakedown. It kept us busy for the first hours of the race but once we were clear of the corner things improved and we enjoyed another fast reach with a rising westerly wind to Barra in the Hebrides.

The finish line was well inside the approach channel, involving a beat into what was now a westerly gale. Under staysail and fully reefed mainsail we tacked in and anchored in the western side of Castle Bay, so named for the McNeil's castle built on an island off the town. Unfortunately, the holding ground proved poor and we dragged anchor across the harbour until we were blocking the ferry from getting into its berth. The engine refused to start so there we stayed until John McNeil, the ferryman and lifeboat coxswain, could come out and managed to get it going and the ferry, indispensable to the island, was able to get alongside.

The Hebrides are lovely and the people extremely friendly. The bare hills and adjacent sea appeal to me and I could have spent the two days just walking, but we had work to do. I was convinced that our poor windward performance was due to a lack of ballast, making the boat too tender so that she heeled too much. The builders and the designer said there was nothing wrong, but I did a heeling experiment and came up with a small metacentric height. We needed more ballast and decided to act.

The jetty had a huge pile of building sand awaiting use and this, we thought, would suit our purposes if we put a couple of tons into the lowest water tank above the keel. The wind was still strong but we motored into the jetty, the shore party failed to catch the heaving line to take ashore the check rope and, despite the engine going full astern, we drifted onto the rocks. To make matters worse the tide was falling. I stripped off, put on goggles and dived down to see how the keel was lying, but apart from a small chunk out of the bottom, we looked safe. We put fenders beneath the shore side to protect the boat as she heeled over, put out the anchor and lines to haul her off when the tide rose again and then rested. Some hours later when *Ocean Spirit* floated off, we went alongside and took the sand with a large group of locals forming a bucket chain to assist. The difference to our performance was quite dramatic and as we headed north-west for St Kilda beating into a fresh headwind we were making 9 knots, as we thought we ought to be doing.

The wind was a run from St Kilda, but gradually veered as we sailed towards the northern island of the Shetlands, Muckle Flugga, or big fly, which it does resemble from the air. We beat round in another gale and luckily called up the lighthouse with the signal lamp and asked them to report us because when we got into Lerwick we were greeted sternly with a demand to explain why we had passed south of the islands, which would have meant we had cheated. I was getting really fed up with this constant critical attitude, especially as neither of us had a clue as to what the official was talking about. It transpired that a naval aircraft flying off the north coast of Scotland had seen a large ketch making its way east between the Orkneys and Shetlands and wrongly reported it as us. In fact, it was American and on its way to Norway. Fortunately, the Muckle Flugga lighthouse was able to confirm the time we had rounded that mark of the course but we never received an apology for the accusation.

The performance of the boat was undoubtedly improved, but we reckoned there was another knot of speed available if we could reduce the drag from the large three-bladed propeller so a visiting frigate's divers obligingly removed it in Lerwick. We set off down the North Sea with a good lead but became becalmed off the Norfolk coast with a forecast of strong westerlies to come. The entrance to Lowestoft Harbour is narrow and we did not fancy trying to tack through, which could be extremely dangerous, so while it was calm I nipped overside and re-fitted the propeller. We arrived in Lowestoft still in first position and motored into the harbour, leaving the organisers convinced we had stopped off somewhere on route to effect the replacement of the prop! We now had a convincing lead and held it for the last leg along the south coast. Our nearest competitor, the catamaran *Apache Sundancer*, capsized off the Isle of Wight which artificially extended our lead to two days. It had been very exhausting but worth it and showed that a hard-sailed large mono-hull could, at that time at least, win the race. Significant development has ensured that multi-hulls have never lost since.

We took *Ocean Spirit* to Cowes and then to my new boatyard where we had some further fitting-out work done before Les and I took turns taking her to Malta, where we were the Royal Naval Sailing Association's entry for the Middle Sea Race that autumn. The main competition was Kees Bruynzeel's lovely ketch *Stormvogel*, which we quickly left behind at the start, but then disaster struck as all our sails, one after the other, tore and left us bobbing along under a staysail and mizzen while we sat in the saloon and sewed and sewed and sewed.

We never recovered from this setback and trailed much of the fleet to the finish. There were some compensations though, not least a Stromboli party on our third day when flat becalmed in sight of the volcano. After a prize-giving party at the finish, Les set out with some new crew members, including a young New Zealander called Peter Blake, for Cape Town for the first ever Cape Town to Rio de Janeiro Race. We covered the not-inconsiderable costs by asking everyone to pay their share of the expenses, giving us an interesting multinational crew of varied sailing experience, but Peter quickly showed his abilities and he became a watch leader for the race.

While Les sailed to Cape Town, back at Mercury on the Hamble we set about obtaining detailed planning consent for the marina and preparing engineering plans to obtain tenders

for the work. The plans drew one protest, from the local secretary of the Royal Society for the Protection of Birds, who
accused me of destroying a bird sanctuary in Badnam Creek.
There was no such sanctuary and in any case we had no intention of building there, but the lady refused to believe me. I told
her to go to the county planning office and check for herself,
suggesting she might like to subsequently return and apologise
for calling me a liar, but I never saw her again.

The council's quite reasonable concern was what might happen
to the regime of the river if we dredged out a large hollow on one
bank. The Hamble river had, according to plans we were shown
in Winchester, been very stable since 1807 and no one wished
to see it suddenly start to wander, eating out existing river banks
and depositing silt at other points. Investigation revealed that
the pontoons would have quite a slowing effect on the water, as
would the boats themselves, and while this would probably help
maintain the river's regime it might cause some siltation within
our basin. This was a risk we had to take. The indicative costs
came out at about £380,000 for the main building, sheet-piled
wall, pontoons, car park and ancillaries and now we set about
finding this money.

I flew out to Cape Town just after the 1971 London Boat
Show leaving Peter Longmore in charge at the yard. *Ocean Spirit*
had gone aground off the south-west African coast and needed
repairs to her keel as a result, so we slipped the boat the moment
I arrived. The crew were kept busy with preparations for the sail
and Clement (Clay) Freud, who came as the cook, worked out
what food we needed. His immediate action on arrival was to
obtain a gift of 200 bottles of excellent wine to accompany his
forthcoming meals, leading to an altercation as I was horrified

by the weight. A compromise was eventually reached that he would help me to stow this cellar low down in the bilges and we would pump overside the equivalent weight of water once the race had started. Next Clay discovered that Eric Tabarly, who was sponsored by an oil company, had welded his disconnected engine to the underside of the cockpit and the race committee were allowing this as their interpretation was that there was an engine on board, as per the rules, even if it was not connected to a propeller. Apparently the rules did not state it had to be capable of motoring the boat.

Clay went into journalist mode and created so much trouble that the engine had to be cut free and connected properly, which did not endear us to the organisers who were bending over backwards to accommodate their famous French guest. With all the boats preparing I decided to indulge in a little psychological warfare and took the crew, less Clay, for runs round the docks just before nightfall. That time was chosen deliberately so that people would see us training while thinking we did not wish to be seen.

If Clay would not come running he was very busy with other issues. His final contribution was to call a press conference to tell South Africa what food we were going to enjoy. The four journalists who assembled knew nothing about boats and their knowledge of cooking was restricted to a *braai fleis*, a South African barbecue. Clay got bored at the rather inane questions and when asked eventually what he liked best responded, green-eyed, oval-faced, sloping-shouldered, red-haired nymphomaniacs. The response was to ask him what he thought of South African girls, to which he answered that he thought they were the answer to a short-sighted man's prayers. When this duly appeared in the local newspaper, I thought we would have to sail early and join the race from outside the three-mile limit of territorial waters!

There were only five yachts in Class One, our class, and the most serious competition was the Canadian maxi-sized racing boat *Greybeard*. They had a large, experienced crew, including three official handicap measurers to whom I presented our International Racing Certificate and asked them whether we were rated with or without our propeller. They unanimously answered it was without, so I dived down and removed it and sent a note to the race committee formed from the Cruising Association of South Africa telling them what we had done. This was to cause trouble later.

The start in Table Bay was in a strong south-easterly so we left under spinnaker and roared into the lead. Down in the galley, as we began to roll in the south Atlantic swell food clattered everywhere as it fell from its storage cupboards. Clay muttered angrily that no one had told him his kitchen would take on an angle like this and bounce so creating meals would be extremely difficult. Nevertheless, the first meal was vastly superior to normal yachting standards and a foretaste of what was to come. As he slowly picked up what this ocean racing was all about, he came out with some cracking remarks that had us in stitches. For example, his comment on the heads at the aft end of the boat, a rather small and unventilated compartment, was that it would make a perfect training for a jockey. You had to adopt a riding position, the heat was sure to make you lose weight and even the handle for the pump was placed where you would normally have your whip!

Fourteen days into the race Clay came out into the cockpit

and gave us a choice of beef, venison, pork or lamb for dinner. When asked why we had the choice he told us we were running out of dry ice and this would be the last fresh meat meal. By this time, I had had to introduce physical training on deck as our waistlines were noticeably increasing. Clay said later that while he had thoroughly enjoyed the whole 21 days at sea, he had found cooking frustrating as, being a restaurateur, whenever he found all his tables booked and every customer so well satisfied, he normally put his charges up!

Although it might appear to be a straight-line trade wind event, the race itself was fascinating tactically. The basic conditions were a run before the south-east trade winds, but the direct line, or rhumb line between Cape Town and Rio led through the zone where the south Atlantic high pressure system hovered. To get too close to this high meant light winds, to go too far from it meant increased distance to sail. The verdict decided the race. Two smallish but lightweight fast racers took the south route and for a while looked as if they might just get into Rio first, while others went north and looked well set at one stage to sweep in first with the stronger winds they were experiencing. Our chosen route was between these two and it paid off in the end as we crossed the finish line almost a day ahead of any other boat, *Greybeard* coming in some 22 hours later in second place and rafting up for a party.

We had won our class, or so we thought. I was minding my own business in the club when I received a message to go to the race office. When I went in I found a panel of committee members, properly dressed in blazers, sitting at a table facing the door. The set-up was rather like I imagined a court martial to be. I was dumbfounded when they accused me of cheating by removing the propeller as, they said, our rating certificate was calculated with a propeller. The measurers aboard *Greybeard* had been quite positive we were rated without it so who was right? There did not seem much to be gained from pointing out that they had made an exception for Tabarly earlier, but there was some shuffling of feet when I asked what had happened to my note telling them I had removed it, or why, as surely this proved I had not cheated. Eventually they admitted my note had been received so cheating was now reduced to an adjustment of the handicap result and they announced a penalty of 11 hours.

I left the meeting very angry at the original implication. I had asked them why, if they had known about this since the start, they had not contacted us to tell us to put the propeller back on during one of the radio schedules, but their only answer was that would not have been possible at sea. It was perfectly possible, as I had shown the previous year. Later I checked the rating certificate and it was clearly stated to be without propeller, but there was no point in taking the matter up again. The committee also had to give consideration to Tabarly's request to have his boat re-classified in our division, because, since it had been a slow race, the handicap system favoured the smaller boats over a longer race in which case he could be declared the winner of Class One (he had finished third in Class Two). They turned down this request so at least they got something right. They ran the race subsequently but after the treatment meted out to us we did not bother entering again.

All this did not affect the celebrations at the Iate Clube de Rio, where a party is seen as an extension of the carnival. The drink prices were so high we took our own bottles ashore, hiding them beneath the Hawaiian skirts we had made for the occasion. The guards, who checked everything, were initially alarmed as they patted us down but then smiled and waved us through when they realised our 'weapons' contained whisky! The party lasted all night. Samba bands were replaced as they collapsed through heat and exhaustion and at some stage everyone started to be thrown into the pool. When the commodore and his wife went in the manager panicked and called the police and it cannot be often that whiffs of tear gas twitch the noses of Rio's high society, nor that they find themselves overrun by 400 armed men. Fortunately, it all passed off pleasantly enough. The next day I flew back home to start work on the Mercury marina project on the river Hamble and Les sailed *Ocean Spirit* back to the UK.

When I got home I was invited by Sir Max Aitken to join him aboard his new 60-footer *Crusade* for the 1971 season and readily accepted. This was an Admiral's Cup year, the most prestigious international competition for the offshore fleet, but we were not in the team, nor was I, with limited experience of this type of racing, likely to find a crew place in the British team. The crew, usually skippered by Max, included the irrepressible Johnny Coote as navigator who used this task as an opportunity to take charge of the cooking. Since he started every dish by putting sherry into the pot, his meals were popular. Hugh Lawson, later Lord Burnham, was another noisy and ebullient member of a team that varied between 12 and 16 in number. At Cowes we either stayed at Max's house, The Prospect, which overlooks the harbour, or on the boat, using the Three Tuns, known as Dot's place, for meals. *Crusade* was a very graceful-looking boat and we had an enjoyable if not overly successful season. For me it was an introduction to Cowes and the racing there, where contrary to popular media opinion, racing was the main occupation, not some swinging social scene.

There were parties, of course. Max was a great entertainer and looked upon his crew as if on unpaid retainers to be used at will to support his social activities. On one memorable occasion of a dinner at The Prospect he had arranged for Uffa Fox to sing as a finale. He then decided that Uffa might not be too well so he should be supported by having the record of his sea shanties played concurrently on a record player in another room. The whole thing was doomed from the start as we had to rely upon a team of signallers to indicate which song Uffa was going to sing and when he would start so we would try to cue in, but Max was deaf to our remonstrance. The chances of ever getting the thing to work in time were remote and, when it came to it, a perfectly robust Uffa started to sing to find himself competing with himself but a few bars behind. Max fumed, Uffa looked puzzled and the song support team collapsed into hysterical laughter.

I learned a lot about what is called ocean racing that summer, which in reality was offshore racing, organised by the Royal Ocean Racing Club. Up until now my sailing had been cruising or real ocean racing, which meant just pushing for the days, weeks or months to grind down the miles to the finish. A complicated new handicap system was becoming popular, the international offshore rule, which was being adopted worldwide to allow yachts of any nationality to race against each other as fairly as possible, but to get the best results you needed a computer.

In offshore racing, few races lasted more than a weekend, the Fastnet being an exception, and the weather played a significant part as there was no time to recover if you got it wrong. The boats, large and expensive for the time, were individually owned, rigged as sloops but occasionally cutters, varying from 30 to 60 feet in length and skippered by their owners and crewed by volunteers. Subsequently, professional sailors started to be bought in as owners realised that the value of their yacht depended on its performance, but this killed the series as the use of money to buy crew put off many owners.

Unlike my sailing so far, the yachts were usually in sight of each other and so the differences made by small changes in sail trim or by the helmsman were immediately visible. This put pressure on the crew and enhanced the competitive element. The need for clear racing rules becomes immediately apparent when yachts are competing at close quarters and a sharp knowledge of these rules was not just desirable, it was essential if collisions were to be avoided among a fleet of perhaps as many as 30 boats, all crowding in on a turning buoy at the same time. A good knowledge of these rules, some calm and determined helming combined with an alert crew could gain yards, and a race could be won or lost at moments like this. It was exciting and fun.

There is an adage that banks would not lend you an umbrella unless there were no clouds in the sky and they had a cast-iron guarantee from God that there was to be no rain. Our efforts to raise a loan to build the marina foundered on the banks' fears that if anything went wrong they would be left owning a muddy hole. This might become true, but this argument could apply to just about any engineering or building project. The fact that the other marinas on the Hamble were full and had waiting lists did not reassure them that our projections of 80 per cent occupancy might be safe, they reduced this to 50 per cent and frightened themselves off. Peter Longmore and I trod through the City but could get no backers.

The project eventually went ahead because I had met the deputy chairman of the Rank Organisation, Graham Dowson, at a dinner and he had offered me a job. While I had turned this down it had opened up an avenue of communication and I arranged to see him and told him of our scheme. He saw the potential at once and within a couple of months the Rank Organisation had become 55 per cent shareholders in the project and, of course, they had no problems with the funding. We built Mercury Marina during the winter and spring of 1971/2 for £385,000, just £5,000 over budget, and filled it completely within three months. Bertie Miller, now redundant as the cadet ships had been decommissioned, joined us to help run the marina, which he did in his own inimitable style. The prophets of doom who had told us we would never find enough customers had been wrong, as they usually are, but, almost by their nature I think they derive some peculiar satisfaction from their failures so they were probably happy!

Back ashore my life was about to make a dramatic change. Sue and I had been meeting whenever I went to collect Sara for a weekend, which was averaging twice a month. Because we did not fight over her our relationship improved, slowly overcoming the bitterness that is left after the judicial system has, by its adversarial nature, forced people to take an uncompromising stand. Thus, when she asked if I would be agreeable to her taking Sara to Lisbon to stay with her sister I had no objection and, after thinking about it, said I was planning to go cruising in that direction anyway and would she like to make the voyage there in *Suhaili*. She agreed and we sailed in August with Steven May, an old friend from school, and Meg Makepeace comprising the crew. Our voyage was quite speedy, only five days, but half of one was spent hove to in a full gale in the Bay of Biscay where *Suhaili* proved her seaworthiness yet again. We arrived at Lisbon at dawn sailing into the sunrise with the city stretching out ahead, an unforgettable sight.

Having no information about yacht facilities we moored in the fishing port and found a bar for a celebratory brandy where we elicited instructions on where to berth. We found a marina up the river at Belém near the statue to the explorers. Steven and Meg returned home and we enjoyed a week of sightseeing in what must be one of Europe's most friendly and attractive capital cities. I left *Suhaili* there for the year and flew home with Sue and Sara as I needed to get back to the marina project.

Our relationship was now back to where it had been before I decided to build *Suhaili* and sail back from Bombay. Our separation and divorce had been a mistake, but I often wonder whether I would have gone off to sail solo non-stop around the world had we remained married and the answer is that probably I would not. Sue and I remarried at Winchester Register Office in April 1972, one of my better moves in life and she and Sara moved back in with me in Hamble. Later that year we flew out to Lisbon to bring *Suhaili* home. We sailed into the inevitable nortada, the north wind that is a feature of the Iberian Atlantic coast and bashed our way motor sailing to Peniche where we pulled in for a rest. Both the girls had been seasick, Sara's little face popped up through hatch with a pleased smile to tell me that 'I've been sick too, Daddy.' In our next leap we made it to Viana do Castelo and then Conception just inside Cape Finisterre. Two efforts to round Finisterre led to a very tired crew and two torn sails so we headed back to Vigo and laid up until I could return with a crew to bash us round.

Sara had enjoyed a relaxed time at the village school in Grantchester but aged seven could not recite her times tables, something I helped her to learn once she moved in, for which she has grudgingly forgiven me, although she became more appreciative when she got older and discovered shopping. We sent her to Rookesbury Park near Winchester, which believed in the old-fashioned but effective methods of teaching, not the experiments which have since proved to be such a disaster for the nation.

It was a fairly strict Church of England establishment and the teachers were shocked when, in answer to a question as to what was the first thing Mummy said to Daddy when he arrived home in the evening, Sara raised her hand and said 'Take your trousers off!' They were not to know I was building a marina and was coming home covered in mud which Sue, not unnaturally, did not want brought into the house. I found the mistresses shying away from me when I visited the school thereafter and it was some time before I realised why! Sara made it worse later in 1972 when we were re-married by answering another question as to what they had done at the weekend with 'I went to Mummy and Daddy's wedding!'

Shortly after my return I was asked to chair a new appeal to be known as the British Olympic Yachting Appeal, BOYA for short. It had a small committee of Robin Aisher, Tony Morgan and myself with the fundraising being carried out by Monica

Dixon. Our task was to raise money to help pay for the Olympic sailing team and we were reasonably successful. When we gave it up in 1977, we had provided funds for two Olympic Games and left £70,000 in the bank. The job brought membership of the Olympic Committee of the Royal Yachting Association so that I could see how the money was spent. This in turn led to the BBC assuming that I knew all about Olympic sailing and asking me to present the sailing games from Kiel in 1972.

My first experience of BBC Sport was at Television Centre when Bryan Cowgill, the man in charge of the Olympic coverage, went through the sports and what coverage they would be given. In turn we were all asked what we thought might be achieved and the number of cameras and time to be allotted was indicated. When it came to my turn I announced that if things went badly, out of the six medals available in the yachting we would get a gold and a silver, but we could get two golds. There was a slightly disbelieving smile and the focus swiftly moved on the equestrians and the number of cameras to be deployed for their faint possibility of one medal.

The initial plan was to send me on my own to Kiel but I eventually got through to them that with no knowledge of the medium I ought to have help. Dewi Griffiths, usually employed at Cardiff Arms Park, was appointed my producer. It was as well. Nothing in Kiel worked and Dewi was driven to making remarks like, 'How you Germans thought you could conquer the world when you are this inefficient beats me,' which I don't think helped, however justified! On the first night we had no idea what film the Germans were going to show as I went live to the UK for ten minutes, which inevitably caused us to look hesitant and disorganised.

Cowgill came on the phone from Munich where he was based the moment I had finished, incandescent with rage and had Dewi white and trembling. It was unfair, Dewi had done all he could, but everyone else in Kiel was up in arms at the lack of the service we had been promised. Then Cowgill started on me and started shouting about my incompetence, lack of knowledge, and we got into a big row. Things improved after the first night and Rodney Pattisson moved steadily towards his second gold medal, while Alan Warren and David Hunt failed to get the gold but got the silver. They should have had the gold but the Russians, who won it, were not protested for being across the start line in one race, so the British had to content themselves with second.

Having left the sea professionally as far as everyone was concerned I was downgraded from List 1 to List 3 in the Royal Naval Volunteer Reserves, unfortunately missing by two weeks the right to exemption to the Navy Command exam. They subsequently gave me an exemption from the navigation part which was kind. I joined the Southampton division of the reserves and enjoyed a number of good outings on their minesweeper, usually sailing as first lieutenant or the 'Jimmy' as he is known. The Ton Class minesweepers were nice little ships of about 350 tons. More than 100 were built in the 1950s when the growing Russian mining threat was appreciated and all 12 RNR Divisions ran one. Their only problem was that they had been designed for a heavy Mirrlees diesel engine but subsequently many were fitted with the much lighter Napier Deltic engines. Despite some additional ballast, they would roll very easily, or on wet grass as some wag put it.

On one occasion we set out on a Friday evening from Southampton to the Channel Islands, straight into a Force 9 gale and once clear of the lee of the Isle of Wight began to roll badly. I was called to relieve the officer of the watch who was down with seasickness, but so was everyone on-board soon after, except two of us and I was not sure how long I would last. For the first time since my first trip to sea I was feeling distinctly queasy. There was no one left capable enough to relieve me, so I had to stay on the bridge all night, my decision to alter the route to reach the shelter of Alderney being greeted by a groan from the other end of the captain's voice pipe.

How the quartermasters managed in the sealed box below the bridge I don't know – on one occasion we rolled so far that a wave smashed the signal lamp on the wing of the bridge. I took it easy, keeping the speed down so we rode the waves more comfortably and at daybreak we crawled at very slow speed past the eastern end of Alderney and into a suddenly flat sea. I called up the buffer, as the bosun was called, and told him to rouse everyone and hose out the accommodation, awash with the regurgitated remains of the previous evening's meal. Then I asked the cook to be turned to and begin making breakfast and all of a sudden the characteristic humour of the British sailor started to reassert itself. We arrived in Guernsey looking as if nothing had happened but that voyage was spoken about for years afterwards on account of the hammering we took.

By the Admiral's Cup competition in 1973 I had become more experienced in offshore racing and happily accepted the invitation to join Robin Aisher and Tony Boyden in their *Frigate* campaign. Designed by Dick Carter and 39 feet in length, she pioneered a number of innovations, not least her spinnaker poles being housed below deck in tubes to reduce clutter and windage on deck, as well as no separate WC and the crew would help to ballast the boat by sitting out to weather when close hauled. I ran the foredeck with Richard Foster, then a bricklayer's apprentice but later he took up yachting as a profession.

The effort to make the boat so streamlined gave us some problems and one of our first demands was that there be a toe rail around the foredeck as we kept slipping overside as we handled sails when the boat was heeled over. We were told we could not have one 40 mm high because it would create windage, but since seven hulking crew were windage on the rail this argument did not hold up. On one occasion when we were waiting for the cockpit to let a halyard go and they were yelling at us to release it, which we could not do as they had not let it go, one of them ran forward and yelled at us in exasperation. I yelled back that he was the one holding things up, demanded a marker pen from the navigator, Dave Arnold, and drew a line across the boat level with the mast. I told them that in future if anyone came forward of that line I would throw back. The line was respected after that!

The Admiral's Cup series was four races in those days, starting with the 220-mile Channel race, followed by two 30-mile inshore races and finishing with the 620-mile race out to the Fastnet rock from Cowes, finishing in Plymouth. There are only three places in a national team for the Admiral's Cup and there were more than 20 British yachts vying for selection. After a hard series of trials, we were selected as the small boat for the team along with Edward Heath's *Morning Cloud* and Don Parr's *Quailo*.

Before the start of the Channel race, 'Aish' had asked me to take charge of the medicine cabinet and make sure I obtained some highly recommended seasickness pills as seven of our nine-strong crew suffered. I managed to get them via the local doctor, put them away and forgot about them. Just before the Channel race after sailing out to the start, Aish asked me to issue the pills to the crew. I got them out, they seemed awfully large, and began to read the instructions. Aish was throwing a wobbler on deck, as he frequently did before a start although he calmed down once the tension really got going. He yelled down to me to get the pills out and I responded that I was reading the instructions. 'Well, hurry up for Christ's sake, or we'll be late for the start!'

What I was reading was horrifying me and I did not know how to break it to the crew. Aish was dancing by now, almost incoherent. 'OK, calm down,' I said, 'and get the crew to drop their trousers and bend over.' Aish looked at me as if I had gone mad. 'What are you talking about?' 'Well, it's simple, Aish, these seasickness pills are suppositories,' I told him. Suddenly we were alone as the entire crew disappeared into Gosport looking for a chemist! We started the series with a pack of 72 and finished with them unopened.

Britain had won the competition in 1971 and had high hopes of doing the same in 1973 but we quickly realised that the Germans had produced a very fine team, led by Berend Beilken's *Saudade*. We lay second to them at the start of the Fastnet race with our old rivals, the Australians, close behind. That year the winds went light just after the three German boats had finished and we and *Quailo* were in and well placed, in fact *Frigate* came second only to *Saudade* in the series. Everything now hinged on *Morning Cloud,* which became becalmed 12 miles from the finish and as we sat in Plymouth watching the horizon hopefully, the trophy slipped away. She didn't make it in time and the Germans won, and even more unfortunately, the Australians beat us for second!

The ebullient Alan Bond, millionaire owner of the Australian entry *Apollo*, had in typical fashion booked a venue for a party to celebrate winning the cup before the competition even started, but despite losing he decided to have the party anyway. The *Frigate* crew were the sole foreign team invited. Towards the end of dinner he got up and made a rousing speech telling his Aussie crews how they had come the furthest, tried the hardest, it was a shame they had not won but they'd be back and win in 1975. He sat down to thunderous applause and yells of 'good ole Bondie'. John Hollamby, one of our cockpit crew, climbed onto the table, called for silence and then said in a perfect RP accent, that we could agree that the Aussies had come the furthest, they had certainly tried very hard as we had observed when we sailed alongside them and we looked forward to seeing them again in two years' time. There was a puzzled silence as the Aussies absorbed the insult. Our rating as a small boat was at least six feet less than their smallest so there was no way we should ever have been alongside them, although we frequently had been. By the time they had worked out the insult the party was finishing.

In 1974, after the success in the 1970 Two-Handed Round Britain race, I was keen to enter again. Of course I wanted to be on a boat that could win, but I would have entered whatever the boat as the race embodied so much that I found attractive: an interesting and challenging course, hard physical work, rewards for well thought through tactics, excellent competition and a very friendly atmosphere. So when Gerry Boxall approached me and suggested I join him in a project to be called British Challengers, whose objective would be to build a very large catamaran, I did not hesitate before agreeing. The British Challengers organisation was chaired by Barry Heath, later chairman of GKN, and the bulk of the money came from the British Oxygen company, after who the craft became known.

Design was in the hands of Rod Macalpine-Downie, whose slightly shy and donnish manner concealed a very creative and alert brain. He had been the designer of *Lady Helmsman*, the first boat to use a wing sail. He had been incensed by the Americans saying after the previous British defeat that there was no point in us challenging again. The upshot was that Rod's designs won the next series eight years in a row. His imaginative mind created *Crossbow*, which held the world speed record of 36 knots over the flying half-kilometre for years. The building of our new machine was in the hands of Reg White's Sailcraft at Brightlingsea in Essex, who had helmed *Crossbow*. The boat was to be 70 feet long and 32 wide, larger than anything else afloat at the time and with a cutter rig. Engineering support was provided by British Aerospace, who also built the hydraulically operated dagger boards and rudders in the middle of the Concorde production line, much to the mystification of their French partners in that project, who were left wondering what *les Anglais* were up to.

Since my experience so far was entirely with mono-hulls I decided to accept an offer from Reg White to go for a sail with him in a Tornado catamaran, in which he was then world champion and shortly to become Olympic gold medallist. Sue, Sara and I travelled up to Brightlingsea one cold, snowy weekend in

February. Reg and I donned wetsuits and he went through the boat and explained the trapeze that I would be hanging onto. Then we wheeled the boat to the water's edge. Before we set out we returned to the nearby yacht club where Reg filled his boots with warm water and put them back on. Baffled, I asked the reason and it was explained that as we were bound to get water in our boots we might as well start with it hot and then the shock would be less! You could not answer this logic and thus prepared we squelched back down the hard and launched the boat. Reg clambered aboard and took the helm, I pushed off, quickly appreciating the warm water in boots idea, and crawled aboard.

We headed off down the river but at the entrance Reg steered straight onto the sandy beach. He instructed me to lift the bow above my head and then busied himself out of sight at the stern from which glugging noises appeared. When eventually I was told I could lower the bow I asked what part of the process this was to be told there was no process, Reg had forgotten to put the bungs in the hulls so we had been filling with water and it would not do for us to sink for that reason!

It was a wonderful afternoon sail. That I was with a master of small multi-hulls was quickly apparent and it was a delight to be making up a two-man team with such an accomplished expert. The final *piece de resistance* came when Reg headed straight for a navigation buoy and casually sheeted in at the last moment so our weather hull lifted over it, just as we seemed destined for a nasty collision. Twenty years later on a race from Calshot to Bournemouth Pier and back, we shared a small Hurricane cat again and by that time our combined ages were well over 100. We felt entitled to an age allowance from the organisers when the best we could do was finish eighth out of a hundred or so. We were not happy mainly, I think, because Reg was not happy that the race was won by his son Rob, by then the British Tornado champion.

Mine and Gerry's plan for a huge catamaran for the Round Britain race was considered somewhat extreme. Although multi-hulls appear to be a recent introduction, catamarans are far from new. A relic of one 20.2 metres long was recently unearthed in the Shandong province of China which dates back to the Sui dynasty between 581 and 618 AD. But long before this, perhaps as far back as 5000 BC most of Oceania had been settled using canoes and multi-hulls by the Polynesians, who discovered Easter Island, Hawaii and New Zealand. Their voyages also explored the area between Palau and the Marshall Islands and the Melanesians, and colonised the islands from New Guinea to Fiji.

The first Europeans to sail these waters were justifiably impressed by the speed and ability of these vessels but failed to respond by copying them. The earliest European attempts at multi-hulls came in England between 1662 and 1684 when Sir William Perry built four catamarans, all of which impressed with their speed but failed to find support from the Admiralty. In the modern yachting sense though, the first multi-hull was crafted by Nathaneal Herreshoff in 1876. The *Amaryllis* was only 26 feet in length but easily defeated a fleet of 33 conventional yachts sailed by the New York Yacht Club and was banned from racing thereafter as a result. Matters had hardly changed 100 years later when prejudice against multis was still strong in the 1970s and '80s, and as a result they were excluded from conventional races on various grounds. The usual and dubious excuse, produced mainly by people with no multi-hull sailing experience, was that they were not seaworthy. They were forgetting Nigel Tetley's voyage. A replica of *Amaryllis* was timed at 19.8 knots over the measured mile and no owner likes to pay a fortune for a conventional yacht he believes to be fast to discover something less costly to build has a considerable edge in speed.

Perhaps the Catamaran's greatest advantage after its speed is the ease with which it can be steered. In large seas, the sort that can make a mono-hull broach and often requires heavy work on the helm, all the cats I have sailed have been extremely light on the helm and never given reason to worry. They are far more prone to bury their bows into the back of the wave in front and come up all standing, but this is a factor of their speed because they can sail faster than a wave.

By today's standards of composite lightweight structures, *British Oxygen* was, at some 12 tons, very heavy, but she was light in comparison to other vessels of her size around at the time and, of course, about a quarter of the weight of a similar length mono-hull. Trials took place every weekend when we could get out and practise, since there is no substitute for time on the water for getting to know the boat, sharpening one's tactical thinking and developing the muscle power for the job.

BO was a brute, the sheets had huge strains which even a coffee grinder did little to reduce. Tacking was a two-man job and left the winchman breathless for some time. Speeds, however, were very satisfactory, 20 knots being exceeded early on, but a squall off the Isle of Wight quickly proved the need for constant alertness. We saw the dark rain approach and waited for it to hit the sails and give us acceleration. The squall arrived but the boat did not accelerate quickly enough and the excess of energy began to heel us over. Ideas vary as to the exact height the weather hull achieved out of the water, but I was quite clear that the very high-pitched cry of 'sheet' which eventually emerged and caused someone to let go the genoa sheet, was mine. It was an abject lesson to us to take immediate action in similar circumstances in future.

Of course, there is not always time to reduce sail sufficiently to avoid a hull emerging from the water and in these circumstances there are three choices: release the sheets, luff the boat to spill the wind, or bear away and allow the speed downwind to reduce the apparent wind and turn the force from one trying to heel the boat to one that is trying to make it pitch, which, as the boat is longer than it is wide, is much less of a threat. I tend to avoid letting the sheets go as I hate the noise and it does the sails, sheets and rig no good to have them thrashing about. In our trial sails around the Solent we did little for the confidence of the mainstream yachtsmen convinced that their conventional mono-hulls were more efficient sailers, especially to windward. *BO* consistently pointed as close to the wind as even the most modern racing yachts but of course, with two long centreboards gripping the water she did not make as much leeway (mono-hulls start to slip sideways when they are heeled over). So although we did not sail closer to the wind, we made good a course closer to it. Sailing close hauled was not very efficient for us though as a multi-hull's speed rises dramatically when she frees off the wind, frequently doubling the speed we could make close-hauled even in those early days of big cats. It was in reaching conditions that we really had the huge advantage.

As the fleet gathered in Millbay Dock in Plymouth for the two-handed race, two craft dominated. The 65-foot trimaran *Manureva* of Frenchman Alain Colas and *British Oxygen*. The next in size was the 55-foot tri *Three Cheers*, being raced by two Royal Marines, Mike McMullen and Martin Read, which seemed tiny in comparison. The press quickly decided that the Frenchman was the favourite, which suited me admirably as it made me angry, the best way for me to go into a competition. The start showed the way things would go, however. The wind was almost non-existent, but by dint of wearing round instead of tacking – turning away from the wind instead of through it when we wanted to change tack – we kept speed on which enabled us to create wind and sail out of the harbour, whereas the rest of the fleet was becalmed by the entrance. We were almost at the Eddystone light before anyone else was clear of the port and led all the way to Cork.

By the second leg it was clear that *Three Cheers* was becoming a nuisance. It had stuck to us like glue. Our greater speed was compensated for by the relative ease with which she could be handled, and an hour and ten minutes at the end of the first and second stops was no margin in a race like the Round Britain. But while we both battled hard at sea, typically we partied together ashore. The Barra Ceilidh coincided with our visit again, not by chance, and Mike and I walked up the hill to buy a bottle of whisky each for the occasion. Later that evening, clutching our opened bottles in our hands, we joined in a 16-strong eightsome reel. We both leaped into the circle simultaneously, hit head on, fell onto our backs and neither of us spilled a drop!

A new hotel had just opened in Barra with grant aid from the Highlands and Islands Board and appeared to be the cause of considerable discontent among the locals. Comments about it ruining the character of the island were to be heard, but when one asked in what manner, the answer was that they all now had to get jobs in the hotel or as taxi drivers, whereas before they had lived off National Assistance. A group of us went out to see the cause of complaint, a perfectly reasonable building with fantastic views west. The locals were obviously still adjusting to their new roles and we couldn't get a taxi to collect us so David Cooksey, who was sailing with the American Phil Weld, and I borrowed bicycles and raced, somewhat unsteadily, back to the harbour.

Lerwick, the capital of the Shetlands, was our next stop as before. We again led the fleet in but the margin with *Three Cheers* remained stubbornly narrow. In the Lerwick Boating Club a fisherman the shape of an Oxo cube announced that all yachtsmen were cream puffs and challenged us to beat him at pull-ups. I was elected on behalf of the yachtsmen and when he faded at 45 I managed a couple more to prove the point but ached for a while afterwards.

Alain Colas in *Manureva* was not performing as expected, she had been forecast to win by a wide margin and the press announced that she was handicapped by carrying too much weight, the inference being that if lightened we would be beaten. Not wishing to be accused of winning unfairly, in response to these media comments we arranged for a BOC van to collect 2 tons of surplus food and stores from her and take it to the finish to make her more competitive. Despite the removal of this handicap her position did not improve.

On the next leg down the North Sea to Lowestoft we took a huge lead of almost 12 hours which gave us a hedge against problems in the final run through the English Channel to the finish. On *Three Cheers* Mike McMullen had accidently fallen overside and Martin Read, with a piece of seamanship that is

223

still not properly recognised, got the boat back, put a halyard around Mike and hauled his not inconsiderable bulk back on board. This caused their delay and we needed all of it. On the final leg back to Plymouth as we were bashing our way into a south-westerly Force 7 off the Royal Sovereign light tower, the Dover area, where they were, was experiencing easterly winds at Force 2. *Three Cheers* romped after us as gear failures began to take their toll on *BO* after being pushed so hard. Eventually we finished with a spinnaker halyard lead behind the mast holding the mainsail up, which put a limit on how far we could press the boat, but even so we managed to overtake the fast lifeboat that came out to meet us. Mike and Martin finished exactly an hour and ten minutes behind us, yet again. We had won, but only by a whisker in the end.

I had hoped to be able to take part in the Observer Single-Handed Transatlantic Race in 1976 but this did not particularly interest Gerry and the boat was sold to the French. Renamed *Kriter 111*, she took part in the race but little was spent on her maintenance and her forward beam failed mid-Atlantic so she was abandoned and lost. It was a sad end to an exciting experiment which, despite the prophets of doom, had proved remarkably successful. Also lost in this race, which was won by the Frenchman Eric Tabarly in a conventional 70-foot monohull after a gale struck the fleet and slowed the favourites, was Mike McMullen in *Three Cheers*. Just three days before the race, his very popular wife Lizzie had been killed when she bent down to retrieve an electric power tool which fell into the water, a loss we, as her friends, all felt. Nevertheless, Mike had sailed, probably the best thing in the circumstances as his instincts as a Marine and a single-hander would have been to survive. He took a very northern route, hoping to get the easterly winds that sometimes occur, but never arrived. Parts of his boat were found in Iceland a year later. We were left regretting the loss of another tough, resourceful friend and very likeable and respected member of the single-handed fraternity.

10

From the docks to the Whitbread

We took over Port Hamble in 1974 and shortly afterwards became Rank Marine International, part of the Rank Organisation. We closed the yard at Mercury, renting out the buildings, and combined everything at Port Hamble. This gave me a boatyard with 200 employees and two marinas to run. It was fun for a time and challenging. A slump was beginning, not helped by the government putting a 25 per cent VAT rate on anything to do with yachting – yet not on any other sport – so people were saving where they could. Work on boats became less available and it was necessary to lay off some men as we were told the yard must make a profit or be closed.

The yard manager had not even stopped the overtime, even though there was no work. Taking advantage of his absence I called the workforce together and told them the facts of life, stopped the overtime and read out a list of 20 people who would be made redundant. I then phoned round the other local yards and found jobs for them all. When they left at the end of the week, tool boxes in hand – a shipwright's pride and joy – they had to walk past the yard manager and the accountant carrying a case of champagne down to one of the demonstration boats in order to entertain the chairman that evening. I was ashamed and resigned as a director. I was out of work for less than two months, though, because Peter Drew invited me to join him in the small team at St Katharine's Docks, next to Tower Bridge in London, to create a marina in the first of the old commercial docks to be redeveloped for leisure purposes.

St Katharine's Yacht Haven can never work as a normal marina from an economic perspective as it cannot offer enough berths to cover the costs of running the lock into the Thames. Its value lay in the increased rents that could be achieved from offices on the site. In those days this was about £2 per square foot. Had this been credited to the marina the dock could have operated on a break-even basis. It would not be easy to market. On the one hand it had an attractive location, close to the City and centre of London, but from a yachting perspective it was a good tide away from decent sailing waters, usually a necessity for a successful marina development. The Haven was popular enough in the summer months when yachtsmen from Belgium, Holland and Germany visited to enjoy the excitement of London, but few visitors came in winter so income fell during that period. The challenge was how to produce steady income throughout the year.

The new marina facility needed to raise its profile and as a way of gaining publicity we started a series of races every Wednesday evening around the basins using Laser dinghies. I enticed teams: the yachting journalists, Olympic sailors, the Thames barge skippers, who were reluctant, and a local team we created to drive the competition. On one occasion the Thames barge skippers beat the Olympic sailors and the resulting party went on all night! I also introduced sculling matches, a difficult skill unless you had been brought up with it. The Thames bargees were not at all keen to show off their prowess until I arranged for beers to be laid on at the halfway mark and then they showed us all how sculling should be done.

A special winter rate soon brought in more than 50 other yachts and we began to feel full. Once people think something is working, they want to be a part of it and we never really looked back from that point. To provide some activity during the winter months we organised a Frostbite race from London Bridge down to Erith Yacht Club on the ebb tide. The accountants told me it was a worthless exercise and doubted I would get six entries but we got 27. At Erith we tried to empty their store of beer but failed. There was ice on the edges of the Thames as we returned to our boats, but the next morning everyone turned out to race back to London Bridge. It was a fun weekend, the berth holders enjoyed it and we repeated it for the next three years but never managed to empty the Erith Yacht Club's cellar!

Among my responsibilities were two Thames sailing barges, the *Lady Daphne* and the *Dannebrog*. There had been 400 of these distinctive craft operating at the end of the Second World War, still bringing cargoes to London. Designed for the shallow waters of the Thames Estuary and east coast, they were shallow drafted, box-like structures, whose motive power came from a huge sprit sail. In the past I had seen them occasionally in the Royal Docks but their main trades were elsewhere, grain for brewing beer being one. By 1975 there were still between 40 and 50, none trading, but they continued their traditional series of tremendously exciting races, which showed just how well a flat-bottomed boat with leeboards could sail. In fact, they pointed up into the wind remarkably well.

The Thames sailing barges were always an attraction but were discouraged by being charged at the same rates as yachts. There were four in the Haven when I arrived so I halved their charges, infuriating the accountants. However, within three months we had 16 berthed, providing a lovely sight and doubling the income from this source. It also brought to the yacht club the people who sailed them, most of whom had been in barges all their lives and were adjusting to the easier task of handling corporate hospitality instead of the search for and delivery of cargoes. They were real characters and great boat handlers, with some wonderful songs about their trade when plied with enough beer.

The barge skipper's normal style of dress was more suited to a farmyard than a boat, but these had been working boats. The *Lady Daphne* was skippered by Derek Ling, known as Spiro, who had started his working life in barges during the war at the age of 14. A colourful chap, short and wiry, I took to sailing with him whenever opportunity offered in the Thames barge matches. When we entered the Brightlingsea match, Derek as skipper and I as mate, we studied the rules and realised that there was nothing barring spinnakers, so I brought up a maxi yacht one and we smuggled it aboard one night when no one could see what we were up to.

Come the match, a light weather race that year, we hoisted the spinnaker on the downwind leg. Although the topmast bent forward alarmingly it held and we ghosted past the rest of the fleet, winning by a nice margin. After we had crossed the line first we celebrated on-board and then went ashore to join the rest of the crews, only to be told by the committee that we had been disqualified for setting 'that there big coloured sail'. We asked under what rule and they said they had just made one. I told them they could not make rules apply retrospectively and the use of the word so confused them that our win remained, but spinnakers were banned for the future. After another match at Southend the forecast was not good and we decided not to remain at anchor in the estuary, but tuck up somewhere more sheltered. We went upriver to Gravesend and with consummate skill Derek wriggled us into a narrow gap between some dumb barges. He was always a lovely boat handler and his knowledge of the river was immense. He knew patches in the Thames where an anchor would hold which did not appear on charts.

When it came time for him to retire I asked an artist friend, Peter Gunnett, to do a painting of the *Lady Daphne* as a retirement present. He did it beautifully, the old-fashioned way, showing the barge at two angles. At the retirement party Derek celebrated, telling the chairman all about the time he had spent at sea. Bargees tended to use almost any excuse not to sail, such as a gleam on the mud indicating strong winds to come or comments such as 'There's a cartful of wind in those clouds' – better stay in the anchorage. I could not resist a little leg pull and asked him how, with all that time at sea, he had managed to sire ten daughters and a son. Without hesitation he turned round and said, 'Well Raabin, I sent me trousers home to be laundered toime to toime.'

I spent two years working at getting St Katharine's going. But as it began to establish its reputation and fill with boats so we could develop the rest of its basins, Peter Drew started to meddle. I liked and admired Peter. He had imagination, it was, after all, his proposal that was accepted for the redevelopment of the dock, but he could be cranky and tended to employ people he could dominate. This leads to eventual stagnation as no one dares make decisions. As far as I was concerned, if he continued to interfere in what I was doing and telling people to do things without mentioning it to me first, we were going to fall out. We had a meeting and I told him that the way he was now becoming involved meant an inevitable conflict, so it would be best if I left so we could remain friends. So I left. Sometime before, I had spotted Troon in Ayrshire as a potential marina project and that is where I went next.

In the meantime, we had more or less the same team for the 1975 Admiral's Cup that had sailed aboard *Frigate* in 1973, but with the addition of Bill Green and we sailed in a new Doug Petersen design, *Yeoman XX*, which unsurprisingly became known as 'Kiss Kiss'. Team training was improved, we went out and did a series of circuits over a very short course in each leg where we were required to change a headsail, which certainly sharpened our sail-handling skills.

During one of these practices, the navigator, David Arnold, was called up to help in the cockpit and, being unfamiliar with the layout, accidentally tightened the spinnaker pole foreguy and eased the topping lift instead of the reverse. I went to trip the sail (let it go), and had climbed onto the pulpit to release the sail and when I did so the pole, with no topping lift, slammed down onto my forehead. I remember nothing except consciousness returning as I squatted on my hands and knees, watching a growing pool of blood beneath me. I felt groggy for a couple of days and then noticed I had lost feeling in my left arm. This clue led to the discovery that my seventh cervical disc was dislodged. It brought my sailing season to an abrupt end, but meant I saw a bit more of my family that summer. Although *Yeoman XX* was fast she was not as outstanding as *Frigate*, but the British team of *Noryema*, *Battlecry* and *Yeoman XX* regained the cup.

On an only slightly less competitive note, there was a race in aid of the Save the Children Fund that year which drew a very mixed bag of yachts to Cowes, varying from the latest ocean racer to out-and-out cruisers like *Suhaili*. It was a short course, but lack of wind made even that only marginally achievable for some of us. Trying to cut back on the leaders I ignored the advice of navigator Jim Weatherall, at that time commanding HMS *Ulster*, the navy's navigation training ship, and took a short cut across the edge of the Bramble Bank. Jim's head had just appeared from below to say that he thought it was getting a bit too shallow when *Suhaili* proved him right. It was the bottom of the tide so we were stuck for about an hour. Without waiting for instructions, the crew started to take down the sails but I stopped them. If we arrived late at the finish having been aground like this, we would be the butt of all the jokes that evening. We put two of the crew on the weather deck with their legs overside and the rest of our weight out of sight to leeward down below to give the impression that we were heeled over by some wind. Six competitors followed us and went aground close by, six who would not be laughing at us that evening!

For 1976, Tony Morgan offered me his Miller & Whitworth 47-footer *More Opposition* for the racing season. The boat had been the Admiral's Cup reserve the previous year. Finding a crew took no time, Roger Dobson and John Hollamby joined from *Frigate* and *Yeoman XX*, Mike Gibson from *Battlecry*, Ginny Bourne, who was a regular, stayed as cook-cum-anything on deck, and we had four first trippers – Dave Mitchell, the Belding brothers, David and Mike, and my brother Mike.

We started training in February, going out into the Channel every weekend practising, practising and practising until evolutions were automatic and everyone knew all the deck tasks. There is a pride in a well-performed manoeuvre and the crew soon realised that they were getting things right, strengthened by observing other boats who were not quite so well drilled. In our first race we took third and that was to be our worst position all season. The highlight was the new RORC Non-Stop Round Britain race where we were up against Don Parr's Nicholson 55, *Quailo*, and Dennis Doyle's *Moonduster*. We came in first by six hours in a time of 11 days which was, surprisingly, still the record in 1998 although eminently beatable. This put the seal on the season and gave us the RORC Class 1 points championship. A side bet of a case of champagne with each of the other boats gave us the basis for a great crew party in an Indian restaurant at the season's end.

I had become aware that what was essentially a fibreglass version of *Suhaili* was being built in California when the owners of the company, Westsail Corporation, wrote to me on a technical point. Early in 1976 they asked whether I would go over as their guest and speak at a few conferences. Since Sue and Sara were included in the invitation, I readily accepted. We flew over in July and were met at Orange County airport and driven to Lynne and Snider Vick's house at Newport Beach, a very plush resort where each house had its own dock, or pontoon as we would call them. Even better, the house was being extended and the builder, who just happened to live aboard his Westsail 42, had daughters a year either side of Sara's age so she had company immediately.

The extent of her temporary adoption of the culture was only brought home to me when I found her with a black mouth caused by liquorice bubblegum ice cream! Riding a bike around the lane she bumped into a boy of her own age who promptly asked her if she was doing anything that evening. When she replied that she was not he invited her round to his house. She refused, but was obviously pleased to have been asked. We were left reflecting that 13-year-olds must mature faster in the US! On a quick visit to Seattle to lecture I met Beryl Smeeton and John Guzzwell and heard first-hand the account of the pitchpoling of *Szu Hang* in the Southern Ocean and how Beryl was washed overside, but the next wave washed her back to the boat. It was an amazing story and John and I have kept in touch ever since.

Next door to the Vicks lived the actor Andy Devine and his delightful wife Dogy. Andy had played the high-voiced stage-coach driver in the John Wayne film of the name. Chatting one evening he asked me whether I had ever met a real sheriff and when I answered no, invited us to a barbecue the next Sunday to which he also invited the sheriff of Orange County, a very bright law officer who sported a huge ten-gallon hat. Dogy, through her friendship with Virginia Knott, arranged a trip to Knott's Berry Farm and then we were given tickets to Disneyland. As a piece of organisation it was brilliant, as a day out it was too large and totally exhausting – at least for parents. By 4 p.m. we had three highly flushed children demanding to see whatever we had missed. Sue and I were amazed there was anything left to see after eight hours and we were desperate for a cup of tea. We, or rather they, did one more tour and then we headed for home, the youngsters falling asleep as we drove.

It had been a wonderful four weeks and a marvellous way for our daughter to mix with young Americans of her own age and discover the real United States for herself.

On our return from California I started working on the project at Troon Harbour in Ayrshire. It came about almost by accident. While at Ranks I had been asked to look at a marina proposal at Irvine and flew up in the HS-125 with a member of Rank City Wall, the property company. Coming into land at Prestwick we flew over Troon, which from the air showed its sheltered harbour to perfection. We drove to Irvine, realised that it might have potential but a long way in the future and decided to take a look at Troon on our way back. By this time the tide had ebbed and the inner harbour was nothing but mud, however it had a number of interesting features as far as I was concerned. It was well sheltered, opened onto the Firth of Clyde and its spectacular sailing waters, had good railway, road and even air access and was close to the town. On my return I made a few enquiries, established that the owners were Associated British Ports and the mud in the harbour appeared quite deep, thus the harbour could be dredged to provide a deep water basin, deep enough for yachts anyway, and wrote up my recommendations for the board. Given the collapse of the property market, my suggestion of further investigation was turned down.

Resigning from St Katharine's left me free to pursue Troon. Associated British Ports were prepared to give us a lease over the inner harbour, bore holes indicated that the rock level was sufficiently low to allow deep water if the mud was removed so we formed a company. At this stage we were told of an existing tenant, the Troon Cruising Club, who would have to be removed. Although legally this was not difficult, they had only a six-month lease, politically it would be dynamite. These were, after all, the sort of people one would be looking to in order to provide a nucleus of customers so to alienate them right at the start was stupid. I asked ABP to arrange a meeting so that we could sit down and try and see where we and the club could work together since, properly negotiated, there were benefits for both parties in our proposals. Sadly, no progress was made over the next three months in arranging the meeting and inevitably the news got to them that someone was going to expel them from the site.

The ensuing uproar was predictable. Everyone seemed to want to be seen damning us, including the local MP and even Willie Ross, the MP for Kilmarnock, who described me as a 'money maker' in the House of Commons. (I took this as a compliment!) An interdict was sought in the local sheriff court to block us going ahead and we were advised by the club that unless we saw them right we would not get planning permission, a far from meaningless threat as we were to discover. Suddenly we were friendless. With hindsight I now know I should have walked away from the project then, but the blanket opposition from people who were not even prepared to listen to what we had in mind made me angry and I put my head down.

Our legal advice was that the club would succeed with their interdict but only perhaps for a short time, so we could forget about building in 1977. This gave time to manoeuvre. I learned that the local shipyard was likely to lay men off, so I asked them for a quote for some yacht berthing pontoons. At the beginning of 1977 the club's interdict was granted and Ailsa's laid off one third of their work force. The front page of the local paper had three headlines: the success of the interdict, considered by the local MP to be a personal success, the layoffs, greeted by the same local MP as an obscenity, and my comment that I was sad the interdict prevented me supplying work to keep the men employed at Ailsa! The phone rang almost immediately, could the MP convene a meeting between me and the club? Their entire committee of 16 attended.

We got off to a good start when 'Big Ian', a shop steward from a nearby works, accused me of being a capitalist, a derogatory word in those days, and looked to the MP for approval, who nodded agreement. I looked him straight in the eye and said, 'Yes, I am a capitalist, but it is capitalists like me, who risk their necks earning their money and pay their taxes, not hiding it offshore, reinvesting it in this country, who provide jobs for people like you and that is not to be taken as an offer of a job!' This was not what anyone wanted to hear and Big Ian started to lose his temper. His colleagues looked worried which indicated that he probably habitually did this if he did not get his way. 'We're tired of you English coming up here and helping yourselves to what you want.'

All I wanted to do was provide better facilities for yachts and business for the town, something they could have done for themselves, but that was not the point any longer. I looked at him again, angry, rolling up his sleeves in an aggressive manner. 'You're quite right,' I responded, which puzzled him. The whole affair was a pantomime, but at least it led to further meetings and we were eventually able to come to a reasonable agreement with the club.

The development plan was simple, seal off the walls round the inner harbour and dig out the silt, sand and clay using shovels and trucks, dumping it on a tip nearby which the Scottish

Development Agency agreed to landscape for the local council. Work started that autumn but ran into immediate problems. We had engineering difficulties, the hydraulic pressure proved too much for the walls, one of which collapsed. Then the planning office told us we needed their permission, and, off the record, we would not get it. We got round that by discovering that ABP, being government-owned, were Crown and thus did not need planning permission. Then the planners set themselves up as experts on silt and refused permission for us to dump it elsewhere, despite the fact that the real experts said otherwise. We stockpiled it in the basin and re-spread what was left of it before we finished. Despite these difficulties we opened in 1978 at a cost of just over £1 million, but we had space and piles in place for 720 berths eventually.

The excessively high interest rates meant that we did not make a profit for the first two years but at least we survived, which was more than much of British industry was doing and after some necessary management changes, entailing getting rid of the two other executive directors, we turned the corner and showed a steady increase over the next three years. Sadly, the main investor, Bob Bell, wanted quick money and marinas, certainly at that time, really deserve to be treated as a property enterprise. He replaced me with the two ex-directors who had told him they could make the changes to improve income that he wanted. On advice from my lawyers we took the company to an industrial tribunal to test our case and we eventually won a very high award. In the meantime, their management of the business was a disaster. They lost £60,000 in the next year and Bell sold us all out at a loss, his being the greatest.

*

To fill the year of waiting for the interdict at Troon to expire, I took part in the Whitbread Race. The first Royal Naval Sailing Association Whitbread Race for fully crewed boats had been run around the world in 1973. It was inevitable a fully crewed race would be developed once the Golden Globe had shown what could be done by a single-hander. Nevertheless, that first race was more of a fast cruise than a flat-out race and was won by a Mexican entry *Sayula*, owned and sailed by a washing machine millionaire. This 1973 event established the race and it was repeated it in 1977.

Les Williams suggested we enter and the design was entrusted to John Sharp and building to the Bowman yard in Emsworth. We plumped for a maxi, a boat where a number of factors in the design gave her a handicap at the top limit of the International Offshore Racing Rule, and the 77-foot long hull was soon under construction using cold moulding of a number of strips of mahogany glued together. It creates a very strong structure, plus it allowed the hull to be finished off varnished which was striking. Perhaps the most risky but interesting development was the decision to try out a carbon fibre mast, considered exotic at the time, which brought a penalty of 3 per cent on our rating. It was built by Vickers and showed an enormous saving in weight with consequent increase in stability and reduction of pitching moment. At 102 feet it was tall, but not ridiculously so.

Heath's Condor, with the sail number K707, was launched during the summer of 1977 and almost our first trial sail was the Fastnet Race where, not surprisingly since both boat and crew were just getting to know each other, we did not cover ourselves in glory, finishing third in class. We were not displeased with the performance, though. We had learned a lot about how to sail the boat but were concerned that there did seem to be a tendency for it to create a rooster tail at the stern when the speed got to about 14 knots and this speed was a barrier we had to force the boat through. Much later we discovered that this had shown up during the tank tests of the hull. I have seldom seen Les lose his temper, it is not a pretty sight, but I was totally on his side when he blew up at Sharp over this matter. We found out too late to do anything about the problem and spent the Whitbread forcing the boat to go over this hump with all the attendant additional strain on the gear that this involved.

By the time the race started I had moved the family to Scotland and was occupied with building the marina at Troon, so it was agreed that Les and I would take it in turns to skipper the boat so we invited Peter Blake over to be mate and provide continuity for the crew. On the first leg Les led from the start, but as *Condor* came into the headwinds of the south Atlantic and began to pitch, the carbon fibre mast buckled level with the headboard of the reefed mainsail. Disconsolately, the boat motored to Monrovia, while at home we got a replacement aluminium mast built in sections in record time and arranged to have it flown out to them. We had hoped to do it in six days, but the promised plane did not fly on schedule and then it demanded higher freight, so it was two weeks before the new mast even arrived. All that time the race clock was ticking, time we knew we could never recover. The new mast, when it was eventually delivered, was bolted together and stepped in a day and the voyage resumed, but our race time had 18 unnecessary days added to it.

In Cape Town, where I took over, we strengthened the new mast and prepared for the Southern Ocean. The late arrival allowed only one day for training but it showed that the boat was sailing well and the crew were keen to try and regain some of the lost ground. My tactics were simple, dive south after the start and head into the roaring forties to find the stronger favourable winds and within two days we had taken the lead. Progress now was fast, speeds averaging more than 10 knots were maintained day after day, but trying to achieve anything above a 300-mile day was blocked by the hump at the stern.

With *Suhaili*, in strong winds down here the sea soon built up to the point where I had to reduce sail and stream warps, but in the much larger *Condor* we had the size and speed to keep going and outrun the seas. It was not always easy. The boat would surf down the front of a wave going so fast that the turbulence round the rudder gave it no bite and without this control she would suddenly swing round beam onto the oncoming wave. The resulting broach, with a wave breaking over us, frequently breaking gear, meant then waiting until the boat eventually could be brought back onto course and we going off again. Since I was the only person who could splice wire on board, I found myself spending far too much time below at the vice re-splicing broken spinnaker guys. Eventually, after two had broken within minutes, I leaped on deck, had the spinnaker taken down and we boomed out two headsails instead. The crew were convinced that this was a cruising technique and unworthy in a racing boat but we were much steadier and, when we came to calculate the day's run, it was proved that we had covered 17 more miles towards the finish line than on the previous hell-for-leather day. It also meant I could allow the less experienced crew to learn to steer the boat.

Our southerly route, a composite great circle course, going

down to 53 degrees south to cut the distance and keep with the stronger winds, became a bit worrying when boats behind and to the north of us reported icebergs around them long before we saw any. But it was cold. The sails were icy, ice formed on the mast spreaders and occasionally fell in lumps onto the deck and the lookouts, posted to ensure we did not bump into a berg when conditions were misty, had to be relieved every half hour to avoid hypothermia. Repairing sails in these conditions, where gloves made work impossible, was torture. Nevertheless, we hung onto our lead and even extended it to 200 miles from Rob James in *Great Britain 2*.

One morning as we were tidying up the deck after a gybe in reasonably light conditions but in a heavy sea, Bill Abrams was moving a block from the gunwale. The spinnaker suddenly filled and the lazy guy tightened beneath him. He was thrown into the air and landed in the sea alongside the boat. When he passed the stern he was thrown a lifebuoy while the klaxon sounded to bring all the crew on deck. Our first task was to get rid of the spinnaker, whose huge size would hinder manoeuvring, and while part of the crew did this, others went to get the engine started. Initially it wouldn't start, and when eventually it was coaxed into life, the folding propeller which had not been used for more than two weeks, was jammed. We got the staysail on deck so we could sail back, but the propeller suddenly opened and we spun the boat round to retrace our course.

Bill could no longer be seen. When last sighted he was supporting himself on the lifebuoy so we knew he would not sink, but the water was very cold, close to zero, and we had no idea how long he could hang on. We set a reciprocal course and quickly noticed a number of albatross circling about a mile ahead. We motored straight for them and eventually picked out a speck beneath. It was Bill, who waved feebly. We brought the boat up on the windward side of him and as it rolled its deck downwards, grabbed him beneath the arms and hauled him aboard. Bill had been in the water almost 20 minutes and was frozen so he was hurried below, stripped and towelled and put into a sleeping bag immediately.

With Bill back on-board we turned our attention to rejoining the race but when we put the engine into gear to turn round there was a clunk and the engine stalled. In concentrating on recovering Bill no one had noticed the staysail sheet fall overside and now it was wound around the propeller. 'Someone,' I said, 'has to go in to clear it.' Suddenly the crowd on deck had something more important to do. I went below and pulled on a wet suit, the only protection available, and jumped in. The water was freezing and however good the suit is, water gets in somewhere and makes its way agonisingly towards your warm stomach. Within seconds my feet, face and hands, which were exposed, lost their feeling. I took a huge breath and ducked beneath the boat to see if the rope could be unwound. No chance. A hundred and fifty horsepower had gone into tightening it around the shaft so it would have to be cut away. Surfacing, I was handed a knife and went under again. My wrist was numb from the cold and would not produce a cutting movement so I was reduced to working my whole arm back and forth to cut the rope. Eventually, after increasingly short spells beneath the water as the cold sapped my stamina, the last strand came free and willing hands hauled me back aboard. One of the crew handed me a brandy, not always recommended for situations like this, but it had the effect of speedily changing the colour of my exposed flesh from blue to red.

We held our lead and as we approached the longitude of Australia I began to work on when we should make our spring to the north. This time the second leg finished in Auckland instead of Sydney and we had to traverse the Tasman Sea and pass around Cape Reinga, the northern cape of New Zealand on the way. The Tasman Sea can be a bit of a bastard, but it can also harbour highs with light winds. Our lead of 200 miles was slightly less than a day and therefore fragile so the decision on when to go was vital. Unlike these days, there was little meteorological information available to us, no facsimile machines, and the only clue was the weather we had and what we could learn from others – if they were telling the truth! We made our choice, sped north into the Tasman Sea and ran into a high right in the middle, but as the rest of the fleet found it as well they did not close on us. By the time they got clear of the light winds we were round Reinga a day ahead and held this to the finish. The big bird had proved she could fly.

Our welcome in Auckland was magnificent. We carefully dressed so the crew were in uniform and crashed across the finish line at 12 knots, then sailed up harbour towards our berth escorted by two tugs with fire hoses playing. Marsden Wharf, where the fleet was to berth, was crowded and among those greeting us was Pete Montgomery, whose first question was to ask me about my much-vaunted response to the T-shirt produced by the New Zealanders for the recent Lions tour, which advertised 'Bash a Pom a Day'. I went below and changed, to re-emerge wearing my T-shirt which simply stated 'Have a Good

Day, Pluck a Kiwi'. Honour was restored. The Aucklanders gave us a magnificent reception and most of the crew were invited back to homes or went touring for Christmas. A small piece of opportunism gave us the pleasure of taking the pop group Fleetwood Mac for a sail, followed by being backstage at their concert. Skip Novak, joint skipper of *King's Legend*, had met the pop group's manager and invited them down to see his boat, saying to look for the best-looking one in the fleet. I ran into them walking along the quay looking for his boat and when they asked for the best-looking boat naturally took them to *Condor* ...

After overseeing the haul out I handed over to Les and flew home. When I rejoined the boat in Rio a package from an anonymous New Zealander was waiting for me. I undid it to find yet another T-shirt, this one with a picture of a kiwi with feathers flying and beneath this the legend 'Pluck me Gently'. The New Zealanders had clearly won the war of the T-shirts!

Les got caught the wrong side of the low pressure systems and lost time on the third leg so morale had sunk a bit by the time *Condor* arrived in Rio. My morale was suffering even more as I had picked up shingles during the winter, an attack on the nervous system that very nearly took my left eye completely and caused it to see double for some years until the retina sorted itself out. I was kept on 12 pain killers a day for three months and lost two stone in weight. I was far from cured when I got to Rio and left the re-fit to Les who, we agreed, had better come along on the next leg in case I had a relapse. I stayed in a darkened room in an apartment resting.

Eric Tabarly joined the race in Auckland with his maxi *Pen Duick V*, which had a spent uranium keel, banned by the rules as it gave a considerable advantage being denser than lead. Given our 3 per cent penalty on account of our carbon fibre mast, also banned at the time, we suggested that Tabarly be given the same penalty rather than be disqualified as seemed likely. The race committee turned our solution down, but later, when the race was in full swing, announced they had disqualified Tabarly on account of our protest. We had not made a protest, only a suggestion, but this did not stop the French ostracising us in Rio until they discovered the truth of the matter. We were keen to race against Tabarly, but on level terms, and were delighted when he announced he would still accompany the race as an unofficial entry. We had a race, boat for boat, and the winner would be the first across the finish line.

At the start *Great Britain 2* tacked on top of us so we hardened in the sheets and pointed higher until he lost power and we could sail out of his lee, yelling all the time for him not to sail below his course. Once out to sea there were few tactics along the Brazilian coast until we turned north when the choice became whether to stay inshore and get a slight current advantage or head offshore for a better wind. Clare Francis in *ADC Accutrac* took the inshore course, giving her the lead for a day or two, but the rest of us went out and benefited long-term. At the equator we were sharing the lead in sight of *Great Britain 2* and *Pen Duick V*, but the latter tore off once we got into the headwinds of the north-east trades and had a lead of 100 miles as we approached the horse latitudes, home of the Azores high pressure system.

With three large boats of reasonably similar performance, the leg from Rio to Portsmouth was always going to be decided by the Azores High and Tabarly had a nice start. For a couple of weeks, I took one of the crew off the watch system to concentrate on receiving the shipping weather forecasts, transmitted at high speed in Morse code. We recorded it on a tape recorder, halved the speed, translated the code and got our weather picture twice a day. The most significant factor this showed was that the centre of the Azores High appeared to move eastwards every five to six days. Plotting ahead, it was clear that if it kept to this schedule it would pass over our course through the Azores just as we all arrived there. The race would be a drifting match for a while, decided by luck with cat's paws – ripples on the sea when a gust of wind touches calm water – and we would be starting 100 miles behind.

I had faith in our crew to perform well in these conditions but even so luck would be the major factor. An alternative, admittedly a risky one that would take us further from the finish line and meant oblivion if the high did not move as usual, was to head out to the west clear of the back of the high, and hopefully pick up the westerly winds sooner than the others. After agonising over this for a couple of days, I called the watch leaders and Les together and told them this was my intention. There was much sucking of teeth, the crew clearly thought that shingles had affected my brain, but we paid off 60 degrees and headed north-west.

For the first day the other boats made good progress, on the second they slowed a little, on the third they were still moving slowly but Tabarly had stopped. On the fourth *Great Britain 2* had Tabarly in sight, so perhaps we should have gone that way, except, they were becalmed as well. In the meantime, after three days of moderate speeds to the north-west we were clearing the high and experiencing a light south-wester coming in from behind. This slowly strengthened and we paid off before it under spinnaker and set a course straight for home. We had 300 miles further to go than the others so all now depended upon how quickly the high released them from its grip.

One of the rules of the race was that we had to send in a position twice a week and, of course, the whole fleet could hear what was being said on the radio. I did not want to let the rest of the fleet know what we were doing as this was a handicap race and the slower boats behind would benefit if they followed us. But we had to make a position report and safety demanded that it be accurate. After thinking about it for a while I called Sue on the radio and told her to take the day of her birthday from the four figures of latitude and longitude that I then passed along. I told her to wait two days and then phone the race office with the position, but give the correct date for it.

We knew the race committee were focused on Tabarly, as they had a guilty conscience about disqualifying him. So confident were they that Tabarly would win they had even had a special line honours award made for him to try and make up for their attitude towards him before. So I gambled on them plotting that position for the day Sue phoned it in rather than the date it was given, which is exactly what they did. The French navy meanwhile proudly announced that Tabarly was winning as usual. Cashing in on the forthcoming publicity Kriter offered 200 bottles of champagne to the first boat home and everyone was happy, particularly us, as the position given for Tabarly was 40 miles behind and we knew we were as fast downwind. A severe gale on the approach to the Channel gave us as rough conditions as we had had in the Southern Ocean but our crew were now highly experienced and we crashed on under our bulletproof heavy spinnaker.

South of Looe we put a call through to race control, who were not particularly interested in our position but excitedly told us of their plans for the reception they had laid on to celebrate Tabarly's victory across the finish line the next day and the special prize they had ready for him. We asked when he was due and were told 1400 hours. They asked us where we were and I told them truthfully that we were 40 miles south of Looe. 'Jolly good,' they said, 'and what's your ETA?' I told them, again truthfully, 1000 hours. The line went quiet and then an incredulous and very peeved voice asked us if we were sure. Oh yes, we were sure all right, barring accidents. The line went dead. We charged on overnight and at dawn passed the Needles into the Solent. Off Yarmouth a boat full of incredulous French journalists came out to us. *'Mon dieu, c'est* Condor! *Ou est Tabarly?'* they asked. 'Can I tell them?' asked Peter Blake. I nodded and he climbed onto the weather rail, pointed behind and yelled, 'He's 40 miles back there!' It was a sweet moment.

We finished shortly after 1000. We would have finished a few minutes earlier but the race committee had not noticed that a buoy had been changed in the approaches to Portsmouth. We rounded what we thought was the right buoy but found the name was wrong, gybed, split the mainsail in the process, went down to the next buoy which was correct, and gybed again, now under only a headsail, and sailed through the finish line. I put it to the committee that they had got it wrong and we deserved redress. Errol Bruce agreed and said if we had seven minutes would we accept it, and I agreed. Then, out of pique we supposed, the committee re-imposed the carbon mast penalty for the whole race so I challenged it. The chairman told us that if we did not like it we could protest. We did protest, despite the chairman telling us it was ungentlemanly, and of course we won.

Poor Eric Tabarly arrived when our party was four hours old and he looked very tired. He asked how we had got ahead of him and I took him down into the navigation area and showed him the chart of our route. That was very clever was his response. It had been a gamble and was only clever because we had pulled it off. We never received the prize for being first over the line, nor the 200 bottles of champagne for being first home! But we did not care.

1978 was a Round Britain year and although the Whitbread had kept me too busy to focus on a really competitive entry I did not want to miss my favourite race. After our victory in 1974 it was obvious that a large multi-hull was required to win but there was nothing available. Les and Peter planned to take *Condor* so I chartered *Great Britain 2* from Chay Blyth, with Billy King Harman as crew, to make a really interesting race of it. Sadly, *Condor* did not enter in the end, so we battled round losing to the multi-hulls. *Great Britain 2* had been built for a crew of 16 paratroopers and her deck layout was primitive, everything appeared designed to be a challenge to sheer muscular strength. It took us five hours to set the spinnaker first time and the spinnaker pole only went up when we thoroughly lost our tempers with it. A graceful-looking craft, solidly built, slightly out-designed by this time, but a really nice sea boat as we learned while passing Muckle Flugga in a wind-against-tide situation.

The race is memorable for two reasons, as well as the fact that it started to bring my strength back after the shingles. From Black Head in Northern Ireland to Barra Head we raced neck and neck against Nigel Irens and Mark Priddy in their 31-foot trimaran *Gordano Goose*. They started a cable astern and finished a cable ahead, we had lost time when the genoa split. The sight of their craft, hull and weather arm bouncing clear of the water with Mark's enormous bulk stuck out on this weather arm to keep the boat upright, looking like an aquatic motor cycle and side car, is one I shall always remember.

The other memory is being becalmed off Beachy Head when we found ourselves just 100 metres ahead of Martin Read in his 30-foot trimaran. I was steering when Martin called over that it was ridiculous to be becalmed this close together in a race when normally we would have rafted up for dinner. This seemed a good idea so I called back that I was putting the fenders over and expected him and his crew in ten minutes. I woke Billy, who was confused by being told we had guests for dinner when he was quite sure he was on a boat in a two-handed race. The rules did state that no boat could have more or less than two crew, but neither of us was moving so we could hardly be accused of racing, nor were either of us well placed enough to win anything so had nothing to lose. In any case Martin was on the race committee so I felt safe! Dinner – smoked trout and stew, followed by port – was interrupted when the wind came up. Both of us thought the conditions favoured ourselves, so selflessly encouraged the other to take advantage of what obviously suited them! Martin beat us home.

The two incidents go to show the progress that was being made with multi-hulls at that time. Admittedly multi-hulls are good on a reach, so Nigel holding us was perhaps not such a surprise, but by Beachy Head, 2,000 miles into the race, he was ahead of us and Martin Read with us, both in 30-foot trimarans holding an 80-foot mono-hull. The lesson was there for all who wanted to see it.

On our return to Plymouth the commodore of the Royal Western Yacht Club, Lt Colonel Jack Odling-Smee, came up and asked me about the dinner incident. When I had finished the tale, he harrumphed a couple of times and then said, 'Well, I don't know what the rules ought to say about this, but it was bloody good form!' Jack had been in at the inception of the race and that attitude explained why it had such a good atmosphere.

11

RIDING THE BIG CATS

The west coast of Scotland is one of the best-kept secrets as far as sailors are concerned. We had started to explore it in *Suhaili* while living in Troon – first the Firth of Clyde and the anchorages at Brodick and Lamlash on Arran and then round the Mull of Kintyre and up the Firth of Lorne and through the Sound of Mull. One season we left *Suhaili* at Kerrera, the island off Oban, and used to drive up on Friday evenings, returning on Sundays having explored quietly all weekend. The beauty of the coast, the bare hills and the lack of people made this a perfect place to relax.

Chris Bonington joined us in August 1979 while he was researching his book *Quest for Adventure*. We sailed up to Scavaig in Skye to climb the Cuillin ridge together, memorable as far as I was concerned because we found at one stage that we faced an 80-foot drop and the way round would have taken an hour. Chris explained that we would have to abseil down then, in response to my query, explained what this entailed. It all sounded very unseamanlike to me so I told him I would get myself down using a bosun's chair lowering hitch, which jams if released rather than letting go as in abseiling. As I disappeared from view he asked if the knot was safe and I told him not to be impertinent. Five minutes later we were rolling with laughter at the foot of the drop.

The anchorage was nicely sheltered, but when the wind went back to doing what it ought, blow from the south-west, the entrance proved rather difficult and our first attempt to motor against the wind failed. Remembering someone telling me that there was usually a lull for a few minutes either side of high water, we tried again the next day and got out, but I am still unsure it was due to this magical high-water effect or just luck. We decided to head for Rum and on the way across Sara, at the helm, called out that she could see a ferry. Somewhat surprised I asked her what colour. Blue, she responded. The Caledonian MacBrayne ferries, which connect all the islands, are black and I knew her eyesight was good. How many masts? I called out. When she replied with three I knew what she had in sight, the Royal Yacht *Britannia*. We motored over and waved to the entire royal family before making our way into the main bay where we spent the next day.

Chris had to return, so we headed back to Tobermory where he caught the ferry to Oban. By this time there were storm warnings for the Sole and Fastnet shipping areas, moving north-east towards us and concern being expressed for the Fastnet race yachts. Tobermory did not give much room if the wind got nasty, so we motored down the Sound of Mull and anchored at Ardtornish, put out all 22 fathoms of anchor chain and went to bed. I stayed up listening to the news coming in about the carnage in the Fastnet race as the wind howled through the night, thankfully well above us. After a short sleep at daybreak we awoke to a placid calm and Sara reporting otters playing around the anchor chain.

Away to the south, 15 people had lost their lives in one of the worst disasters ever to hit a yacht race. The problem was, as much as anything, that the most recent races had had calmer conditions and this had given inexperienced people more confidence than they should have had. From the tragedy came an excellent report commissioned by the Royal Ocean Racing Club. This report resulted in tighter standards and the insistence on more experience among the crews, which has benefited all sailors since.

Fishermen are renowned pessimists and the west coasters were no exception. They seemed to spend much of their days making long and morose comparisons with each other on the VHF radio about how poor the fishing was and how they would have to sell their boats if matters did not improve. We would happily leave them to it if they did not monopolise one of the main 'chat' channels for their prolonged complaints.

To give me some practical support I had invited Dave and Jan Mitchell to come up and join us at the marina. Dave had worked with me at Mercury and Port Hamble and was a typical raw Hampshire lad, well over six feet tall, who I had got to know very well and trusted completely. They moved north. With Dave ensconced, Sue and I had a bit more time in the summers to spend cruising with *Suhaili* on the beautiful west coast of Scotland, but once I was ousted and without the attraction of a business to run I decided to get back into serious racing.

By 1980 I was missing the international racing circuit and decided it was time to rejoin with another multi-hull. As usual, I was unable to make any progress obtaining sponsorship and so

I took out a large mortgage from Mercantile Credit to build a new boat, hoping that sponsorship would materialise once the boat existed to cover her costs. *British Oxygen* had shown the way to go: bigger, however much harder the work, was likely to be better. The problem with *British Oxygen* had been our lack of knowledge at the time about the engineering of such craft, so she had been built rather stronger than was necessary in places. This had added to her weight making her, at 12 tons, very heavy by later standards. The hulls, however, had been lovely and since the mould for this still existed I decided to start from there.

I went south and met with Rod Macalpine-Downie and he drew up a new boat based upon the hulls but otherwise very different. For a start we increased the freeboard at the bow to avoid ploughing into the waves. By now better resins were available, meaning that greater strength was possible for less weight and we made the main beam out of timber not aluminium. As with *British Oxygen*, the boat was controlled from a central nacelle as I liked being in the middle. Some of the newer French boats were adopting two control positions, one in each hull, but I saw no point in duplicating the steering, winches and instruments that this involved as it increased cost and weight.

The new boat was built by Reg White in Brightlingsea, launched as *Sea Falcon* by Sue and Sara simultaneously breaking bottles of Auchentoshan whisky on each bow, and towed round to Cowes where Spencer's stepped the mast and put up the rig. Aside from the sheer freeboard forward and less aft, the engineering was much improved and the whole boat when launched weighed just 4.25 tons without her rig. At 70 feet in length and 32 in beam, she was smaller than the new 80 footers being built in France, but she was a lot stronger and proved to be a superb sea boat. With a larger rig than *British Oxygen* and being much lighter, she was a far faster boat. We ran her up to 32 knots in one burst in Portland Harbour. Of all my big cats, she remains my favourite.

In February 1981, we sailed her round the coast to Troon with a mixed crew of locals, including the actor Iain Cuthbertson who claimed the trip cost him a great deal of weight. Then Billy King-Harman and I took her out into the Atlantic in order to qualify for the new two-handed transatlantic races. As we ran out along the Ulster coast I took some sleep only to be awakened by Billy saying we were doing 18 knots and he thought we might have too much sail up! So our hopes were high when the race started in June.

New and exciting equipment was becoming available. A fax machine that could download weather forecasts was a huge advance, enabling us to try and predict the best route to take, and we fitted a brand new piece of equipment that was just coming onto the yachting market: a satellite navigation system, made by Walkers. The frequency of fixes varied considerably owing to the lack of satellites at the time and would provide a fixed position within 15 minutes off the UK coast, but there was a gap of up to eight hours off the United States. It was accurate to within a couple of miles and saved a great deal of time previously spent with a sextant and calculations.

The TwoSTAR Two-handed Transatlantic Race started on 6 June 1981. The first night was a beat into a strong south-westerly. We took it carefully, not pushing too hard and we found ourselves in the lead the next day. Looking at the faxed forecasts we plumbed to go north of an oncoming low pressure system, thereby keeping the winds behind us, our best point of sailing. Sadly, our forestay – a new type which consisted of an aluminium extrusion with bearings at each end, allowing it to roll up the headsail – jammed its upper bearing. We dropped the sail since the wind had risen to Force 7.

The next day I spent two hours at the masthead reconnecting the bearing as the low closed in on us and we missed getting the right side of it by a few miles. This made the difference between a strong following wind to the north and a strong headwind to the south and as we couldn't get that little bit further north we got the latter. This meant we had to heave to for almost a day and cost us any chance of winning. We tried, though, and during the next days achieved the best distance covered in 24 hours by a good few miles. We pushed so much that in the last couple of days the whole boat was leaping out of the water and thudding back down so hard that water flew through the trampoline and eventually began to loosen the central nacelle from its fastening behind the main beam. This forced us to slow as the nacelle contained not just all our instruments but, more importantly, the hydraulic pump for the steering. We closed the gap, but we had lost too much time earlier and could only finish fourth after 15½ days at sea. We found a race to get us home. Sue and Rod Macalpine-Downie joined the crew in a course that took us via the Lizard to Brest. We came third, our time from Ambrose Light to the Lizard being 11 days 7 hours.

Our speed towards the end of the TwoSTAR race attracted attention in France and I received a request to charter her to a French team. Having negotiated a good rate, I agreed but as they could not get insurance unless I was aboard I was forced to sail with them. Their race was from La Rochelle to New

Orleans so we went to France and trained there. There was a lot of posing, not too much sailing, but our skipper obviously thought he was the new Tabarly and adopted an arrogant attitude. We made a disastrous start, his navigator even missed a mark off the course so we had to go back and do it again. Then, instead of letting the boat rip by easing the sheets and taking advantage of a multi-hull's ability when reaching, we sailed hard on the wind for a point in the Atlantic that he decided he had to round.

On the way the navigator altered the clocks, as one does an hour for each 15 degrees, but he altered them the wrong way so we had breakfast before it was light, lunch at elevenses and dinner mid-afternoon! Since it was my turn to prepare the meals that day, I served them at local time, to suit the sun. The navigator quietly corrected it the next night. Having reached this mysterious waypoint, we hung around for nearly a day because our skipper could not decide whether to take the northern or southern route and was waiting for advice from a meteorologist. Eventually we started on the northern route then he changed his mind and we went south. By this time, we were lying about 14th.

We chugged across the Atlantic with our skipper pouring scorn on the boat, which he was sailing like a mono-hull. I found this hard enough to take as, despite the fact they were paying for it, I had pride in my boat. But when they cheered at the news from Argentina that HMS *Invincible* had been sunk in the Falklands War, I became a very unpleasant person to live with. I had put up with their arrogance and incompetence until that point but now I really was angry. I went on the offensive by criticising everything and anything they did – there was plenty of scope.

There were five of them and as I did not trust them I slept with a winch handle in my open sleeping bag. To add to their discomfiture, the Argentine forces on the Falklands surrendered just as we finished in tenth position. I think the crew were relieved to get to Gulfport, Mississippi!

The contract called for them to ship the boat home but they claimed they had no money. It was a clear breach of contract but that was secondary to me as I wanted to get home to participate in the next Round Britain race. I asked around for crew to help me and Marc Pajot, who had won the race, introduced me to a young rugby player who wanted to get into sailing. Bernard Gallay was 23 years old, 6 feet 4 inches tall, and played flanker for the French junior international team and the Army. His English was poor, so was my French, but 21 hours after arriving in Gulfport we had stored up and departed together to sail the boat back to England. This was to be the beginning of a long partnership and a friendship that continues to this day.

The voyage from Gulfport back to Plymouth took 23 days. Early on, I introduced Bernard to the mysteries of my main meal at sea: Pot Mess, similar in construction to bouillabaisse but with meat instead of fish. He watched incredulously as item after item was tossed into the pressure cooker. I usually start by frying some onions and garlic in butter, adding whatever meat is handy – corned beef, stewed steak, fresh meat, etc. – and then I throw in a choice of vegetables. A tablespoon of pepper, a couple of bay leaves if one is feeling sophisticated, an Oxo cube, a couple of slices of bacon, which for some reason seems to act as a catalyst, then put the top on the cooker and stew for 40 minutes. Ideally one eats no more than half at a sitting so that the remainder acts as a basis for the next meal. Thus fortified we had some brilliant sailing, 84 miles in four hours on one occasion, but as we approached Plymouth the mainsail tore, a few hours later the spare went the same way, and then we were faced with calms.

We eventually staggered into Plymouth on 9 July, 17 hours before the start of the race. A tired boat, she had just done more than 9,000 miles with just a 21-hour break, and a similarly exhausted skipper were handicap enough, but the Royal Western Race Committee also gave me a 19-hour penalty for being late! Effectively this put us out of the running as there was absolutely no way we could make up that amount of time in a race that would last eight days or thereabouts, it meant sailing 15 per cent faster than any other boat and there were some fast ones entered, but the Royal Western committee did not seem to grasp this point.

Really there was little purpose in taking part with such an enormous penalty, but Billy King-Harman had taken leave from the Army to do the race so we made the effort. Billy and Bernard rushed around to get sails repaired and Sue bought fresh stores while I dealt with the scrutiny, my temper not being helped by the club's scrutineer asking me if I knew how to use the sextant! We started well, but any chance of success was wiped away when the tired mainsail split off the west coast of Ireland and we spent eight hours sewing it back together. Fortunately places like Barra in the Outer Hebrides take a practical approach to problems. We took over the village hall, courtesy of Father MacLennan, and while Billy repaired the mainsail there I did some essential tightening of bolts on the mast. We caught up a little thereafter but could only finish fourth.

*

Sue and I did a short cruise towards the Western Isles in *Sea Falcon* that August, taking Sara and my nephews to Appin. We were struck by a nasty Katabatic wind off the Mull of Kintyre on the way back, which lifted a hull and sent the speed up to 29 knots before we bore away and got under control. A less speedy craft would probably have gone over. It was *Sea Falcon*'s acceleration that reduced the sting of the squall by quickly lowering the apparent wind. Then it was over to France, sponsored by Olympus cameras, to take part in the second Route du Rhum, a single-handed race from St Malo to Guadeloupe.

Most attention before the start focused on a new proa, to be sailed by Guy Delage. It made Meccano look simple, with a long rakish hull and small pod out on a beam on its starboard side. The pod could float and be swung about its axis and although the reason for this was never made clear it created great media fascination. All through the week before the race this moveable pod was demonstrated daily to an admiring throng of press. However, when I sailed out for the start just ahead of this contraption I was no more than a mile towards the start line when there was a tremendous commotion behind me. Delage's boat had broken up. It was as well it happened within a mile of the port as he was hardly inconvenienced. His sponsors were quite happy though, they got more publicity from the incident than they could have hoped for if he had won. It was estimated that more than 200,000 people saw the start of the race and French television was following us for a day in a ferry. Sailing, of this type anyway, was big news in France hence why they had so many entrants and sponsors prepared to back them.

The first night, half the fleet went into Brest for shelter from a full gale, the remainder of us plugged away, making miles that those sheltering would never make up. By the fifth day I was sharing the lead with Marc Pajot, with three other large multi-hulls close behind, averaging between 6 and 10 knots as we beat out to the west. I steered whenever I could, enjoying the sheer pleasure of sailing fast in a well-balanced boat, sensing her surges and compensating lightly in advance for any slews she might wish to make to reduce the resistance created every time the rudder is used. A human can anticipate these moves whereas an electrical autopilot can only react when it senses the boat is off course. However, single handing a 70-foot catamaran is hard work and would be quite impossible without an automatic pilot to provide time to cook, sleep, navigate and do all the maintenance tasks that arise when crossing an ocean.

Like most of the boats, I had an Autohelm system, which worked off the batteries. Maintaining a charge was essential, so the small Honda generator had to work at least eight hours a day if I was to have any time away from the helm. So the appearance of thick brown smoke from the nacelle on the fifth afternoon out spelled trouble. The source of the smoke was the heavy duty battery connections which had burned off their plastic covering and were glowing red hot. I dived beneath the smoke and tore off a terminal with a spanner, then crawled back coughing into the open air. The automatic pilot had stopped so I took over and steered while the smoke cleared and I tried to figure out what had gone wrong. I never did work out the cause of the problem, there was no logic to it, but by dint of steadying the boat on course, diving into the nacelle and disconnecting all non-essential electronics, I was able to restore the pilot. Its performance was lazy, not surprising given the drain the batteries had just had, so I put the charger on. I would have been lucky to get away with such a serious problem – I didn't, the batteries refused to take a charge. This was calamitous. In order to rest or work I had to have the automatic pilot, which now only ran when the charger was on, but I had insufficient petrol to keep the charger running all the way to the finish on the other side of the Atlantic.

Withdrawal was the obvious course of action, but not attractive. However, to continue I needed new batteries and more petrol which meant a 400-mile diversion to the nearest land at Madeira, and by the time I had done that the rest of the fleet would be too far in front to hope to catch up. Just the same, the other two British boats in Class 1 had withdrawn and I did not wish to join them. I sent a message to my sponsor and sailed to Madeira where Chris had made arrangements for me to pick up new batteries and petrol from the pilot boat off the harbour, and sailed on. My position had gone from first to 22nd, so, angry at the delay, I set out to catch up as much as I could. For five days we flew, covering 1,750 miles and pulling up to 14th place, but then the winds steadied all the way across the central Atlantic and none of the top 16 positions changed to the finish. My automatic pilot failed three days from the finish and I arrived at Guadeloupe so exhausted I did not really appreciate the wonderful reception the organisers had laid on.

The Atlantic sailing record of 12 days, 4 hours and 1 minute had been held by the schooner *Atlantic* since 1906. To work up some interest in it, the *Sunday Times* announced a prize for the first person to beat the *Atlantic*'s time. Sadly, they announced this when there were no British boats around capable of beating the time, both Chay Blyth and I were between boats, so the

Frenchman Eric Tabarly in his hydrofoil trimaran had no competition. His time was not that fast, averaging only about 12.5 knots, but fast enough to beat the *Atlantic*. Shortly afterwards Marc Pajot brought the time down to 9 days, 10 hours and 6 minutes, an average speed of 13.268 knots in his catamaran *Elf Aquitaine*.

Sea Falcon had shown that she was as fast as *Elf Aquitaine* during the Route du Rhum, so I decided to have a go at the record on the way home. The secret would be to await a suitable weather pattern. What was needed was a depression that was heading towards Scotland or Iceland and not Labrador – more likely in the winter but not easy to predict. For such an attempt I needed crew who came from the services, with one exception, Arthur Gibson, whose speciality lay in aerial photography. Four of us flew to Nassau, recommissioned the boat and set out for Norfolk, Virginia, where the rest of the crew were to join.

Since the radio was away for an overhaul we did not receive any warning of the hurricane that struck us off Cape Hatteras. Very shortly we were hove to as the seas built up extremely quickly, fuelled by a northerly wind and a north-going current, the Gulf Stream. For eight hours we lay a-hull. Sailing down the waves just slammed us into the back of the wave in front, sailing with the waves on the beam, since they were short, was asking to be capsized, so we held her with the waves coming from the quarter. The only consolation in all this was that at least the Gulf Stream was warm so that as waves broke over the boat we were soaked but not frozen.

Arthur, whose first experience of sailing this was, expressed some concern when he realised that unlike flying we had not had to file the equivalent of a flight plan and there was thus no authority who would, in due course, organise a search for us if we sank. Oliver Stanley, a guards officer, refused to be put off at all and maintained a constantly cheerful demeanour, the other crew member broke down and crawled into a corner, sobbing that he was a broken man. On two occasions all that saved us from going over as we were tilted by an oncoming wave was the weight of the water on the deck when the wave broke over us. When the wind slowly eased, apart from a parted forestay which did not dismast us because we had led the spinnaker halyards forward as a precaution, we were unharmed. We crept up to Cape Henry, the entrance to Chesapeake Bay and the US Navy sent a launch to tow us into Little Creek, an amphibious base where we were to berth and the remainder of the crew awaited us. They had been about to report us overdue to the US Coastguard when they heard we were coming into the bay.

Our hosts were Assault Craft Unit TWO and the US Navy lived up to their generous reputation as hosts. Within hours the Seabees arrived with two cranes and hauled out our rig and placed the cat ashore on improvised chocks. Everyone seemed to want to help, even the fire brigade who got the job of 'laundering' the sails. With repairs made we sailed up to Atlantic Highlands and awaited the next depression. Ideally one needs to wait until a clear pattern of favourable weather is approaching, but we had the pressure of servicemen needing to get back to their units, so we took the first promising weather and sailed on 4 April 1983 as the wind turned westerly. It was soon clear that our depression, far from heading north-easterly, was heading south of east. We had one good day of winds when we averaged 14 knots, but then it turned easterly and died. What in meteorological terms is called an omega block, after

On board *Ocean Spirit*, with Les Williams and Clement Freud, sailing from Cape Town to Rio de Janeiro, 1971.

Sara, safely harnessed, on our journey to Lisbon in 1971, during which we sailed into a gale – but happily her mother and I were soon back together again.

Sue and Sara during our visit to California, where we had such a wonderful time in 1976.

With Bertie Miller, who had been my seamanship instructor when I was younger. He was one of the strongest men I ever knew, and remained a good friend until his death. (Bill Rowntree)

British Oxygen cuts through the waves in the 1974 Round Britain.

Part of the crew on *Frigate* during the 1973 Admiral's Cup.

Sea Falcon remains my favourite of all the catamarans I sailed – we took her up to 32 knots in Portland Harbour on one occasion in 1981.

Cooking on *Suhaili* – but the weather was about to get much worse when I crossed the Atlantic back to Europe in November 1990.

A battered *Suhaili* limps in to the Azores, after being hit by a huge storm which broke her mast.

Suhaili moored up in among all the ice during my visit with Chris Bonington to Greenland in 1991.

Base camp, with our objective, the Cathedral, behind.

There's no one better to accompany you, if you're climbing up ice or a sheer rock face, than Chris Bonington.

ENZA New Zealand coming in to Brest after breaking the Jules Verne round-the-world record, completing the journey in 74 days, 22 hours and 17 minutes.

Celebrating our new record, Peter Blake and I.

On my way to Tora Bora in Afghanistan, for a BBC programme.

With my hunting trophy, Sir Ranulph Fiennes.

The Three Dogs, as the programme was called: me, John Simpson and Ran in the Arctic.

Saga Insurance completing the Velux 5 Oceans Race in 2007 when, at 68, I became the oldest man to complete a solo round-the-world race.

The 'Indian rope trick' to repair *Saga*.

Working an astrolabe, to try to work out how Columbus had navigated his way to America 500 years before.

With William Ward, who has worked with me on the Clipper project for many years.

The Clipper project has been one of the most important projects I've worked on, but things don't always go to plan, as when one of our boats ran aground near Rio in November 2015.

its horseshoe shape of isobars around a high pressure centre, formed in the mid-Atlantic and we all but stopped in the calms.

Runs of 11, 15 and 18 miles per day meant the record was unthreatened, but our survival was. We had food aboard for 18 days, but by the 14th day at sea we still had half the Atlantic to sail and the menu was limited. It was obvious that we were going to starve if we did not find more supplies, so I started to call up passing ships and eventually got a response from the Norwegian bulk carrier *Tongola*, which stopped and waited for us to row across. Oliver and I set out across three-quarters of a mile of ocean in the Avon inflatable, came alongside the pilot ladder that had been lowered for us and I flung myself across as the swell lifted the dinghy up. I nearly bounced off again, the six water containers festooned around my neck hit the hull first and sprang me back, but I had a grip and climbed up, securing the painter so that Oliver could follow. The Norwegians were extremely generous, supplying us with enough food for ten days and filling our water containers. They even supplied 600 cigarettes, which was a great relief to the smokers. We rowed back past three large whales and had our first proper meal in a few days.

If ever there was an example of the old adage that sailing ships have destinations and not estimated times of arrival, this was a classic. Eventually, an easterly wind arose and we reached Plymouth on 30 April, our 26th day, out of power, with water and food rationed. Forecasting was not as developed as it is today, when we can predict the path of a depression with reasonable accuracy, but even a large, fast, light catamaran cannot be moved if there is no wind at all.

*

The same problem, a lack of wind, prevented us from taking part in the Three Peaks race that year when we drifted around for four days off the entrance to the Bristol Channel. Sue phoned the coastguard to find out if they had heard from us and someone in their station, quite disgracefully, contacted the *Daily Mail* to tell them we were missing. No doubt they earned themselves £25 for the information. We only discovered what was going on when the collier MV *Portrush* stopped to tell us there was an all ships message out about our absence. They reported us and that was the end of the matter, but it should never have happened. What with one thing and another we missed the start of the race so returned to Troon.

Our final race that year was a new one, a two-handed affair from Plymouth to Vilamoura in Portugal, organised by the Royal Western Yacht Club. Sue and I decided we would do this one together. We were third at the end of the outward leg, not bad since it was Sue's first experience of helping to handle a really big cat with just two crew. At one stage she had to help haul me up the mast to clear a tangled sail while she continued to steer the boat, a very testing task. The return passage was our chance to catch up and we sped off up the Portuguese coast, beating, but *Sea Falcon* was fast in these conditions.

Off Finisterre we ran into fog and when this cleared we were nicely north of the cape and able to make a course directly for the finish line. That night Sue called me up when the mainsail halyard winch collapsed and I crawled beneath the sail with a torch and spanner to put it together again. My next recollection is of a bang and being flung sharply through the air and then I hit my head and passed out. When I came to Sue was bending over me. Neither of us knew what had happened so we crawled back into the cockpit and tried to make sense of the situation. Sue had noticed the mast creaking and we noticed the port backstay was loose and there were splits around the nacelle.

We began a check around the boat and soon discovered serious damage: a split right across the deck on the starboard hull halfway between the main and forward beam. The cracks descended down either side of the hull to within a foot of the keel, a large section was missing from the inside of the hull, which was full of water. The crack was opening up each time the boat rose on a wave so, to stop it getting worse, we attached a spinnaker sheet to the forward beam and cranked it in as tight as possible, but it still flexed each time the boat pitched. Attempts to check the inflow with cloth failed and the whole forward section of the hull slowly filled through the access holes.

The boat was noticeably bow down and it was then that we discovered a similar crack in the port hull, which was flooding as well. Clearly we were no longer seaworthy so we set a course towards Corunna, but within a short time both bows were awash and the rudders out of the water so sailing became impossible. At daybreak we were able to get a better assessment of the damage. The mast was swinging back and forth as the boat pitched and there was an indentation just above the upper spreaders which worsened as we looked at it. Rather than wait for this to collapse and possibly cause injury, I slacked off the backstays and let the whole mast fall. We were now an unmanoeuvrable raft but not in danger, our raft still had plenty of buoyancy and the aft part of both hulls was dry.

We were having a bite to eat (with aspirin for me as I had a splitting headache) when a Spanish fishing craft came towards us. They suggested we abandon the boat, but I persuaded them to take Sue aboard and take us in tow to the nearest port, Corme, which we reached at 1500 hours that afternoon. The next day we made a deposition to the port captain and began to collect our personal gear. Lloyds had been informed and were trying to discover what vessel might have hit us but without success. They sent a surveyor out to view the mess and bargain with the fishermen, offering them £12,000 for the tow. This was refused by their bank manager, who had taken charge of affairs, so we removed what we could carry and flew home courtesy of Jeff Houlgrave and Colt Cars, who sent their private aircraft to fetch us. We never saw *Sea Falcon* again.

Bargaining for salvage cost the fishermen dear as Lloyds paid me out for a constructive total loss and left them with the hulls, which was of no value to them at all. I felt really sorry for the fishermen, they were decent people misled by a sharp bank manager who, while trying to be clever, lost them a fair sum at no loss to himself. The whole business had been one long nightmare from the moment I had been thrown against the mast. People's word means nothing once you are in a salvage situation and all for no purpose as there were no winners: we and the fishermen were the losers and I lost a wonderful boat.

Two years later Clive Jacobs, ex-presenter of the BBC's motoring programme and a contemporary at Berkhamsted, introduced me to Lord King and Colin Marshall and within three weeks we found we had a sponsorship arrangement with British Airways for a new boat – a 60-foot catamaran specifically designed to break the New York to San Francisco record via Cape Horn. Again Rod Macalpine-Downie was the designer and the building contract was placed with the Ipswich Boat Building

Partnership. With hindsight, it is obvious that they were experiencing difficult times, but how difficult did not come out until the bank brought in the receiver before we had even got a keel in place. Rather than let the project stagnate I moved up to Ipswich, re-hired the building team, took over the shed, an old maltings, and we completed the boat in four months and launched her in the autumn of 1984. Bernard came over to give a hand and, of course, join the crew. Sailing trials proved her to be a handy little boat, not as fast as the latest lightweight machines, but she was built for a particular job that needed strength, namely to beat around Cape Horn.

Having learned from *Sea Falcon* the disadvantages of having the galley and heads away from the control centre, the new boat had her accommodation in the four-foot high extension behind the main beam. The WC came from a Trident aircraft that was being broken up. We removed its holding tank and fixed the seat and bowl down to the flap valve in the extension. The contents thus dropped straight into the sea below which would have been bad luck for anyone driving a boat beneath us at the time! It was very practical however, being placed in the galley, we could use it as a rubbish chute when cooking.

Our first race was from Benalmádena to Santo Domingo in an event called the Ruta Descubrimiento with Billy King-Harman and Bernard joining me. We sailed out, pausing in Gibraltar where the crew disgraced themselves by picking up a car and blocking the main street, then, pleased with the effect, doing it again and being arrested. A journalist who had tagged along saw the potential dangers of the situation, walked into the police station and, ignoring the sergeant on duty, verbally tore into the crew who sat shamefaced throughout the tirade.

The sergeant was so impressed by the 'Skipper' he let them all go uncharged!

When we left, a navy launch took us in tow and made an appalling hash of it, such that she eventually caught the tow rope round her propeller and the chief petty officer stood and shouted at everyone in sight. Since we were drifting onto a rocky wall, I ignored him while Bernard grabbed a line and swam it ashore so we could hold ourselves safely while we sorted out the problem. I then turned to the red-faced chief who exploded with a long list of his miseries. There was no point in listening, I stripped, dived into the water, removed the rope from his prop and told him to try his engine again. Sullen and quietened, he towed us out of the harbour. He had hardly impressed his admiral, who was in my crew.

The race was one of a series that were being run at the time from and to ports that had been persuaded to pay to host the races in exchange for the publicity. It ran out of the Mediterranean, down to the Canary Islands, then across the Atlantic to San Salvador and back to Santo Domingo. Starting in December, it should have been clear of the hurricane season and provided an escape from cold and windy Britain to warmer, balmier climes. The first flaw in the plan was a gale that hit the fleet as it passed the Canary Islands. The leaders got clear, the smaller boats like us got caught and lost time. Before the next gale our generator decided to put its connecting rod through its crank case and expired.

Without electricity we lost radio, weather forecasts and lights. Four solar panels provided a tenth of their advertised output and only gave us instruments. The only purpose of these was to frighten us with the wind speed when, halfway across, we ran into another gale which quickly rose to more than 50 knots. We turned downwind and ran before it, not being helped by the mainsail jamming up the mast so that we were unable to reduce sail below the second reef, more than enough in the circumstances. We didn't know how many miles we sailed like that during the night, more than 120 anyway, during which we nosedived twice and I was washed off the helm on each occasion. *British Airways* had recovered and continued her headlong progress well before I had waded back to the helm! Bernard and Billy shared the vigil with me, standing by to cut the mainsail free if it proved necessary. At daybreak we were tired, the wind was coming from the west and we just put the boat onto port tack under easy sail, had a meal and then grabbed some sleep in turns to recover.

Eventually the proper winds re-established themselves and we headed to San Salvador with no idea of what had caused our problems. We were soon to find out. Halfway to the eastern end of Hispaniola the wind came up and, having enough battery power saved by then, we switched on the VHF only to receive a hurricane warning. This was 23 December – very, very late for a hurricane. It caught us late on Christmas Eve and we spent Christmas Day hove to, in lovely sunshine, with waves breaking into the cockpit, listening to the progress of the beast and learning of ships close by, such as the huge liner *Norway*, ex-SS *France*, which was hove to less than 100 miles away. Eventually, we detected a slight moderation in the conditions and when the wind fell back to a Force 8 we decided that it had inconvenienced us enough and it was time to make a Christmas lunch. In a bouncing galley I produced one of my better curries, if I say so myself, and then Billy and Bernard disappeared into the galley and produced a fried fruit flambé, which was absolutely delicious. Aside from with my family, I have not spent such an enjoyable Christmas with more congenial company.

We arrived third in class, not particularly good but not bad in the circumstances. We stayed a day in Santo Domingo and then sailed to Montego Bay where Sue and new crew joined. Among these were two people with cerebral palsy who we were giving a lift to the Bahamas to join Operation Raleigh. My respect for people with this disability rose to new heights from this experience. A bright mind encased in a rebellious body has to be one of the most frustrating conditions I can think of, and yet they both remained incredibly patient and persistent in their efforts to make themselves understood. At one stage, because it was so hot we anchored in the lee of a small cay and I allowed everyone to swim. One of the two, Robert, wanted a go as well as he was tired of us throwing buckets of water at him. We rigged the bosun's chair from the end of the spinnaker pole, swung him outboard over the sea, and lowered him chest deep into the water. He kicked around happily and then, catching me watching him, yelled 'Robin, I know why you're doing this!' 'What's that, Robert?' I responded. 'You're using me for shark bait!'

We dropped everyone off at Freeport except Bernard, Sue and I and we sailed on to Fort Lauderdale in Florida, coming in towards the brightly lit skyline towards dawn. We had been warned about the drug runners and so when we heard the sound of very powerful outboard motors and detected a long, low, mean-looking powerboat approaching, we feared the worst. Bernard was loading our rifle as the craft came alongside and challenged us. It was manned by five heavily armed men, carrying everything from a Browning automatic rifle, through

Armalite rifles to Magnums. I told Bernard not to bother, one Lee Enfield was out of its class against that sort of arsenal.

Nervously, I walked over to the side of the boat and told them who we were but I was much more concerned to know who or what they were. DEA they responded, Drug Enforcement Agency, and we want to search your boat. They produced their badges, which, as I had only seen these sorts of things in films, did not mean much, but there was no point in arguing so I invited them aboard and hoped they were who they said they were. A few minutes later, we were all sipping coffee together in the cockpit as their boat, lashed alongside, provided us with the power to enter the harbour, the wind having died. They explained what they were doing, how they had missed two drug runners that night and they were heavily armed because the smugglers would get life if caught and so would be willing to kill to avoid capture. They towed us to the marina and were a quiet, pleasant bunch of people doing a very nasty job.

1985 was a very busy year for us. We sailed to Martinique for a speed week, took four sailors from HMS *Fearless* on our crew back from there to Freeport via the Virgin Islands, and laid up there for three months, courtesy of Sir Jack Hayward. In spring we sailed to New York and broke the British record for a crossing of the Atlantic with a new time of 10 days and 14 hours, but it wasn't good enough for the world record. We had a visit to La Trinité-sur-Mer on Quiberon Bay for the annual multi-hull regatta, where Sue gorged on *moules* and I starved begging for *fromage*.

Next we prepared for the Round Britain race, with Billy as crew again. Looking at the competition it was obvious that we ought not to come in better than about sixth if every boat sailed as they should and we were tenth into Cork. However, the Round Britain is an obstacle race and it is always worth pressing on as the opposition might run into difficulties, plus the second leg suited us perfectly. We had strong reaching conditions, which enabled us to average more than 17 knots for more than a day, so we pulled up to fifth in an elapsed time of 41 hours and 8 minutes and the new leg record. By Lerwick we lay fourth, Lowestoft, second, but the best we could manage at the finish was fourth.

There is a short entry in the logbook which states: 'Crew in tears – knocked over his consolation whisky', which is the sole cryptic announcement of what has become known as the Headland Policy. Off the southern entrance to Lerwick, we ran into a flat calm and drifted slowly into a bay. We tried to tack to sail clear in next to no wind, but the boat would not come round. Inexorably, we were drifting towards the rocks and while Billy got the anchor cleared away we tried wearing round, sacrificing the remaining gap between ourselves and the rocks in a final gamble. It worked, the sails half-filled on the other tack and we slowly crept out of the bay. As we passed the headland that marked its western extremity I asked Billy to bring up the whisky as I felt we had earned a tot. And thus began the Headland Policy. The rules are simple: a drink can be taken whenever a prominent headland has been passed. A 'headland' can be almost anything, just so long as the crew, the skipper and the owner, each of whom has one vote, all agree that whatever the object was, it was a headland. For purposes of vote counting, the crew have one between them but I cannot recollect a dispute when a vote has been taken.

After the Round Britain race we sailed to Kiel to participate in the first Round Europe race, taking a short cut through the Kiel Canal. The canal rules state that craft must motor, but we were so much faster than the dinghy and outboard under sail that in fact that is how we completed the bulk of the transit, starting the motor every time a police launch appeared. The first leg to Holland was a demolition derby, five yachts being dismasted, and it was some time before the fleet steadied. The race finished in Porto Cervo, Sardinia, where we were second in class, but finding the prices astronomical, breakfast for two cost £60, we sailed at once for Monaco where our next event, a race to New York, was due to start in mid-October. For this I decided to take Sara as I felt her education would not be completed until she had crossed an ocean. Her response was, 'Great, when do we start?' I told her I expected her to ask what about her job, but she responded that she could always find another one of those!

I augmented the crew with a friend of Bernard's, a trainee lawyer, Philippe Guesnier. His first task was to get sailor Josh Hall off a charge of breaking a street lamp, which he backed into with our van. I have to say that when the police first arrived to apprehend him I burst out laughing as it did not seem a very serious crime, but in Monaco damage to municipal property is taken very seriously. No wonder Johnny Coote kept quiet, or as quiet as he was able to, when there. As second hand of a submarine during the war, they had sent a torpedo straight through the harbour entrance into a German minelayer that had exploded with dramatic effect. Many years later, he bought a newspaper from a kiosk in that corner of the harbour and was regaled with an account of how the Germans had nearly killed the owner, saved only by being in his friend's cafe having a coffee, when the German minelayer had exploded and flattened the kiosk. Johnny wisely kept schtum about his part in that particular incident! Philippe got Josh off the charge just before we sailed.

By 21 October we were within 20 miles of Cape Trafalgar and, despite the fact that one third of the crew were French, I decided to have a celebratory dinner. Bernard and Philippe kept asking what we were celebrating as they helped prepare the feast, but I kept the truth from them until we were sipping a quiet cognac afterwards. Their joint response when they learned the truth that it was the anniversary of the Battle of Trafalgar was to almost, but not quite, throw their cognac overside with yells of 'Merde!' Bernard got on the radio to ask for a British defeat by the French to celebrate before the race finished.

The race eventually hinged on the interpretation of the weather pattern in the mid–Atlantic, when all three of the multi-hulls in Class 2 were in sight of each other. Something nagged at me about the forecast and eventually I thought I had it. I asked Bernard to check my thinking and he agreed with me. We took the tack for the northern option while the others went the southern route. The wind rose, as predicted by our forecasts, and we soon put the others 200 miles behind us. We would have finished that far ahead, too, if the mast had not cracked at the upper hounds and we were forced to finish with just a fully reefed main and partially furled headsail with the top of the mast in a splint made from bunk supports. But we won our class and that gave us the points to win the Class 2 world championship for the year, during which we had spent 185 days at sea and covered 22,000 miles, most of it racing.

We left the boat in Newport, Rhode Island, for the winter

in the care of Peter Dunning at Goat Island Marina. We collected her again in the spring and sailed home. With Bernard we entered and came fourth in the next TwoSTAR and then delivered her home again before setting out to break the Around Ireland record with a new time of 76 hours and 5 minutes. Apart from myself, Bernard and Josh Hall, the crew for this were largely Dubliners, including John and Jennifer Guinness, Jenny having been freed from her kidnappers just two weeks before. Appearing on the Gay Byrne show after we returned, the boat captain of Denis Doyle's yacht, which had held the record, called in to say that I had not broken the record, I had only sailed around Ireland faster than they had. Gay Byrne and I did not dare to look at each other!

We stayed in Dublin long enough to give people a sail on the boat in aid of the RNLI and then headed for home. Halfway across the Bristol Channel there was an enormous bang and the mast fell down. One of the shrouds, the wires that hold the mast in place, had parted although only five months old. We got a tow from a fisherman into St Ives, towing the mast behind us. There we discovered an unexpected problem as St Ives has very narrow streets which made it very difficult to get an expensive crane down to the water's edge to lift the mast out. We would have to think outside the box so I looked for a busy pub, went to the landlord and offered him the price of two pints of beer for every volunteer who would come down to the harbour, pick up the mast and carry it through the streets to the awaiting lorry. Twenty-four of us were enough. The mast got to its lorry, the publican sold 50 beers – well, I had to join in, but I had a difficult task explaining to British Airways that 50 pints of beer was a hundred times cheaper than the cost of a crane!

This, plus three Atlantic crossings in five months, left me tired and I was glad to lay up and have a rest. My real sadness with *British Airways* was that we never did what she had been built to do. When I proposed it to the British Airways PR department after the first year that we should go for the New York to San Francisco record they told me there was no value in it and in any case they thought, now, that it was a bit risky – had I ever been near Cape Horn? I controlled my response but realised that with this sort of unadventurous attitude, we were never going to provide the publicity return I had hoped. With the contract at an end, I sold her to Dutchman Henk de Velde, who did take her off around the world in an attempt to break the record, but was thwarted by the necessity to pull into New Zealand for repairs when the cockpit sole began to delaminate.

12

ARCTIC ADVENTURES

With *British Airways* up for sale, I recommissioned *Suhaili* in 1987, moving her from Woolverstone to Chatham, Kent, for a major re-fit. My objective was to enter her in the 1988 Original Single-handed Transatlantic Race (OSTAR), knowing full well that we were hopelessly uncompetitive, but I felt like a voyage sailing on my own after all the responsibility of having a crew on a fast multi-hull. I enjoyed the start and forgot I was in an uncompetitive boat for a few minutes but quickly realised the true situation when most of the others sailed off ahead. For a day I kept pace with *Galway Blazer*, Bill King's boat from the Golden Globe Race, but then the wind increased and she left us, too. For a week we worked our way west, keeping up a twice-daily chat with Nigel Rowe, who was having a race against his son Anthony (who won on handicap), and James Hatfield until *Suhaili* suddenly started to take on water and I lost the radio as well.

The problem was easy to find, the caulking forward had dried out completely while the boat was out of the water and had not swollen properly again. It had washed out of the seams and I was sitting in a sieve 700 miles from the nearest land. I turned for home, the prevailing winds made that the only choice, and pumped every half an hour or so for the next seven days as I motored and sailed back to Plymouth, arriving totally exhausted. My efforts to cross the Atlantic east to west, as opposed to sailing up and down it north to south in *Suhaili* had been frustrated. I re-caulked her and started to plan what to do next.

For my sixth two-handed Round Britain race in 1989, I teamed up with Bob Fisher in *Barracuda*, star of the BBC TV series *Howards' Way*. Although very different in character, we made a competitive team. Bob brought his golf clubs and to be sociable I joined him on the course at Cork during the stopover there, despite only ever having played once before. I lost count of my score, became thoroughly frustrated, and decided that there was not sufficient time left in my life to master the game. I accidentally left my Guernsey sweater behind in Cork and asked Ewen Southby-Tailyour to bring it on to Barra. We left Barra before he arrived, but in Lerwick I received a ransom note saying that if I did not leave a bottle of whisky there for him, Sue would receive the left sleeve as a ball of wool!

My lawyer, James Trafford, was in the boat behind and we arranged a summons to be handed to Ewen on arrival, but while doing this we discovered a package from Gieves addressed to Ewen. James muttered something about interfering with Her Majesty's mail as I opened the package, but I told him I wanted constructive legal advice not negativity. Inside the package was a brand new yachting hat which I removed and replaced with a counter ransom note. Ewen arrived eventually to find a large crowd awaiting him on the quay.

The local policeman approached, identified him and asked for a chat in private. Ewen said he supposed this was one of Knox-Johnston's jokes, but was immediately rebuked by being asked if he thought the police had time for games on the day that the Princess Royal was visiting. Chastened and convinced he must have done something stupid like leaving his military ID card in Ireland, Ewen invited the policeman below and was handed my summons. When he got over being the butt of the joke he went to race control, picked up his package and returned on board, looking forward to trying on his new cap. It was not his day! We exchanged hostages after the race.

Bob and I in the meantime were working our way up through the mono-hull fleet and eventually finished third over-all, having beaten all the boats in the three classes above us. It was enormous fun and thus encouraged we entered the next Three Peaks race, an event, established by Major Bill Tilman, which requires boats to sail from Barmouth and drop off run-ners near to the highest peaks in Wales, England and Scotland. We had a marvellous team of runners and came home second overall, the first mono-hull to finish.

Ever since I first climbed Table Mountain in 1957, I had been rather drawn to climbing. Mountaineering and sailing have much in common: both are practical outdoor sports, slightly hazardous, that involve physical effort and the use of ropes, although most sailors, brought up to look upon safety as the epitome of good seamanship, would look askance at some of the risks mountaineers like to take. Perhaps the best exponent of combining the two sports was Bill Tilman, who was also at Berkhamsted, so I was aware of his mountaineering and later sailing. He, too, liked the more remote areas of the world and his interest in the polar regions excited a personal desire to see them for myself. His apparent indifference to the cold I could easily put down to living through a winter in an unheated boarding house in the Tring gap in Hertfordshire. After that the Antarctic in winter must seem like a holiday camp!

After our little excursion in Skye in 1979, Chris Bonington and I discussed going mountaineering again, but we wanted a special objective, something off the beaten track requiring a proper expedition and where the easiest access would be by boat. There are not many areas of wilderness left, which is obviously where unclimbed peaks are more likely to be found, but there were quite a few in Greenland which satisfied both our wishes. I checked the coast for good landing places with sheltered anchorages because we needed a safe place to leave the boat while we were away climbing, and then gave him the list so he could study aerial photographs of likely objectives. To add expertise of local conditions, we asked Jim Lowther to join our team. Jim had sledded 500 miles across the Greenland ice cap and his knowledge of ice travel and mountaineering was to prove invaluable.

Gradually our list narrowed to one prime objective with three other peaks to fall back on. Chris had found two routes to a large virgin mountain called the Cathedral, just over 2,400 metres high, both of which involved sledding inland up glaciers. The question was whether we could land at the foot of the glaciers since any other route was blocked by mountains. The whole operation depended upon the ice conditions we encountered on arrival. These are not predictable but, in general, the sea ice usually cleared from this area by late July which would allow us to approach the coast. The sea access lay just north of the Arctic Circle on the east coast via a fjord called

Kangerlussuaq. This extends inwards, joined by Watkins Fjord, named after the British explorer and leader of the Cambridge Expeditionary team during the 1930s.

As most of my service was in the tropics, I was unfamiliar with ice navigation, sighting the odd berg in the Southern Ocean does not count, so I was very keen to see what it was like. The Admiralty publications give good advice, but there is nothing like listening to those with experience so I spent some time with Captain Tom Woodfield, who had spent 16 years with the British Antarctic Survey, pressing him with questions. *Suhaili* was the obvious choice for this expedition since her Colin Archer shape resembled Nansen's *Fram* in some respects. The disadvantage is she is small, which meant we would be crowded. A small boat is also fragile when faced with ice as hard as floating rock.

I chose the crew carefully, because I would be leaving them in charge of my most valued possession for the best part of two weeks while I was climbing. Perry Crickmore, ex-merchant navy, was a member of my regular cruising crew and James Burdett came highly recommended. Jim and Chris were the climbers and John Dunn, freed from the tyranny of the radio studio, joined us as far as Reykjavik in Iceland where we intended to collect the latest ice information and pick up a TV team. We had not intended to take cameras, so when the BBC first asked if they could come, we said no. When they offered to pay their expenses we still said no, it was only when the offer reached the point where it covered the costs of the entire expedition that we gave in. The fear was that their presence would spoil the purity of our intentions, but in fact the team of Allen Jewhurst and Jan Pester, the cameraman, fitted in very well and never once forced us to change plans.

By the time we were ready to sail from Whitehaven in July 1991 *Suhaili* was loaded down. The fo'c's'le was packed with sledges, skis, camping and mountaineering equipment. Every locker was full with the food necessary for seven people for two months and we solved the problem of stowing our personal gear by leaving it in waterproof sailing bags across the middle of the cabin. The mini mountain this created gave us all exercise every time we moved and proved my sole training for what lay ahead. Chris and I had intended to go to the Alps and practise but there had not been time, but the London Royal Marine reserves taught me to abseil which turned out to be extremely useful.

The trip to Iceland went smoothly and took nine days. Chris, John and Jim knew little of sailing but quickly settled into the routine and shared watches with James, Perry and me. The worst weather was a Force 6, on the beam so did not worry us. The gradual increase in daylight hours and drop in temperature were the only signs that we were moving north for the landsmen, while the sailors confirmed progress by watching Polaris rise higher in the sky each night. In Reykjavik we enquired at the meteorological office about the ice conditions, but the Denmark Strait between Iceland and Greenland had been covered by fog for the past month. However, there were signs of free icebergs indicating the pack ice was clear of the coast which might give us the opportunity we were seeking so we sailed within two days.

For the next three weeks we enjoyed extremely pleasant weather. The wind never rose above Force 4 and was so light on the outward passage that we did most of the trip under power. Our arrival at the Arctic Circle coincided with sighting our first giant iceberg, which we approached at a safe distance. This one had rolled over already so we kept clear. There was no telling when a part of it might break off beneath the water and come shooting to the surface, as well as causing the berg to roll again as it readjusted its buoyancy to a new shape. The second berg we approached was more interesting so we lowered the dinghy and explored its face, removing some ice for afternoon drinks in the process. It hurt to hit this ice with a pick; it was as hard as any granite and if the *Titanic* could be opened up like a sardine can, what chance would the inch-and-a-quarter wood-planked hull of *Suhaili* have? It was a sober warning and we steered away from further bergs which, fortunately, were not profuse.

The abnormal refraction in these high latitudes has been reported by seamen for 400 years and it is quite fantastic. The 8,000-feet-high mountain range, white tipped but brown below, along the eastern seaboard of Greenland came into view at 80 miles. To the north, especially in the twilight, there was a long, dark mass suspended above the horizon. Later this splintered and we realised we were seeing icebergs way beyond normal visible ranges. We motored in towards the coast. As the light improved, the mass of white against the brown and white mountains, indicating heavy iceberg concentrations, Kanger-lussuaq came into view. It was not too crowded initially. We worked our way into the fjord through the ice and located the small bay protected by islands that we had picked out from the charts. The islands, which were little more than well-worn rocky outcrops, would prevent the large bergs from entering. This was to be the safe haven for *Suhaili* and the boat party while the climbers were away. Having established where our boat base would be, we started up the main fjord into steadily thicker ice to get to the landing point for the mountaineers. Progress soon slowed to a crawl.

Navigating in ice-filled waters, where the density of surface coverage increased to 50 per cent, was a new experience for all of us so we proceeded with great care. We took it in turns to look for the best route from the upper mast spreaders, 30 feet above the deck. Chris's diary brings back the joy of this first encounter with the fjord:

> The first time I climbed the rope ladder it was quite scary but now I'm going up easy peasy, one rung at a time! It's good training for the arms this, climbing high up towards the sun. It's a lovely day. There's high cirrus cloud but plenty of blue sky as well. The sky here in the Arctic is a gentle pale blue. The land is incredibly arid though. The rocks on the immediate shoreline wouldn't be good climbing. They're basalt, very mucky and broken. Once we get inland to the Lemon Mountains it's gneiss and much better. It's immensely exciting. I have a wonderful sense of contentment having got so far – having managed to get here without being seasick and having learned a little bit about sailing.

The quantity of movement among the bergs in the fjords was a surprise. There were clear tidal streams and the ice moved with these, fastest in the middle and almost stationary near the shore. We quickly learned how to use these to our advantage, edging *Suhaili* into the middle on the flood, and the sides on the ebb. It was tiring and cold up the mast and from time to time we just drifted while we brewed a cup of tea to warm up and discuss progress. I quickly appreciated that Perry and

James were to be totally trusted with the boat, they treated her as if the hull were made of eggshells and this put to rest any lingering fears I might have had at leaving *Suhaili* in their care while I was away climbing. Gently advancing, we took three hours to cover the six miles to the entrance of Watkins Fjord and six to traverse the next four miles to the Sidegletscher, the glacier that was our route through the mountains to the interior, where we anchored. Offloading with the dinghy proved fun as it bounced off bergs, but once all the equipment was ashore – sledges, skis, tents, food, climbing ropes – we made an evening meal and rested. The next day I returned *Suhaili* to the anchorage where we moored her securely with three anchors and a long line to the shore as insurance against Katabatic blasts. As I returned by dinghy, Chris and Jim were taking equipment up the moraine to the glacier proper where it would be possible to ski.

When I got back I took two loads up, hard work for which my legs were unprepared, and we camped. The next night we started the haul, our sledges, or pulks, loaded with about 80 kilos each. At these high latitudes there was no real night, it was twilight at midnight but still possible to see quite clearly. We covered eight miles before the warming sun of morning made further progress difficult. Travelling at night was not only easier, it was safer, the snow froze to make the bridges of snow across crevasses strong enough to bear our weight. There was something immensely satisfying about this form of travel, although it was very difficult physically. I was lagging behind, as much as a mile in the early stages as I learned how to glide my skis, which was frustrating for the others. The high mountains on either side of the glacier were pristine, the air was cool and fresh, the landscape unsullied by human influence. With the scenery constantly changing ahead, we would be anticipating the next glorious view the whole time. We were all deeply contented, a bit like schoolboys let out to play in a fairyland.

The next night we joined the Frederiksborg Glacier, about five miles wide at this point. We camped among crevasses on the rubbly surface where the glacier rolled over obstructions below. The following night was hard work, getting through the rough stuff involved numerous diversions, adding miles to the distance to cover, but I was beginning to understand the technique and was keeping up now. We camped with our objective, the Cathedral, in view. Chris, like a thirsty horse that can sense water, was impatiently awaiting the next evening when we would reach the foot of the mountain.

My previous experience of climbing with Chris had left me with two familiar feelings: fright and exhilaration. Hanging by one's fingertips from a tiny ledge on a vertical face 200 or more feet above the ground is frightening if you are not used to it, but reaching the top is incredibly satisfying and, of course, since you have reached the top and the fear is behind, you can be very brave once again. I suspect that this euphoria dulls the memory so that the fear is forgotten in time. Fortunately, fright didn't come until well into the climb. The first 1,200 feet was up an ice wall, crampons on boots for grip, ice picks in each hand and we were roped together to prevent one of us slipping all the way to the bottom, Chris telling me encouragingly that my clothing would wear through very quickly if I slipped that far and my body would not last long either. It was interesting and the view steadily improved.

Then we started to climb, the others choosing the route and taking it in turns to lead, frequently out of sight. It was not until I came round a corner to find a vertical wall ahead that I began to question what I was doing. Chris was already 30 feet above, clinging like a goat and told me to follow. At first I could not see a grip, then I realised that he meant me to entrust my life to a narrow shelf, and by narrow I mean five millimetres wide. This was unseamanlike but I stepped out gingerly, looking for a hand hold. Impatiently Chris asked what I was doing and when I told him, said I did not need a hand hold. I looked down at my boots, barely holding on the ledge, and below them at the 3,000 foot drop, and yelled back that he might not need a hand hold but I bloody well did!

The peak turned out to be a disappointment because a few hundred feet away, but separated by a chasm, was one slightly higher. We had been climbing for 14 hours and were tired. We had brought only light food, chocolate bars and the like, and Jim was beginning to worry about the dark cloud closing from the north. Chris pondered for a bit and then said we ought to go back. Although the real peak looked so close, it was probably at least four hours away by the time we had abseiled ourselves down to the ridge that connected it with ours and then climbed up again. More than 36 hours without food and a proper rest plus a nasty sky did not seem very sensible and so, reluctantly, we started to descend. It took us 12 hours and, as we abseiled down the lower part of the ice wall, we realised how right he had been. Gone was the excited chatter of the previous morning, we were tired, cold and quiet and snow was falling.

Chris and Jim made one more attempt unhampered by me while I took the TV crew down to Watkins Fjord to meet the dinghy called up by radio. We set out in *Suhaili* the next day for the rendezvous, the ice noticeably thicker, and arrived just as Jim and Chris returned, having found yet another peak higher than the one we thought was the summit, so the Cathedral remained to be conquered. The voyage back was uneventful except for the series of nasty depressions which swept over Iceland from the Atlantic and forced us to take shelter five times before we got a westerly and were able to break for Britain. One could begin to see why Iceland was colonised, it is easy enough to sail to but very difficult to get away from.

Two months before setting off to Greenland, I was reappointed as managing director of St Katharine's Yacht Haven. The business had gone downhill during the previous 15 years and was in urgent need of revitalising. On my return from the voyage everyone concerned with the marina seemed distracted by the politics that can bedevil a large company. The failure to exploit the asset was so unbusinesslike as to be almost criminal. Peter Drew was now chairman of the whole Taylor Woodrow group and more time seemed to be spent by people positioning themselves to curry his favour than getting on with the job.

I began by building up the morale of the staff, the prime requisite for making the place attractive again. I introduced many changes, including a uniform to make everyone recognisable – practical as befitted our task and comfortable. Everyone took their VHF radio licence to improve our communications with boats in the river and to give them confidence. We started manning the marina full-time at weekends when the customers were expected, which had, incredibly, lapsed in my absence. Slowly word got out that St Katharine's was operating for the boat owners. not its own convenience, and the visitors began to increase. Activity begets activity, within a year St Katharine's ceased to be a boat park and had an exciting boating atmosphere again and the turnover figures reflected the change.

Later that summer we arranged to sail our Thames sailing barge, *The Lady Daphne*, to attend the festival being organised in Brest, known as Brest '92. Derek Ling, like all the real barge-men, could almost sniff his way around the Thames estuary in thick fog, but going further afield made him nervous and he preferred to keep one foot on the kerb and keep as close to the coast as possible. Brest, he decided, was best reached by nipping across the Channel at Dover and crawling down the French coast. I eventually persuaded him that a GPS made it perfectly safe to go out of sight of land, which happened after we departed from Weymouth, but he was enormously relieved when we sighted France. *The Lady Daphne* was 70 years old and worked a lot so we spent much time at the pumps and even had water sloshing around the hold, where we were living, for an exciting moment but a good diesel pump, taken for such an emergency, soon dealt with the problem.

The festival was spectacular, more than 2,000 craft attended, mostly old craft, and over 800 came from Britain, which led to the question being asked of why not do such an event in the UK, in turn leading to the International Festival of the Sea in Bristol in 1996. The bravest Briton to attend Brest was undoubtedly the owner of the Trafalgar Gun Company, Martin Bibbings, with his full-size naval guns of the Nelsonic period which he fired at regular intervals to enliven proceedings. Chatting to him one evening, he complained that he never fired his cannons from a boat because yachts were too small and larger vessels had high gunwales. Thames barges have low gunwales of course, so we arranged to pull alongside and load one of his guns, a six pounder, the next morning. We sailed into the middle of the naval harbour and fired off five charges, which set windows rattling all over Brest. In no time a smart launch came heading towards us with an immaculate French naval captain in the stern. He pulled up alongside and yelled across, 'You bloody English pirate!' I responded that it was a national habit and would he like a drink. 'Of course,' he answered and enthusiastically joined us for the last salvo.

By now I was enjoying being back in harness at St Katharine's, but the job far from stretched me. Organising the design, build and planning permission for a river pier gave me something interesting to do for a while, and adding it to the ill-fated river-bus schedule was pleasing, but in general I was under-extended since I was not interested in the scrambling for position and status in the company, usually exemplified by the totally unnecessary working of long hours to give the impression of loyalty. I have always taken the view that anyone who needs to work excessive hours, except when there is a special hurried project, is disorganised and not really up to the job and therefore should be replaced.

In the middle of our time at St Katharine's, we sold our house in Putney and bought a flat overlooking the marina as a temporary measure, as Sue had set her heart on moving to Devon long-term. She went house hunting and eventually we put in an offer on a cottage in the small village of Torbryan, near Ipplepen, about four miles from Newton Abbot. Despite the fact that it was six miles from the sea, it was in a lovely small valley, with two farms and about 40 inhabitants. Our offer was accepted and we moved to one of the friendliest places you could ask for. I took to driving down from London whenever I could. Then Peter Drew left Taylor Woodrow and the new chairman decided that I was too expensive in salary terms, so I left and we moved to the country.

We had some five acres including two fields which one of the farmers used for his cattle and we left that arrangement in place, focusing on the remaining two acres. Sue and I were probably happier here than anywhere else we had lived and we stayed in Torbryan until she died. She took to exploring Dartmoor and its fascinating history while I joined a local shoot, based on Staverton, where we jointly made our pens, reared the birds and took turns beating and shooting. We never had large tallies, usually a brace each weekend which was fine for the pot, but it was a lovely day out with congenial company. A new Labrador grew up with these outings, both on Dartmoor and shooting, and eventually got the message that I expected her to collect the occasional pheasant that strayed into my shot.

We had a small stable block which was the garage and became my workshop but I always thought that as the evening came on it was more pleasant to sit and chat to Sue in the kitchen as she made dinner. Rather than be idle I would bring some work in with me, but a gearbox being stripped on the kitchen table was taken as a bit of an affront. Sue refused to accept that I was only trying to be sociable and in any case the kitchen table is the perfect place to apply varnish as it is warm and dry. I took the hint!

13

ENZA

Right from its inception in 1973 the Whitbread Race had appealed to me, taking place every four years since. As the sixth in the series approached, Admiral Sir Jeremy Black invited me to join the committee for the 1993 event and I readily agreed, having fond memories of my effort with *Condor* in 1977. There had been a lot of friction during the previous race between the sponsors and the Royal Naval Sailing Association, who ran the race, and a split was widely forecast, but Jeremy soon put the two back together.

From my point of view the task did not involve much except helping formulate the rules and acting as a scrutineer before the start. If ever there was a case of a poacher turning gamekeeper this was it. I never had any real problems with being scrutineered, which means checking the boats are sound, seaworthy and have the right equipment aboard, which most boats should be able to prove easily. What was never checked were some of the emergency procedures, so for once we actually made the boats perform a man overboard recovery, show how they would jury rig the boat in the event their masts broke, and demonstrate their system for jury steering if they lost their rudders.

Peter Blake was also a member of the committee and a fellow scrutineer. He had dominated the previous race, winning every single leg, so he brought some up-to-date practical experience to our discussions. It was as we were leaving a meeting that he asked me whether I was going to Paris for the announcement of a new French government-sponsored trophy, to be called the Jules Verne, offered for the first boat to sail around the world without assistance in under 80 days. The record then was 109 days, so to reduce the time by 29 days called for a massive increase in boat speed. However, this record was held by a single handed 60-foot mono-hull, so a larger boat, or a different type of vessel, with a full crew might just have a chance. In France there were some very large multi-hulls that could produce the speeds required, but doubts were raised as to whether a multi-hull could survive in the huge waves of the roaring forties.

Remembering how Nigel Tetley had almost completed his solo circumnavigation in the Golden Globe in his 40-foot cruising catamaran *Victress*, I thought it could be done and the French would certainly rise to the challenge. I replied that I was thinking of attending the meeting to find out more about it. It was obvious that we had both been thinking about it and the conversation drifted towards what sort of boat we thought stood the best chance. Peter's plan was unusual and imaginative, calling for a large lightweight mono-hull, designed by Bruce Farr, to have large pods out on either beam which could be filled with water to provide stability and reduce the keel.

My ideas were slightly less extreme, more along the French lines, just a very large catamaran – perhaps 90 or so feet long if possible. We discussed sponsorship, essential for such vessels, agreed it was hard to find and Peter suggested we join forces. It took us five weeks to produce our proposals which we sent to five companies, two in New Zealand and three in Britain. Only one in Britain even replied, saying there was no publicity value in it. Both the New Zealand ones did respond, which led to a meeting with New Zealand Apples & Pears Inc., a marketing board, in London. As we left the meeting, Peter turned to me and asked how I thought the meeting had gone. I said, honestly, that it had gone far better than I had expected and things looked very positive. 'Yeah, I think you're right. Oh Lord, what have we done?!' was his response.

It was now early September 1992 and, with two French projects already announced, there was no time to build either of the boats we had planned, so we had to find something that already existed and we might be able to modify. Looking at what was available there was only one possible choice – *Formula Tag*, designed and built in Canada by Nigel Irens in 1983 for Mike Birch but now laid up in Rhode Island. Originally 85 feet long, she had been cut down when the French decided that 80 feet was expensive enough and made that the upper limit for their races. The last we had heard was that she had been chartering in the Caribbean, but had disappeared since. We eventually tracked her down and, while Peter flew to New Zealand to complete the sponsor negotiations, I slipped away one weekend and flew across to Portsmouth, Rhode Island, to make an inspection of the *Tag*.

Any hope of secrecy evaporated when an American friend, Mike Plant, wandered into the yard as I was crawling under the boat. 'Hi, Robin, what brings you over here?' he said. I muttered something about looking at the boat for a friend, but I don't know if I was very convincing. The boat had been on the market for a while and needed a lot of work, but if the owners had found out what we had in mind they would have demanded a higher price. In the event, we bought her pretty cheaply and Nigel Irens started to plan the re-fit while we organised delivery across the Atlantic.

We kept our plans secret so we could make a surprise announcement in October at the public launch of the Jules Verne Trophy in Paris. At the conference I asked to speak and was told I could do so when everyone else had finished. Three government ministers spoke, followed by various French sailors, some of whom had nothing to do with the project. Our request forgotten, the floor was opened for press questions. I waited for 20 minutes and then stood up. I said I had a small announcement to make on behalf of Peter and myself. Then I told the assembly of sailors and media that Peter and I had teamed up again, had bought *Formula Tag*, were off the next day to collect her from America and we would be re-fitted and ready to start at the beginning of January. There was a satisfying stunned silence.

The rules for the Jules Verne were delightfully simple. The voyage must be non-stop, around the world south of the three great capes of Good Hope, Leeuwin and the Horn, and no outside assistance apart from weather information and advice. The start line was to be between Ushant and the Lizard, a heavy bias towards the French end, so in effect competitors would start out of Brest. There were no plans for scrutiny, it being assumed that those who would enter were experienced enough to know what they were doing. All an entry had to do was advise the organisation of their plan and intended start date so they could be timed as they left. If the 80-day target was achieved, then the trophy would be awarded subsequently to whoever sailed around the world faster.

Routiers were allowed and we asked Bob Rice in the USA to be ours and advise us on what the weather was going to do and the best courses to take. For the speeds we expected, this was essential and we just would not have the time on board to download and analyse all the information required. He was very much a part of our team along with the experienced sailors we recruited as crew: Paul Standbridge, Don 'Jawsie' Wright, Ed Danby, David Alan-Williams.

We collected the boat with a delivery crew, put in her mast and set off at the beginning of November. Had *Tag* been a small mono-hull, I would never have dreamed of crossing the Atlantic that late in the season, but a large multi was more than capable of running fast enough to avoid trouble from the big waves. In the event, a brief touch of force 10 gave us no problems but instead a lot of confidence. Indeed, those conditions were helpful because we were able to learn a great deal about her handling character-istics. As a result of this trip, we scrapped the French system of a steering position in each hull, which was very exposed, and built a small central nacelle. Apart from saving the costs and weight of duplicated steering, winches and instrumentation, it was much drier.

Five feet were added to her length and the old aluminium mast thrown away and replaced with a longer one of carbon fibre, which saved three-quarters of a ton. It was the single most expensive item of the whole re-fit but the effect was almost magical. Its prime advantage was that it weighed half as much as the aluminium one, the equivalent to removing an Austin Mini car from 30 feet above the deck. This not only saved weight, it hugely decreased the pitching moment. Put simply, there was much less weight aloft tending to force the bows down every time we pitched and less weight to heel us over. Storms delayed the work. At one point the sheds at Hamble Point flooded, but we launched in early January and immediately started trials. It was obvious the first time we set sail that the overall performance was greatly improved, which encouraged us to think we could take on the latest French monster multi-hulls.

We had two French competitors, Olivier de Kersauson in his 90-foot trimaran *Charal* and Bruno Peyron in his 80-foot catamaran *Commodore Explorer*. Both were highly experienced, but neither Bruno nor any of his crew had been in the Southern Ocean before so they would take time to acclimatise to the conditions. Kersauson refused to comply with the Jules Verne rules and sailed a week before us, but had trouble making the necessary average of 332 miles per day. We agreed to sail at the same time as Bruno, but when he delayed six hours for TV we went anyway and got a good start. We covered the 380 miles from Ushant to Cape Finisterre in 23 hours, passed the Canary Islands in four days and crossed the equator nine days, six hours out. This is where we made an error and went too far east and Bruno overtook us. The two boats raced through the South Atlantic and into the Southern Ocean with his lead varying between 100 and 250 miles, narrowing when the stronger winds reached us and opening up again as they passed over us and reached him. Then news came that *Charal* had hit ice and lost the bow of her starboard float. Kersauson's race was over and he diverted to Cape Town.

We were comfortable at the back, sailing well within ourselves, not breaking anything and holding onto *Commodore*, which was reporting new damage every day. I established a daily radio chat with one of their crew, where we openly exchanged positions and news, and discussed such matters of interest as the price of dry socks. Our tactics for the time being were to maintain the necessary average speed and just sit on *Commodore*'s stern, keeping up the pressure while sustaining no damage ourselves, as we could press harder later if need be, but in the meantime they might break something serious and be forced out.

It did not work out that way. Shortly after midnight on 26 February, we felt a slight bang and almost immediately Jawsie erupted out of the starboard hull saying that his bunk was almost under water. The immediate response was that this was not a funny joke, but he insisted and we discovered to our horror that he was right. Every means of bailing was brought into use and, as we reduced the water level, we found the cause – a large tear in the hull. We never established what had happened. We must have hit something but what we will never know. Not that it mattered what had caused the damage as we could not race the boat with a jagged hole exposing the honeycomb core of the hull. So we too had to retire and head for South Africa. *Commodore* slowed once we withdrew and it seemed she had no chance of beating 80 days, but then, during the last few days she got perfect conditions and crossed the finish line six hours inside the limit. It was a great effort and we went over to France to congratulate them when they docked.

*

Our dream of being the first to circumnavigate in less than 80 days had vanished and it looked as if *Enza*, as *Tag* had been renamed, would be laid up and sold. Then the sponsor realised just how much publicity our attempt had generated and asked us whether we would like to try and win the trophy away from *Commodore*? Is the Pope a Catholic? Of course we would. Planning started at once for another attempt in 1994, just seven months away. *Enza* was towed from her berth at St Katharine's to Tilbury and loaded aboard a P&O container ship for shipment to New Zealand where she was to be re-fitted. A whole new underbody was added to each hull, partly to give more protection against any future collisions, but also to smooth out the shape as the hulls were also extended, five feet at the stern and two at the bow. The bows were also given more freeboard to increase buoyancy forward.

The crew gathered in New Zealand in the autumn and we made a tour of the major ports, sailing from Auckland to Wellington, Nelson, Christchurch, Dunedin and Napier, giving local fruit growers a chance to sail in their investment. As a country New Zealand is very like Britain and seems more like a natural addition to England, Ireland, Scotland and Wales, the people having an admirable independence and self-reliance. I would like to have spent longer there and travelled ashore more but time was short and we had a deadline. *Enza* was shipped back to the UK, re-rigged and prepared for the next attempt.

Olivier de Kersauson had also decided to have another crack at the record and as soon as he knew we were up and running suggested we should make a race of it. The competition was a natural. We, the Anglo Saxons, had the largest catamaran in the world at 92 feet; he, the Breton first and Frenchman second, had the largest trimaran, named after her sponsors, Lyonnaise des Eaux, at 90 feet. The differences did not stop there: our crew was now eight, we had lost Paul Standbridge but gained Barry McKay, George Johns and Angus Buchanan, whereas de Kersauson was sailing only five up.

On 16 January 1994 we towed out of Brest together into a rough sea, which quickly sent the escorting powerboats back into shelter. We made a sail change which gave *LdE* a lead and she crossed the start line seven minutes ahead and tore off on a broad reach. We lost sight of him but now we were racing and going well. The passage south was remarkable for the lack of delays. We overtook Kersauson off the Spanish coast, passed the Canary Islands three days after the start, at an average speed of 17.6 knots. We crossed the equator, 3,223 miles into the race, in 7 days, 4 hours and 24 minutes having averaged 18.706 knots – the record for some years – and had the luck to shoot straight through the doldrums without any calms.

We were south of Cape Town, 7,600 miles from the start, on the 20th day, our average now 15.83 knots. During this passage we achieved a distance of 521.8 miles in 24 hours, an average speed of 21.74 knots – a new world record at the time. De Kersauson had kept up with us until the South Atlantic high when Bob Rice guided us expertly through a very narrow band of wind into the Southern Ocean while Kersauson was left becalmed for three days, complaining that the only thing missing were the flies! By the time he got moving again we were 1,200 miles ahead, a three-day advantage.

*

The Southern Ocean provided the real test. When making the voyage plan, I had allowed for us to average just over 17 knots through it, or 410 miles per day, and we knew this was where we had to really push for all we were worth. The winds would be there, it was up to us to exploit the opportunity and force every possible last mile from the boat. The usual pluses and minuses of a large, fast boat applied: because you can go so fast you can outrun most waves, but the speed means that you occasionally overtake them and run into the back of the wave in front. This was where the danger lay and provided us with the real check on progress as when the bow buries itself in the back of a wave the boat stops hurriedly, in fractions of a second. The deceleration is a major threat to the rig and sends everything loose tumbling forward.

It was when we hit one such wave and dropped from 27 knots to zero in a second that Peter lost his grip climbing out of the pod and was flung eight feet forward to hit his back on the chart table. Doubled up, he got into his bunk and we fed him painkillers until the pain and bruising began to ease. We lost him from the watch on deck for ten days, although he still participated in the decision-making. The benefit of having a large crew showed during this time as our watches were reduced from three hours on and five off to four off, no real strain, and we covered 4,473 miles, an average of 18.3 knots for the next ten days, which put us south of Adelaide in 30 days from Ushant. Subsequently we discovered Peter had chipped a vertebra so it's not surprising he was in pain.

Just as Peter recovered enough to take the wheel once more, the weather began to behave in a strange way. When sailing east in the Southern Ocean, the trick is to keep the high pressure to the north and the low pressure systems to the south, thus keeping in the westerly airflow between the two. What was happening now was that the low moved north, giving New Zealand hail and snow in mid–summer, and south of this a ridge of high developed all the way to Cape Horn. The choices were not attractive. We could either go north of New Zealand and add miles or dive south. We took the latter course. Down and down we went until we finally levelled out at 63 degrees latitude, where we found a moderate westerly wind but paid a price for it.

Icebergs appeared, not small ones but great islands, 400 feet high and half a mile long. We picked these up on the radar but the small growlers did not show at all and we were forced to keep a lookout from the bow, a freezing task during which half an hour seemed like a century. On one occasion we thought we had steered between two growlers only to discover, as the bow passed between them and it was too late to do anything about it, that they were joined together out of sight under water! Fortunately, the join was more than five feet beneath the surface or it would have damaged our rudders.

We were desperately awaiting a return to the normal system but it refused to happen. Behind us it did, allowing de Kersauson to catch up remorselessly. By Cape Horn our lead was reduced from 1,500 to 300 miles and a storm off the Cape slowed us even more to a mere eight knots, most of which was in a southerly direction, as we were forced to turn off down sea to ride the waves safely. The high pressure system accompanied us around the Cape leaving us no choice but to keep heading east or stop dead if we wanted to try and cross it. Although this was not immediately disastrous, as the sailing ship route recommends a wide swing to the east to pick up the south-east trades, de Kersauson gambled and took the direct line and so appeared, to the non-sailing observer, to have caught up – or at least his distance to the finish line was the same.

This caused great excitement in France and some consternation among our supporters, at least for those who did not understand the Southern Atlantic weather systems. After stating that he was about to eat apples, a reference to our sponsorship, de Kersauson ran into the inevitable head winds while we were freed off and arrived at the equator more than a day ahead. De Kersauson next announced that he was not disclosing his position again until the finish, leading to a French journalist asking us whether this worried us. 'Not in the slightest,' we replied. 'If he is quiet we know he is behind because he will be the first to shout if he is in front.' This message must have got back because the next day he gave a position, well astern of us. We now had a sufficient lead to know that if we kept the boat in one piece with no breakages, we had victory, and a new world record, within our grasp.

Progress was delayed by the doldrums jumping ahead of us when we thought we were through them, then an unexpected move of the Azores High to the east, and finally a storm as we came up channel. This latter event forced us to put out all spare halyards and the anchor, its warp and chain to provide a brake as we did not want to pile into the back of another wave and risk being dismasted this close to home. Even with this drag astern, we still surfed at up to 17 knots. We really needed even more warps out but there was nothing else available. We crossed the finish line with this encumbrance being towed astern, probably the first time a world record can have fallen to a boat attempting to heave to! Our official time was 74 days, 22 hours, 18 minutes and 22 seconds, two days less than the time we had predicted and taken food for but five days more than what might have been had the weather been as kind in the second half as the first.

We received a great welcome in Brest where our families were waiting for us. De Kersauson's arrival, two days after us, was the cause of an even greater welcome. He might not have beaten us but he was the fastest Breton, which was more important in Brest than being the fastest Frenchman! We went down to greet him as he docked and I jumped aboard and congratulated him. As we shook hands he said, 'Robin, I hate you' and grinned broadly. He had his compensation but I suspect that had he sailed with the same number of crew as us, the finish would have been very much closer and perhaps the positions reversed.

He continued to try to win the outright record and was rewarded in 1997 when one of the weather systems changed in the run to the finish and allowed him to cut 1,200 miles off the distance. He got round in just under 72 days but with an average speed less than ours, which emphasised the part meteorology plays in ocean racing. In the New Year honours list at the end of the year both Peter and I received knighthoods, a wonderful reward made even more satisfactory because our wives, who provided us with so much support to allow us to go sailing, officially became 'Ladies'.

In the past 20 years, the out-and-out record has been reduced to 40 days, a phenomenal reduction. This is down to the boats, all multi-hulls, becoming larger and benefiting from new designs and materials and some awesome sailing. The Association Tour du Monde en 80 Jours continues to govern the rules for the awarding of the trophy, the current president being Titouan Lamazou, and the two vice presidents Olivier de Kersauson and myself. Rather sadly, the only non-French team to have held the trophy is still our *Enza* New Zealand team.

14

SINGLE HANDING

Despite the fact that it had been shown possible to circumnavigate the world solo non-stop in 1969, there was a 14-year gap before another single-handed around the world race was organised. Perhaps the dramas of the Golden Globe made it look bleak, but I had finished, Nigel Tetley very nearly so, and Moitessier probably would have finished as well if he had wished. Then in 1978 I received a transatlantic telephone call from David White, an American single-hander who had participated in the 1976 OSTAR in a Westsail 32, asking if I would be interested in entering such a race again. I wasn't really. Having been there twice I was not particularly keen, even with a faster boat, but I told him I would consider a two-handed race.

I heard from him from time to time as his plans progressed. He set up a committee in Newport, Rhode Island, created some rules and even started to get entrants, but aside from a small amount in entry fees, he had no funds for real promotion or organisation. Then one of the entrants, Richard Broadhead, approached the BOC group for sponsorship. Nigel Rowe, the company's chief of corporate relations, did not want to sponsor an individual, but he was interested in the race as a means of connecting the company's principal subsidiaries around the world – in the US, South Africa and Australia. He eventually agreed to provide funds provided the race changed its name to the BOC Challenge and he could make changes to the composition of the race committee. He invited me to become chairman, as he said at the time 'to help give the event international credibility and be its spokesman'.

To organise a major event like this was exciting and can be great fun provided you have the right team and we did: Freddie Alofsin, an ex-mayor of Newport and chairman of Rhode Island Yachting Committee; Dr Robin Wallace, a Brit who had stayed on after being the doctor in one of our America's Cup Challenges and served in Vietnam; Peter Dunning, another expat Brit who ran Goat Island Marina; Pete Hegeman, commodore of the Goat Island Yacht Club; Nigel Rowe; and Dick Kenny, ex-*Chindwara* and now an offshore yachtsman. Our first action was to make some minor changes to the rules, mainly removing the restriction on sailing through the Bass Strait, changing Hobart for Sydney, Buenos Aires for Rio de Janeiro and bringing the start date forward a month. The purpose was to try and get the boats around and clear of Cape Horn by the end of January, considered at that time a wise and seamanlike precaution. The remainder of the rules were left intact. The maximum size allowed was 56 feet, *Gypsy Moth*'s length, the minimum 32 feet because that was *Suhaili*'s length. Starting from Newport, the yachts would race to Cape Town, then across the Southern Ocean to Sydney, from there around Cape Horn to Rio de Janeiro and then back to Newport.

While I happily attended to the details of the race, Nigel and Dick Kenny organised the shore arrangements in Newport.

As a part of this they sought proposals from US PR agencies. I attended one such presentation out of curiosity. The team were three: a small, very sharp man, a woman and the male leader – smooth, blazered, with a New York Yacht Club tie. The small man did all the talking, introduced 'Joe' as a member of the NYYC and therefore someone who had the experience to advise us and introduce us to the right people. The paean of praise continued, Joe, shooting his cuffs modestly, decided he ought to say something and after clearing his throat, asked if BOC had any interests in the USA. Nigel responded by mentioning 'Airco' whereupon they asked if BOC was a subsidiary. 'No, we own it,' was the answer. There was a stunned silence, they knew they had lost it. Lack of reconnaissance!

Eventually Newsom and Company got the job, represented by an ex-Marine Rid Bullerjahn, who fitted in with the organisation from the start. He took his duties very seriously and was even reluctant to hand over the press desk to any of us to go for a quick break. Early on he left it to Dick Kenny and me and as he came back he asked if anyone had phoned. 'Only some guy called Cronkite,' I told him. 'But don't bother, we told him to call back later if his question was really important.' Rid went purple, but it was the last time we caught him out.

The fleet that assembled in Newport in August 1982 consisted of 17 entrants from eight countries. Most were standard yachts, not built for racing, but one stood out from the rest the moment it arrived in Newport, Philippe Jeantot's *Credit Agricole*, designed by Guy Ribadeau Dumas. Built of aluminium to save weight she had a sleek shape, water ballast tanks that could be filled with sea water to increase the weight on the weather side when beating to windward, thus holding the boat more upright and getting more power from the sails. She also had small fins in the transom, copied from sail boards, to keep the boat on a straight course in rough conditions, which were to prove highly successful. The remainder of the boat showed similar careful thought, designed to make the sailor's life as easy as possible so that he could conserve his energy for hard sailing. We did not appreciate it at the time, but we were looking at the prototype of what was to become the most successful style of boat for solo circumnavigations for the next 30 years.

But even if *Credit Agricole* had to be seen as the favourite, the margin was small. There were six other 56 footers in the race, two new and the others being sailed by experienced sailors so the competition would be intense. They were a very mixed bunch, some brash and noisy, some quiet, some like David White and Desmond Hampton I knew, others like Dick McBride from New Zealand unknown to me. I have always liked Kiwis' attitude, their no nonsense get-on-with-the-job approach appeals to me and Dick and his back-up team had this aplenty. They became known as the 'Trevs', after a fictitious sheep-shearing character in New Zealand, but got even with me by telling me to remove my shirt as I was showing the governor of Rhode Island around the fleet and giving me a sheep shearer's armless sweater to put on. They revealed their own similar garments, each with 'Trev' embroidered across the chest, but across mine was 'Robin Knox-Johnston's Trev'. Thus adorned, I continued to escort the governor!

The last few days before the start drew a large number of spectators down to the pier at Goat Island, many of whom knew little about yachting and saw the event as a maritime equivalent of those magnificent men in their flying machines. In some ways this was appropriate as this was the first solo around the world race where all the contestants would start together. There was an air of excited anticipation on the docks and of apprehension on the boats. Well-wishers are all very flattering but they get in the way; at times like this one needs to be left alone to concentrate on the final preparations, but the sailors were unfailingly polite, answering even the most bizarre questions such as 'How do you anchor in deep water every night when you go to sleep?'

Sixteen boats arrived safely in Cape Town, *Credit Agricole* winning by six days. After a rest and re-fit 15 restarted, soon to be reduced to 14 when David White dropped out. The next casualty was Tony Lush, who discovered his keel was coming loose and abandoned his boat and joined fellow competitor Francis Stokes for the remainder of the leg. Unlike the organisers of the Route du Rhum, we gave Francis the time back that this rescue cost him and did not disqualify him from the race because he had two crew aboard. Desmond Hampton sailing *Gypsy Moth V* gave Philippe Jeantot a real run for his money until he slept through his alarm and piled into Gabo Island at the eastern end of the Bass Strait. The rest struggled into Sydney, battered, all relieved that they had made it halfway, some grinning as always like Bertie Read, some exhausted. All were conscious that although they had already achieved a great deal, the largest hurdle, Cape Horn, was still ahead of them.

Nigel had chosen Pier One in Sydney as our base there so as to allow the public access. The characters and modest behaviour of the sailors soon elicited a number of invitations from yachting clubs for lectures, which we did our best to fulfil. Yuko Tada from Japan, sailing *Koden Okera*, even found some

Japanese fishing boats to help him throw a sake and fish party, which finished when he insisted on playing his saxophone. His musical performances were more notable for their exuberance than ability!

The next leg nearly ended in tragedy when, on 18 December, Jacques de Roux sailing *Skoien II* was dismasted and the remains of the mast, held alongside by the rigging, knocked a hole in the hull. The retired French naval commander bailed for his life while Peter Dunning in the Newport race control tried to contact other contestants to go to his assistance and then guided the nearest, Richard Broadhead in *Perseverance*, back up wind for three days to effect a rescue. Richard nearly missed him. He was down below obtaining Jacques's latest position by radio as he sailed past less than a quarter of a mile from the stricken *Skoien*. Jacques, who was shouting for all he was worth, nearly gave up in despair as he watched his rescuer sail away. By the time Richard came back on deck there was no sign of *Skoien*, but he saw what looked like an iceberg to the south and decided to head for it. The berg proved to be *Skoien*'s jury sail. Two days later a French warship rendezvoused with *Perseverance* and took Jacques off, he was the first to admit he doubted he would have survived long enough for them to find him had Richard not reached him. Richard's act of seamanship rightly earned him the award of Yachtsman of the Year in Britain in 1983.

This was the last of the dramas as, by the time the fleet arrived in Rio, Philippe had built up a sizeable lead and he held this to the finish, getting around in a sailing time of 159 days, almost halving the time it had taken me, admittedly in a much smaller boat. He also achieved a best day's run of 240 miles. Ten of the starters had completed the race, more than most predictions and no one had lost their life. The race had been a profound success, giving single-handing an event to compete with the Whitbread race. Dick Giordano, then chief executive of BOC, announced at the prize-giving that they would sponsor the event again in keeping with the four-year programmes for all the classic races. In order to provide an event that would not clash with others, and give potential entrants plenty of time to plan, we announced the second race would take place in 1986. From a personal point of view, organising the race had been a thoroughly enjoyable experience and I willingly accepted Nigel Rowe's invitation to organise the next one.

Before the finishers left Newport we held a wash-up to obtain their views on the race and find out what lessons could be learned and applied to future rules. We were criticised for not including a designer in these discussions, but we did not see the need. The group comprised all the modern experience of solo sailing in the Southern Ocean. As sailors, we knew what we wanted, it seemed to us that it was up to the designers to satisfy our needs, not try to tell us how to sail our boats. Furthermore, we knew what the conditions could be like and they didn't. The basic rules needed little change, although we agreed to increase the maximum length to 60 feet, the largest we felt should be taken to sea single-handed. The most significant rule change was the introduction of the requirement to have watertight sub-divisions in view of Jacques de Roux's exhausting battle to stay afloat. Three bulkheads were required in future, placed so that if the hull was holed anywhere it should not sink. Jacques had not taken to his life raft, but he had only kept his boat afloat by constant pumping. As the 1979 Fastnet storm had shown, it is far safer to stay with the boat if possible rather than take to the raft which is a smaller target for rescuers.

Before the 1982 race we had received drawings of two projects that had been designed to depend solely upon water ballast for stability, no keel being fitted. Even as the first race finished we received a third such proposal. Designers may have thought these safe but we didn't and to prevent it we agreed to introduce a rule that no entrant should heel more than ten degrees with all its tanks on one side full and on the other side empty since the only way to achieve this was to have a substantial keel.

The question of the legality of long-distance single-handing was given an unwelcome boost by the success of the first BOC Challenge. The criticism of single-handed sailors lay in the fact that they must rest sometime and therefore they cannot comply with Rule 5 of the International Collision Regulations, which states that a lookout must be kept at all times. This is of course true and one of the reasons why the single-handed races kept the maximum length of craft allowed to enter to 60 feet. It was felt that by keeping to this size, large enough to be reasonably safe in a rough sea, but small enough not to pose a threat to other vessels in the open seas if they should hit them, that single-handers were accepting responsibility for their own actions with their lives. There are few small vessels in the open oceans, even the fishing boats are 300 tons or more, so the likely casualty of a collision would be the single-handers themselves. Close to land there are more small vessels, fishing boats and other yachts, but the need to navigate, and self-preservation, keep single-handers on watch in those areas. Of course, guard-zones on radar are now enabling single-handers to give themselves much more warning of approaching vessels, which provide a degree of compliance. This attitude was tacitly accepted by the authorities, but not by some in the media and among sailing authorities who campaigned for a total ban.

Unfortunately, the world is full of those who love to ban other people's sources of enjoyment rather than tackle the very real problem behind any collisions that might occur. A collision is not caused by one vessel, it takes two. Rule 17 of the collision regulations states that where a collision cannot be avoided by the action of the giving way vessel alone then the other vessel shall take avoiding action. This is quite clear and means that a large ship seeing a yacht bearing down on a collision course and observing no attempt to alter course is obliged to alter course herself. If she does not and a collision results, she shares the responsibility. But not the risk, of course, indeed they might not even realise that a collision has taken place. During the Second World War the liner *Queen Mary* sliced the light cruiser HMS *Curacao* in two and barely felt anything. The single-hander accepts this risk as the price paid for the freedom to carry on their sport but what of the watch-keeper on the other vessel? They are professionals, qualified by their governments and paid to be there, and just as specifically bound by Rule 5.

I have always felt that the media and authorities who criticised single-handers would achieve a great deal more if they concentrated on ensuring that watch-keepers on large ships complied with the rules since there are far more of them and, with no lookout, they are a real threat to yachts, single-handed or not and, naturally, each other. When I was at sea we had a minimum of two people on the bridge at any one time, now it is often one and what happens when that person is navigating, writing the log or dealing with a distraction? Technology will help of course, and already there are alarms fitted to radars that will sound when an echo comes within a pre-set range, but the target must return an echo. As we move into an era where human-free vessels are being planned one wonders how the authorities will overcome their objections and re-define Rule 5.

We had 25 starters in 1986, 11 in the new Class 1 for yachts between 50 and 60 feet in length and 14 in the second class, which was open to yachts between 40 and 50 feet. The minimum length had been increased from 32 to 40 feet for safety reasons in order to keep the fleet closer together, since there are few ships in the waters we were sailing and the nearest help would almost certainly come from another competitor, as Francis Stokes and Richard Broadhead had shown. The new breed of BOC 60s, also known as the Open 60, showed the wisdom of this decision. There was a fascinating variety of craft with some very imaginative ideas to make the boats easier and safer to handle. It was single-handers who produced self-steering gear and roller furling. Now watertight bulkheads had been added, twin rudders made their appearance and alarms on radar range rings too to awaken a sleeping sailor if a ship came within a pre-set range. Once again the yachts were fitted with the Argos satellite tracking system, giving their positions every four to six hours so we could keep an eye on them.

Newport was a perfect host once more, taking the sailors to its heart and many of them into their homes. A range of activities were organised from parties to sport. I have never been particularly good at cricket and life at sea does not allow many opportunities for team games. I enjoy watching and listening, though, and playing the occasional game as a medium-pace bowler, indifferent fielder and terrible batsman. My best score ever has been 36 runs scored while playing for the *Dwarka* against the agents in Basra and I have never been able to explain why that happened. In the week before the start we decided to form a single-handers cricket team and took on a local Newport side, worryingly strengthened at the last minute by the inclusion of three Australians. We played at Goat Island, supported by cheerleaders. We won, just, and Philippe Jeantot to this day does not understand why we were so delighted when he connected with the ball and sent it over the boundary to give us a victory. We played again at Constantia in Cape Town, winning by a few runs owing to a vital contribution from Eddie Barlow and the fact that the other side did not notice we had 13 batsmen! But our team was being decimated by the withdrawals from the race and that was the last appearance of the solo sailors.

There was drama right at the start when Titouan Lamazou of France rammed Warren Luhrs of the USA, who was forced to return for repairs, but this was just the beginning of a demolition derby which was to see six yachts drop out before Cape Town. The first to arrive there was John Martin, 16 hours ahead of Philippe Jeantot in second place with Jacques de Roux coming in fifth overall and leading Class 2.

As the yachts headed off on their second leg into the roaring forties, it was immediately obvious that the boats were being pushed a lot harder than they had been in 1982. Just as the second Whitbread was more of a race, the novelty and extreme caution were gone for our second race and performances were much better. Average speeds of ten or more knots became the norm, not the exception, as the fleet sped towards Sydney.

But the progress was bought at a high price as we received report after report from the boats of knockdowns and damage. Lamazou led the way into Sydney with Jeantot closing to within 40 miles at the finish.

Tragedy struck towards the end of the leg when we noticed that the Argos track of Jacques de Roux, sailing *Skoien III*, was not following a logical route – very unlike him. We watched it for two more position reports and then, as it was still not taking the direct route to Sydney, I phoned the authorities and advised them I was concerned. Canberra were not at all helpful, the thrust of their refusal to launch a search was based on the fact that Jacques was single-handing and yachties like myself usually panicked far too quickly. I realised I was going to get nowhere with them and rang off. Next I called the New South Wales police, who had been extremely helpful to the whole organisation and they promised to get a boat out the next morning. Later I learned that Warren Luhrs' back-up crew, led by Bill Biewenga, were planning to go down the coast to help him rig a new mast and I agreed to hire an aircraft so they could go and check the boat. I needed a sailor's view of what was happening and Bill was highly experienced. His news was far from encouraging when he called me over the aircraft's radio. The boat was drifting, her sails untrimmed and there was no response to their fly-pasts.

We now needed to get someone on board to check whether Jacques might be ill below or dying, but Canberra still refused to react. My hopes now lay with the police and other yachtsmen and while we waited to hear what the police were achieving, Canberra suddenly phoned and said they were taking over. Better late than never I suppose, they asked a merchant vessel to divert and lower a boat to check Jacques' boat. It was found to be empty, a half-finished meal scattered on the deck. His last log entry gave us some idea as to where he might have gone overside and a search was mounted, but nothing was ever found. *Skoien* was towed into port and laid up and the Royal Australian Navy allowed us to hold a very private memorial service in their base chapel overlooking the Pacific Ocean, which seemed totally appropriate. We all felt the loss. Jacques was a true gentleman, always courteous and a very fine seaman and if he had any enemies I never met one.

This tragedy undoubtedly had an effect upon another contestant. Harry Mitchell, the oldest person in the fleet, was sailing the old *Yeoman XX*. He was trailing way behind and his track started to show aberrations as well as he left the Bass Strait so we spent almost a day agonising as to whether to call the rescue authorities again as we could not make contact with Harry on the radio. His track eventually began to show movement towards Sydney and we were relieved when he arrived. On the next leg he went aground on the New Zealand coast and having been towed off, motored in the direction of Cape Horn, an action not allowed under the rules (contestants are allowed to use their motors to take them in and out of a place of safety and they must restart from where they started their motors). By the time he had effected repairs he was so far behind that he could not have completed the leg within the limits and so was disqualified for his breach of the rule. In my heart of hearts, I think we did the right thing, but Harry was not a quitter. His attempt to enter the next race were thwarted by a collision in the mid-Atlantic on his way to the start, but he was back again in 1994 at the age of 70. On the third leg, en route to Cape

Horn, a bad storm swept over his position and contact was lost. He was never seen again.

We 'borrowed' the Australian Prime Minister Bob Hawke for the restart from Sydney, which he performed with typical enthusiasm from HMAS *Fremantle*. Helping to keep the spectator fleet at bay was the Port Captain John 'Abbo' Briggs, who I had lowered into Durban Harbour from the *Chindwara* all those years ago. We managed to find time for an evening out together, the intervening 30 years might never had passed.

The yachts headed out into the Tasman Sea and then along the most lonely and dangerous leg of the race to Cape Horn. Canadian John Hughes was dismasted early in the third leg, but rather than return to the nearest land in New Zealand, he sailed under jury rig 4,400 miles around Cape Horn to the Falkland Islands where a new mast awaited him. Jeantot beat Lamazou into Rio to take the lead.

Rio was desperately hot, near to 30 degrees Celsius most of the time, which was enervating and shortened tempers. Nothing happens quickly, but we were lucky that our local chairman was the retired head of the Brazilian navy and had his own highly effective methods of getting things done. It never happened immediately, but it seldom took more than three days. Another of the committee was a neurosurgeon who, noticing the bumps on my cheeks which I had been trying to get the National Health Service to deal with for two years (they said it was a dental problem), identified them as cysts and whipped them out one afternoon. Sue, arriving at the airport, was met by a husband without a beard she hardly recognised. Since I found the heat delaying the healing process, we took an excursion for a long weekend up country to a town called Ouro Preto, where the temperature was much cooler and the people very friendly, a welcome break from the coast.

Jeantot was not unassailable at the start of the final leg, but Lamazou needed to gain nearly four days in order to catch him, a considerable margin. None of us were convinced Jeantot had the fastest boat and his performance was impressive. Part of the secret to his success was that he liked to do everything himself, his re-fit, preparation, storing and planning, while others left it to their back-up teams. He was right, of course, it was his reputation that was ultimately at stake and he wanted to make sure that everything had been covered. He came home the winner in a time of 134 days 5 hours, 3½ days ahead of Lamazou overall. Interestingly, if one ignored Hughes' time because of his long slow period under jury rig, the slowest boat took 175 days to get around, so the margin between first and last was just manageable from an organisational point of view.

In 1987, Philippe Jeantot phoned me and asked if I would object if he established a solo non-stop race around the world using our BOC rules. Of course there was nothing I could do to stop him, and it was the next obvious race to have, but it was typical of Philippe's good manners to call me. This became the Vendée Globe Race, now the pinnacle of solo sailing and the toughest challenge in sport. Philippe and I shared thoughts about the rules and discussed changes with contestants, based on everyone's experience and adapting where necessary. But, almost inevitably, an organisation called International Mono-Hull Ocean Class Association (IMOCA) was established specifically for the new breed of 60-foot yachts whose rules largely mirrored the ones we had created over five races. Although the concept of a class association was sensible, it soon turned into a trade union and started to dictate to race sponsors.

At the end of the second BOC Challenge in 1987, although I had thoroughly enjoyed the two races, I felt I had had enough influence on the event and to avoid it becoming perhaps dangerously dominated by my views, it was time to allow other people to take over and maintain the dynamism that was part of the event's success. The American Mark Schrader was chosen to succeed me because he had taken part in the second race and knew what the sailors would have to go through, a vital attribute in any sporting event but particularly so in a race like this. Mark ran the next two BOC Challenges and then carried the race forward as Around Alone when BOC decided to discontinue their sponsorship in 1995.

The race looked like it would die after that, but I could not accept that Around Alone should disappear. I discussed the situation with William Ward, a property developer I was working with on another project, and we took over Around Alone. The first race we organised was in 2002. Although Around Alone still used the rules we had developed over 20 years by discussion with contestants, we ran into immediate problems with IMOCA. Our advisors told us we should abandon our rules and accept the IMOCA ones. We did and it turned out to be a very serious mistake as it left us vulnerable to that organisation with disastrous consequences down the line as we had abandoned our only bargaining chip.

The 2002 race attracted eight entrants and we started from New York, raced to Brixham in Devon, then on to Cape Town. Tauranga in New Zealand was our next stop, then Salvador de

Bahia in Brazil and then back to Newport, Rhode Island. The race is indelibly printed on my mind thanks to the weather forecast in Brixham which showed a small but nasty low developing just as the race was due to start. The skippers and I gathered all the weather information we could and discussed it, coming to the unanimous decision to postpone the start by a day to allow the low to move on. Unfortunately, the wife of the commodore of the Brixham Yacht Club announced this before we had got the message out to partners and sponsors and all hell broke loose, mainly from PR people worrying about their guest executives. To make matters worse the original day for the start dawned with a flat calm in Torbay and I came in for a lot of criticism. However, by midday, when the boats should have been towed out to the start line the wind was howling and waves were breaking over the coast road. If we had started in those conditions, we would have risked lives.

We made nothing financially out of Around Alone 2002, but we had kept the event going. It was a less expensive way for ambitious sailors to get the recognition they needed to allow them into the top level of solo racing. But to run it again we needed a sponsor and we found an excellent one in Velux, the Danish manufacturers of windows. The next race eventually attracted seven entrants, a disappointingly low number, but the sponsorship enabled us to give the race good coverage. Michael Rasmussen, their marketing director, proved a tough negotiator, was always clear about what he wanted and kept his word. This led to an excellent relationship. The race was rechristened the Velux 5 Oceans and started from Bilbao in 2006 but reduced the stops to Fremantle, and Norfolk, Virginia, in order to reduce contestants' port costs.

*

By 2005, I knew I had to get back on my horse, and the best thing for me to do was get back to what I did best, go to sea and race solo. Clipper now ran Around Alone. We already had some good entrants in Alex Thompson and Mike Golding, so this seemed a race worth doing. I discussed it with their teams and they told me that the boats were so hard to sail and the modern computer systems so complicated that I would find it too difficult at my age. I hate being told what I cannot do, and I put in an offer, through Bernard Gallay, on a good French Open 60 boat built by the excellent Italian sailor Giovanni Soldini that had won the race six years before and went away lecturing on the *Queen Mary 2*. A week into my cruise I received a message from Bernard that my offer had been accepted. My immediate thought was, 'Oh Lord what have I got myself into now?' And then I started to get excited. But the costs of doing the race were huge. I needed a sponsor to defray them. And then Saga became involved. Well, since they boast of offering their services to the over 50s, at 67 when we began the race I was not a bad example for them! Their initial contribution got me to the start line, but as the race developed they supported me more.

I went over to Lorient where the boat was based and with a small team took her over and sailed her back to Gosport. It was a learning voyage. None of us had experience of sailing one of these Open 60s and we were cautious. Nevertheless, the boat gybed on one occasion and I was pushed over. My lifejacket inflated, jamming me under the guard wires and I was underwater and could not get free. Fortunately, the crew realised what was going on and gybed again, pulling me up out of the water. If I had been single-handed I would have drowned.

Time was now of the essence. We had a limited budget and

a lot to do to get ready in just months and I had to get a quali-
fying voyage across an ocean to do in that time. Our first issue
was to replace the swinging keel which had done more than
80,000 miles, the limit of their safety. I found a new one in
France and we shipped it over. We were learning on the job and
did not know any of the short cuts when it came to removing
and replacing the keels but Greg North and I did it.

In the middle of all this activity I received a letter from
Vice Admiral Manohar Awati of the Indian navy telling me
that they were planning to send one of their officers on a solo
voyage around the world and what would I advise. I responded
that the best thing they could do was to send the officer to join
me and he would learn all there was about solo racing around
the world. Commander Dilip Donde, a specialist diver, joined
me a couple of months later. It was rough introduction to solo
sailing for Dilip. We were working seven days a week when he
joined our team and, as he said afterwards, I gave him one day
off throughout our preparations. But he dug in.

Since I decided to enter we had brought in an experienced race
director in Australian Dave Adams, who had previously competed
in the BOC Challenge. I had to qualify for the race of course,
after all I had made that rule, and so I planned to sail with crew to
New York and then sail back solo, which would qualify me. We
set off well enough but halfway across had a whale strike which
hit us on our port side and then on the starboard quarter. I was in
my bunk when the collision occurred and was thrown onto the
deck by the collision. The person on watch put his head through
the hatch to tell us that we had hit something. That was pretty
obvious! We checked the boat, no leaks, but we needed to get her
checked so I changed our destination to Halifax as it was closer.

A proper check told us that all the damage we had was a couple of dents in the hull, which did not affect her integrity, so the crew left and I set off back to the UK alone. It was not a fast trip but it was a useful one as I learned more about the boat and my ability to handle her. We were short of time when I got back, but hauled out to fix the dents and then we were on our way to Bilbao where the race was due to start. On the way down I slipped in the cockpit, fell on my back, and fractured my coccyx. On arrival in Bilbao I saw a doctor who identified the problem but told me that it would hurt for a month, and I would not be able to heave huge loads around for a while, but otherwise I could sail in the race. That was all I wanted to hear.

We cracked on preparing the boat – my group of enthusiastic volunteers versus the professional *preparateurs* for the heavily sponsored boats. I was focused on getting the boat ready to sail, not necessarily ready to race, but when one of the *preparateurs* said they would see me in Australia if I got there I responded, 'Oh I will get there, I just am not ready to race there at this moment.'

In fact, neither Alex Thompsons's boat nor Mike Golding's made it to Australia as both had problems on the way, Alex's keel breaking loose which made the boat unmanageable and then Mike being dismasted after he had picked up Alex. I had enough problems apart from my slowly recovering coccyx, as I approached the equator one of those sharp squalls, typical of the area, hit and the autopilot switched itself to standby. The boat, without direction, went straight over on her side. I crawled out of the cabin, hanging onto the upper winches and let go all the sheets but she remained stubbornly with her mast on the sea's surface. When the squall passed she came upright and I was able to get back on course, but the thrashing had broken all the battens in the mainsail and I did not have spares for all of them. I considered going into Cape Town to get new battens, as without them the mainsail was not even half effective, but decided the loss of time would be too much and so pressed on. I got to Fremantle eventually, three weeks behind the leaders.

My priority on arrival in Fremantle was to sort out my automatic pilot. Fortunately, I now had a back-up team, led by Simon Clay, joined by Dilip and others, to tackle what became a mini re-fit. The autopilot was my main concern as its failure is what had caused the knock-down at the equator. We thought it was fixed but within hours of the restart from Fremantle it failed three times and I knew that I could not sail in the Southern Ocean with a pilot like that. So I turned back to get the problem sorted. The local Raymarine agent came aboard and quickly decided that the problem was a lack of power to the steering rams. The connecting wires, put in professionally while in Gosport, were like those used in a bedside table lamp and could not provide a large enough avenue for the power the rams required when under a heavy load. This had been the problem all along. The wires were replaced with much heavier ones and I restarted, nearly three days later than the rest of the fleet, but at least I now had a reliable autopilot.

I headed south to get into the stronger westerly winds which were essential if I was not to lose touch with the rest of the fleet. Confident in my self-steering now I pushed hard to catch up and slowly overtook the two tail-enders. The sailing was fantastic. I watched as we slowed down between the wave crests and the sails were slightly shielded. Then, as the next wave came up from astern and lifted the boat she would accelerate, just enough so that the wave crest did not quite break over the stern. Then of course, she did not move quite fast enough and the wave came into the cockpit where I was having my evening 'think' with a glass of whisky and a cigarette, both of which were soaked in salt water!

Weather information is vital in modern ocean races and there are some excellent systems out there but they require a satellite connection. Suddenly I did not have one, my Fleet 77 system stopped functioning. My back-up Iridium was refusing to connect, which was due, we discovered later, to the wrong PIN being registered by the supplier. I contacted Simon Clay and he told me the advice was to lift the dome off and check the aerial was aligning itself. This was easier said than done as the dome was large, and apart from the risk of a wave soaking what it protected, I had no wish to be picked up by the wind while holding it. Eventually I got a calmer day and took the risk. There was nothing obvious so back went the dome. I was sailing blind now, my only weather information coming from analysing the progress of the other boats in their respective positions. If they were south of me and going faster I headed south, and the reverse. It was far from ideal, and some days I fell back and on others closed in. By Cape Horn I had two behind me, but I had arranged to head in to Ushuaia to get some means of communication working and they would overtake me again.

I rounded the Horn on a fast reach and then hardened up to enter the Beagle Channel. As darkness fell the wind was rising and the waves were short and steep. With a fully reefed mainsail and storm jib set, I beat westwards. However, when I looked at the plotter it was soon apparent that I was being driven north onto the Argentine coast. There was no way I would get the boat to tack in those conditions, so I watched, hoping for a slight shift in the wind direction and knowing if it did not come there was a point where I would have to wear round and head out to the safety of open water. I detected a slight freeing of the wind and hardened up. It was not enough to clear the next headland but it was better. I pressed on and was rewarded by another small freeing of the wind.

We could make it now, but ahead came the necessity to contact the boat that was coming out to meet me as short tacking through some of the narrows was not an option. I detected a light nearby that seemed to be keeping pace. Was it my boat? It did not respond to calls on the VHF radio, but I had a few miles to go before the narrows and decided to sail that far and then, if nothing turned up, I would have to turn round and see whether the Falkland Islands could provide some support. The radio crackled. I was being called. Could I make it a bit further and head into a small bay where it would be calm and they could come aboard? A calm bay in these conditions seemed totally unrealistic but I agreed. And they were right. As I turned into the bay the wind dropped completely. The Beagle Channel is a strange place!

With a tow line secured I was towed to Ushuaia where Simon had flown out with spares to meet me. The Fleet 77 was fixed quickly, its azimuth drive belt had jammed, and a new Iridium phone was installed. I sailed back down the Beagle Channel, enjoying the sights I had missed on my way in because of the dark. I had some catching up to do. I took the Le Maire Strait and steadied on a course for the eastern side of the Falklands at 11 knots where I rendezvoused with HMS *Edinburgh*. Then a few days later HMS *Dumbarton Castle* came over for a chat so the navy was looking after me. Then I made a costly mistake.

The weather system fitted in Ushuaia was new to me and I could not get it to give more than a three-day forecast. But it showed an interesting wobble in the isobars which meant a straight course for Cabo Frio might pay, instead of the more usual sweep to the east. I tried it. The wobble disappeared in the next forecast and I spent a wasted week beating east. As I crossed the equator I celebrated my 68th birthday and reflected that even if my position in the race was not good, this was as good a place as any to celebrate a birthday. I arrived in Norfolk fourth out of the four left in the race and 19 hours behind Unai Basurko overall. There was still a chance.

The start from Norfolk was in a strong easterly. We beat our way out into the Atlantic. Bernard Stamm and Kojiro Shiraishi, pointing higher, managed to get north enough to pick up the westerly winds we all wanted. Unai and I could not point up as well and eventually I tacked north, losing a day in the process. But Unai kept going and I seized my chance. Once into the westerlies I gave it all I could to build up a lead over him and as I approached Cape Finisterre it looked good. But then a small low developed off the Cape, throwing me north and as Unai closed in the low disappeared. I beat him over the line at the finish, but my lead was insufficient to gain the 19 hours I needed and I finished a disappointed fourth. It had been fun. Overall I had enjoyed the race and shown that age might slow one down a bit, but it did not stop a person from sailing solo around the world.

Dilip Donde had returned to India after I left Fremantle to get his boat *Mahdi* ready for his forthcoming voyage around the world. When she was completed by Aquarius Shipyard in Goa, I went out to help to commission her, guest of the Indian navy at their officers' training academy, where I enjoyed the luxury of their Indian breakfasts, slightly chillied and delicious. *Mahdi* was heavy on the helm, but by raking back the mast we removed that problem and got on with checking the boat out.

At 56 feet she was not small, nor was she a racer but she was solid and well built. Dilip set out and completed his voyage, calling at Fremantle, the Falklands, Cape Town and home and was greeted on his return by the president of India. It was a great effort, and more than justified Vice Admiral Manohar Awatis's ambitions. But Manohar was not satisfied. The man who, as a vice admiral, used to ride to his office in New Delhi in full uniform, thereby causing Prime Minister Indira Gandhi to call him in and complain that the sound of his horse distracted her, had more ambitious ideas. He wanted the Indian navy to go further and have one of their sailors go around the world solo and non-stop. As was the case with a person who has a firm belief, he subsequently managed to arrange for Lieutenant Commander Abhilash Tomy, IN, to take Dilip's boat around the world non-stop.

During Abhilash's voyage I went out to India again, and was privileged to speak to the young cadets at the Indian military academy at Pune, a fantastic establishment where young potential officers train together before going to their selected service to specialise. Quartered in the admiral's accommodation I decided that I could live life like this . . . My only problem was that although the young cadets spoke in English it was with such an accent that I had difficulty understanding them and Dilip, on the stage with me, often had to interpret! From Pune we went to Mumbai and I gave a lecture there, again, quartered in an admiral's accommodation. Life does not get much better. Dilip and I took time out to find Darukhana, which was no longer the place where broken-up ships' artefacts could be found and we went looking for where *Suhaili* was built, our only reference in the much-changed Bombay Harbour being the Cross Island fort. We sort of found the spot but could not be certain. We took a trip to Cross Island where there were still two Armstrong rifled guns that I remembered from nearly 50 years earlier lying in the water. Manohar arranged their recovery.

After Mumbai, Dilip and I drove down to Janjira as I wanted to see where we had dived for gold 45 years before. We stayed with his uncle in Janjira, visited the Marud fort out in the harbour and then set out for Goa. Unfortunately, someone told the media of my visit and this led to a headline in the *Pune Times* that read 'The return of the Gold Digger', which I did not appreciate. We spent the rest of our drive to Goa looking into the rear-view mirrors in case the Indian customs thought I had found gold in 1965, hidden it, and come back to collect it 45 years later!

A couple of years later, I was invited to lecture at the Indian Institute of Technology at Kharagpur and Dilip joined me. We took the train from Howrah, Kolkata, to Nagpur, where we were taken to the Satpura Tiger Game Reserve, arranged by Manohar. The rail journey across the Bengal plain was fascinating and I stood for hours at the open door watching the countryside pass by and people working in their farms and rice fields. When we got to the Satpura reserve we stayed at the visitor bungalow built in 1911, high up where the climate was refreshing. We searched high and low but did not see a tiger.

We did witness the efforts being made to grow the right grass to encourage antelope to live in the reserve, which would provide food for tigers, and the villages that had been cleared to provide a sensible-sized tiger reserve and the new, much better, accommodation being built for the displaced villagers. The only wild animal we saw, and that was the briefest of glimpses, was a bear. The numbers of tigers actually in the reserve were unknown. Perhaps 50, maybe 30, but no one knew for sure. But the authorities were making a huge effort to try to encourage them.

One evening when Dilip and I were having a late evening whisky in the visitor bungalow we heard shouts and noisy activity from Manohar's bedroom. He always went to bed early so we wondered why was he creating such a rumpus this late at night. We decided to ignore it and did nothing, but the next morning we asked Manohar why he had been so noisy towards midnight. His response was that a snake had fallen from the roof onto his bed, but it was not dangerous and anyway he had killed it with his stick. We found the snake's lifeless body. It was a viper, but we decided not to tell him.

We left Nagpur on the Indian Railway Express for Mumbai. Dilip took me to see the cooking car where the food was produced as we rattled along. Dante could not have invented anything better. The stoves were within feet of the gas cylinders and health and safety would have had a fit, but the food was excellent. I had enjoyed a wonderful visit back to a country I love, and my Hindi might even have slightly improved.

15

SOME EXPERIMENTS IN NAVIGATION

It is rather difficult to be an ocean navigator and not wonder about who first sailed the seas you are plying and how they managed to work out where they were going or keep track of their position sufficiently to be able to make their way home again. There is some suggestion that the Phoenicians, the greatest of all the maritime exploring and trading nations, sailed around Africa as far back as 600 BC, in an expedition organised by the Egyptian Pharaoh Necho II. They certainly traded with Cornwall and India and may well have ventured as far as America as Carthaginian coins have been discovered on the outermost Azorean islands. Thor Heyerdahl showed with his *Kon-Tiki* voyage that it was perfectly possible for quite primitive rafts to sail across large tracts of ocean. The spread of the Polynesian peoples across the Pacific is more recent proof and the greatest impact on the diffusion of people has come from the migration of the inhabitants of the British Isles by sea and their colonisation of North America, Australia and New Zealand. Did they just sail off into the blue or could they find their way back and if so how?

The Portuguese were the first Europeans to make a science

of navigation in the 15th century as they sought a way to the Indies and it was their technology that Columbus used for his three voyages to islands bordering America. But how accurately could he have navigated? His voyages show that he knew how to get back to the same places in the Americas again, which indicates a knowledge of celestial navigation, not necessarily expected from a merchant and which would have required reasonably accurate instruments. There was not much available at the time – the astrolabe measuring angles and a simpler form known as the quadrant were in use, but nothing as sophisticated as a sextant or even the cross staff that Drake used a century later. The absence of reliable timepieces, they usually carried just an hourglass, meant that only latitude could be established anyway since to calculate longitude accurately, time is essential. Vessels of this period could sail roughly on a desired latitude when they crossed the Atlantic, relying on keeping the Pole Star at the same altitude above the northern horizon, but they had no means of measuring how far they had travelled apart from timing chips thrown into the water passing a known length.

To find out how possible it might have been for people to make landfalls with a reasonable degree of accuracy an instrument could be tried at home, but this would never compare with the actuality of a rolling boat and the real pressures to establish a position when there are no other means available. The test had to be made at sea and since the 500th anniversary of Columbus's voyage was almost upon us, I decided to try to sail the route of his first voyage of discovery.

To replicate the conditions Columbus experienced, I chose to sail at the same time of year. My only instrument was an astrolabe, which was all he had. Furthermore, it would be best carried out alone where there would be no one else to distract my efforts. The National Maritime Museum allowed me to copy one of the astrolabes in their collection, the *Guardian* newspaper and Barclays Bank provided sufficient sponsorship to enable me to hire the Argos satellite tracking system that would enable people at home to know where I was even if I might not be certain. The plan was for me to record where I thought I was and radio this back for a comparison to be made between where I thought I was and my true position to see how accurately I was navigating with the astrolabe. *Suhaili* was the obvious choice of boat because she could average about the same speed as Columbus and I knew her.

I left Falmouth in August 1989 and took 12 days to sail to the island of Gomera in the Canary Islands, from which Columbus had sailed 497 years before. There were still some relics from that era, the house he lived in, the church he and his crew prayed at before their departure and the well from which he filled his water casks just prior to departure. Within two days I sailed and at once started making regular timings of items such as weed or matchsticks along the hull to work out how fast I was going. I had a number of advantages over Columbus: I knew the distance I should sail and that there was a favourable current of between a quarter and half a knot which I could add to my progress through the water to give a better indication of how far along the track I was. For latitude I used the astrolabe, having indexed it before I sailed. It proved awkward at first, swinging wildly in a small boat, but in time I got better at it. On slightly hazy days, though, it was very hard to read accurately as the sun did not provide a sharp image against the brass of the instrument. It took time to resolve this, but I did it eventually by smoking the brass surface with a candle flame, something I suspect that the navigators of the Renaissance period must have done as well but which I could never have discovered in a controlled experiment on land.

As I completed 30 days at sea, my concern as to where I actually was began to increase. My positions were based upon untested instruments and calculations; if I was badly out we could run into land while I was taking a rest. From the astrolabe I felt I had a reasonable idea of latitude but if so, the Bahamian islands were somewhere ahead and they are low-lying. So I did what the earlier navigators had done, concentrated on looking for signs, birds flying towards land in the evening, from it at daybreak, bits of waste like branches floating in the sea that had been wrenched from the land by gales. The Polynesians were capable of sensing land at great distances, reputedly more than 100 miles, by feeling the swell reflected from an island but I was unsure whether I, a modern navigator, would have this sense.

In the event my clearest indication of the approach of land came from the birds, supported by crossing paths with a large cruise liner. Then the next morning I could just make out a small wave formation moving towards me whereas the natural ones were moving in the same direction I was sailing. Within a couple of hours the horizon hardened, became firmer and then land rose above the sea. But what land? The answer came in a radio call minutes later, someone on San Salvador was calling *Suhaili*. The island ahead was my objective and I was coming in about eight miles out in the latitude.

When my positions were compared with the actual ones, the average error was 16 miles in latitude, but this was halved if one ignored the two worst observations, taken on cloudy days. This would have been accurate enough for a vessel making a landfall to pick up an obvious recognisable object such as a hill and find its destination. In distance-travelled terms I was 22 miles out at the finish, which shows how accurately it is possible to judge a boat's speed measuring the time it takes to pass small objects in the water and knowing roughly how much current to allow. The voyage had been fascinating. It showed that the navigators 500 years before could work out their latitude to a reasonably accurate degree, once the sun's declination tables had been computed by the Portuguese in 1485. These tables plotted the movement of the sun on an hourly basis north and south during the year. I wrote up the experiment and was highly gratified to receive the Royal Institute of Navigation's Gold Medal for it.

After a couple of days' rest, I sailed to Nassau, picked up Commander Larry Brumbach, an ex-US navy flier who had handled the communications in the BOC Challenge, and we enjoyed a Verdi concert of a sail up to Norfolk, Virginia, where we berthed in a small marina, part of the enormous naval base where by now Vice Admiral Jim Weatherall had offered accommodation while I awaited the crew for the return voyage to join. Philippa King, David Balls and Chris Hipwell joined two days later, and got straight into provisioning as we sailed on 14 November, already late in the year for an Atlantic crossing

Lloyds had refused to give me insurance for the voyage out to Nassau since I was single-handing, but they covered *Suhaili* once I had crew again. Their underwriters got it badly wrong. We ran into bad weather within two days, a baptism for the others. With all our spare rope streamed out astern and no sail set, we bounced quite safely through the 35-foot waves caused by a storm 700 miles away to the north. Since the path of these depressions is generally north-east I had hoped that our course towards the Azores would diverge from them and the weather would become easier, but we were out of luck.

The next depression started out quietly enough two days later, forecast to pass 500 miles away, but it rapidly deepened into a storm and swung towards us. We altered course to the south-east to move further away from the oncoming storm, but the effect of this was minimal. At daybreak on 21 November the wind was already gusting to 55 knots and the seas were building. The first indication of what was ahead came when three monster waves approached, a combination of a number of different wave formations.

We rode the first, the second sent some water aboard but the third began to break before it struck us and broke as it hit, completely covering the boat. Some of the water, perhaps deflected back by the cabin, hit me at the helm and drove me back beneath the pushpit. I was some feet below the surface, thinking that we must pop up soon as I was getting short of breath, when the water cleared. My safety harness had stopped me from going overside, but this was the first time I had been totally immersed since 1968 and I was not happy with the reminder. Our problem was that although most boats, and *Suhaili* is no exception, will lift their sterns as a wave approaches, these were large and breaking and their tops were falling over us. We started to stream the warps again, but a wave washing over the boat tangled them and we were still sorting this mess out four hours later.

After spending so much of my life at sea, I am used to bad weather. It is not something any sane person seeks, but if you spend a lot of time at sea you are going to run into it sooner or later. Normally one shrugs one's shoulders and settles down for perhaps a day of discomfort, perhaps a lack of hot meals and the certainty of wet clothing and a few bruises. Even in the Southern Ocean, *Suhaili* had bounced over some enormous waves so I was not too concerned but the lack of the warp and the speed with which the waves were building was making me uneasy.

Another wave roared in towards us. We cringed slightly as the wave broke just astern and then crashed onto the deck with enormous power forcing us forward and then into a mild broach. *Suhaili* went over on her side. Chris Hipwell was steering at this stage and had his harness attached to the shroud. As *Suhaili* went onto her side the wave washed him out of the cockpit and out to sea until his harness became taut as it caught the spreaders on the mizzen mast. He was there as *Suhaili* swung back in response to her natural stability and grabbed the mast to find himself hanging halfway up it when *Suhaili* was upright. It made us laugh, which was perhaps just as well as we discovered that the blow had somehow removed the compass, not that we were using it much at the time.

The next one came as David, Pippa and I were below trying to get the latest forecast from the US coastguard. We heard the wave coming, felt *Suhaili* start to lift her stern, then there was a roar as the wave broke and our world exploded. Like three peas in an empty tin we were flung across the cabin, I landed up, winded, in the back of the galley where I would have sworn there was no room for me. Water came through everywhere as the hull sprung with the force of the blow. We picked ourselves up as the hatch flew open and Chris yelled down that we were breaking up. I could not believe it, but pushed my head through the hatch to find out. The mess on deck was unbelievable. The masts had gone, both of them, and were lying, broken, in the water alongside. 'Hold on here,' I said to Chris, 'while we check the hull's OK.' I dived below again to search the lockers and bilges to see whether the force of the blow had sprung any of the planking. We seemed all right, so leaving David below to pump, Chris and I set about tidying up the deck.

Suhaili rode better now. For some perverse reason she lay beam on and the occasional wave rolled over, soaking us as it did so, but we no longer felt as endangered. Our first task was to dump the broken masts before they knocked a hole in the hull. We worked our way round the deck, salvaging what we could and unbolting the rigging screws. We saved the sails, the main and mizzen booms and some rigging but the rest we let go. It floated clear and eventually disappeared from view. We threw out all the rope we had and attached the anchor and chain to it to provide further drag. She rolled sharply, to be expected without the steadying effect of the masts. The motion made cooking impossible so we ate what we could cold, but a cup of tea would have done wonders for our morale. There was nothing else we could do until the weather eased, the glass was now rising indicating that the storm had passed and the worst was over, it was just a question of waiting.

We still had the Argos system on board transmitting our position and in Newport, Rhode Island, Peter Dunning had noticed that we had stopped. He knew the weather conditions we were experiencing and became concerned. Then, a day later, he noticed that we had started to move eastwards again and contacted Sue to tell her that we seemed all right but might have lost a mast or our radio. As the weather got better we had set up the main boom as a stumpy mast, lashed to all that was left of the original mast and set the only sail that would fit, the mizzen, its foot as a luff. Provided we kept the wind on the quarter it filled and sped us on.

Our next task was to get the main engine to work again so that we did not lose power, and after a couple of hours it fired up. This and a hot meal had put heart back into the crew and we now set course for the nearest land, the Portuguese islands of the Azores. At 1,400 miles it was further than America but lay downwind, and as we could not sail the boat to windward with our jury rig we expected to get there sooner. But not soon enough for Larry Brumbach who contacted navy friends and asked for a 3C Orion maritime patrol aircraft to extend its patrol to see if we were all right. It arrived suddenly and flew over us then circled back. Unsure as to its intentions I got out the Aldis signalling lamp and called it up. It responded by flashing its landing lights. I sent a simple message 'Suhaili, Horta, OK' and the landing lights flashed again and it banked away. It was a relief to know that we would be reported and our silence might be explained.

We settled back to our leisurely progress towards Horta, with the stronger than expected winds we were averaging 100 miles a day even under our jury rig. Towards nightfall the aircraft came back, dropping flares as it did so to lead a merchant ship in towards us, but for what purpose I could not fathom. It swung in and nearly rammed us, only by gunning the engine did we avoid a collision that would have put us in distress situation. A loudspeaker blared at us to abandon ship, which we refused and then, to my enormous relief, it left us with a final comment that we were crazy. The ocean seemed much safer when they had disappeared over the horizon. They had meant well but I was not ready to give up *Suhaili* when she was perfectly seaworthy, however bad she may have looked. For the rest of the voyage we avoided drawing attention to ourselves.

We arrived at the Azores 14 days later but had no intention of remaining there as we still reckoned on getting home for Christmas. We found an old mast and set it up but the moment we left Horta we ran into another storm and took shelter in Praia de Vittoria. While there, moored alongside an American army tug, yet another storm came through which reached 98 knots in the harbour and blew away the anemometer at the airport so we took the hint. We laid *Suhaili* up and flew home. It had been a salutary experience, a reminder of the enormous power of the sea and I doubt if a more modern boat would have survived the ordeal. The next spring, when the weather was less vicious, I sent new masts out by sea and then flew out with a new crew and sailed her home for a proper re-fit. The only good things to come out of the adventurous homeward voyage were the opportunity to meet the people of the Azores and the realisation that the North Atlantic is not the place for small boats in November, something that Columbus had also discovered 500 years before.

Columbus had a magnetic compass, but what was in use before its discovery? Experiments with a possible system of direction-finding by the Vikings, in co-operation with Captain Søren Thirslund, occupied me on and off for the next two years. The possibility of making oceanic voyages and maintaining a desired direction using a simple sun compass only came to light comparatively recently. In 1947 half of a small wooden disc, originally 70 millimetres in diameter, was discovered at the site of an ancient convent at Uunartoq, Greenland. For 30 years it was largely ignored, and then in 1978 the Swedish astronomer Dr Curt Roslund noticed that it had a curve etched into its surface. It did not take long to establish that this mark represented the curve to be expected if the shadow of the sun was cast by a small pin at the middle of the disc, a gnomon curve.

The significance of this curve soon became apparent. Bearing in mind that the sun moves north and south relative to the globe, its shadow lengthens and shortens in winter and summer in the northern hemisphere. Thus the length of the shadow will depend upon the latitude and the time of year. It was a simple matter to calculate that this curve represented the sun's shadow for the solstice at roughly the latitude of Bergen. By taking a replica disc to the same latitude at the same time of year it was quickly noticed that provided the end of the shadow was kept on the line, and the disc held exactly horizontal, the point on the disc nearest to the pin pointed steadily due north throughout the day. This discovery of the disc and the detective work to solve the reason for the curve suddenly showed how people of the Viking era could have navigated on any desired course. It was they who colonised Greenland and left the original disc there.

Provided someone went to the trouble to spend the day before sailing marking the end of the shadow on the disc at hourly intervals and then joining those points together, a simple sun compass was created. This would be accurate at that particular latitude for a week or so, depending upon the time of year. It would remain accurate for longer about the time of the solstice as the sun's movement north/south is at its minimum then and June, of course, was the height of the Viking sailing season because the weather was clement at that time. It was the simplicity of the system that most impressed me and it could work just as well on a plain or flat desert.

Had it been known long before the Vikings? So far there is no evidence of earlier discs but if they were made of wood they could not be expected to survive except in special conditions that would allow their preservation. I tried the disc out myself at sea, on a fitfully sunny day, which meant that for much of the time I was reliant on direction by holding an angle to the wind, with occasional checks when the sun showed itself. The result was remarkable, we were less than a mile off our original latitude, having tried to sail due west for 50 miles. The system should become a part of the school curriculum as it would teach children how to orienteer and explain to them how the sun moves relative to the earth.

We did a practical experiment with the BBC using the sun compass to navigate from Bergan in Norway to Sullom Voe in the Shetlands. The boat used was a knarr, a typical Viking trading vessel 60 feet long and not one of the longships used for raids. I set up the compass the day before we sailed and we headed out into the North Sea with a cheerful mixed crew of Norwegians and Danes. After a couple of observations, the sky clouded over and for the rest of the day and night we could only get our course from the direction of the waves. The next morning I got a brief glimpse of the sun, just enough to show that we were steering south of our course so we altered to the north to compensate. Eventually, a large lighthouse came into view and we knew where we were, just three miles out. Any experienced Viking navigator could have achieved the same results.

To make the programme more interesting it was planned to portage the knarr across an isthmus which the Vikings were reputed to have used to save a 60-mile row. This was fine except the knarr is much more heavily built than a longship and did not carry as large a crew. We got over this problem by announcing we were looking for muscled volunteers to help push the boat across the land. Another unforeseen difficulty was the main road which passed across our portage area, plus the land had been raised six feet during the past 1,000 years. We emptied eight tons of stone ballast from the boat, put logs to act as rollers beneath the keel and started to haul. The rope broke. The director was distraught as this was to be the exciting part of the programme.

However, by this time we had amassed an army of helpers and, by putting a strop around the stern, 100 willing Shetlanders soon got the boat onto the road. At this point I was due to fly home, but a friendly policeman suggested that it would not look good if I left a heavy 60-foot boat blocking the main road north, so my flight had to be rearranged. The boat was moved across the road and then gravity took over and it ran away from us down the other side into the water. I doubt whether the Vikings would have bothered to portage a knarr, but we had shown it could be done. As far as navigation was concerned the Vikings could have found a chosen destination with ease.

16

Time for the Clippers

The Clipper Round the World Race has been my main pre-occupation for the past 23 years. The idea came to me while mountaineering with Chris Bonington in Greenland, where we had discussed the costs of climbing Mount Everest. The price seemed high, more than the cost of a small-to-medium cruising yacht anyway. But it got me thinking about the sailing equivalent. It did not take long to conclude it was a circumnavigation, which got me thinking: how much would I have to charge a person who did not have enough money to buy a boat or was not confident in their own abilities to sail around the world, to provide them with the opportunity of a race around the world? The costs would have to include the boats, food, port fees, insurance, the salary of the skipper, repairs and supervision. Some back-of-an-envelope calculations, followed by some discreet enquiries as to the cost of boats, led to a figure of about half the cost required to climb Everest for the whole voyage per person, provided we had 120 crew paying. A plan was put together. Adverts in the newspapers in the autumn of 1995 led to a large response, so there was clearly a market. Once an idea like this has been floated if you don't go ahead with it someone else will, so we got to work.

While we interviewed potential crew, we looked around for the ideal boat, not too small, strong and seaworthy. Colvic near Chelmsford came up with the Camper and Nicholson Bluewater 58 sloop, in fact 60 feet long, which exactly suited our needs. We placed a contract for eight of the boats. Everything was going ahead at breakneck speed. We had planned to enter the fleet in a race being organised by Jimmy Cornell, but were unable to agree terms so we decided we would organise our own event. With money going out at a fast rate, I began to have some doubts about the finances of the person supporting the idea. When payments to Colvic started being late with no good reason for the delays being provided, I became seriously worried. We were committed to a lot of people by now and we had taken money from them so we had to deliver. It soon became apparent that I needed to find the money elsewhere to keep the project running. This is where William Ward, a property developer, came into my life. It did not take long to arrange a share transfer so we went ahead with the project.

We set up our base in Plymouth and the first person I took on was Andrew 'Spud' Spedding, an old friend and author of *Sod's Law of the Sea*. He became the senior skipper and was able to support me in supervising the build and specifications of the boats. Inevitably there were a few issues to resolve. To start with, the boats became almost unmanageable in a squall and would round up to windward however much helm was applied, but by raking the mast back a little we removed that problem. Colin de Mowbray came next to join us and then other friends from sailing, mainly ex-services, soon followed. As the boats were completed. we sailed them down from Ipswich to Plymouth and began crew training, taking on additional skippers as we went.

While this was going on I took off around the world to arrange the port facilities for the route we had chosen. This ended up being transatlantic to Florida via Madeira, then through the Panama Canal to the Galapagos Islands. The Pacific leg went on to Hawaii, Yokohama and Hong Kong. Singapore, the Seychelles, Durban, Cape Town and Salvador in Brazil followed and then back to our starting point in Plymouth. In all, with time allowed in ports, its duration would be almost ten months.

The original name of the company was Maiden International, which meant nothing. We had long discussions about the names for our eight boats and eventually decided to call them after the sailing Clipper ships that used to take tea from China to London, as half our route was the same. This led us on to using the name for the company and it became Clipper Ventures Plc, since a venture is an adventure and our race was certainly going to provide plenty of that.

The Maritime & Coastguard Agency had recently decided to set up standards for building and equipping commercial yachts. We came under that category as we were charging the crews for their voyages. One could see the logic in having rules as it provided assurance and guaranteed safety standards for customers. However, the requirements were based on those for a Class 7 merchant ship, a typical dry cargo vessel. This led to some bizarre demands. One of these was that there should be body bags for everyone on board. I phoned the MCA and queried this. They told me it was so bodies could be stored in a freezer. I pointed out that a 60-foot yacht does not carry a freezer and if it did it would be too small for a body. I also asked whether the final bag had the zip on the inside as there would be no one else left to zip it up! Body bags were removed from the requirements, my sole success.

The Class 7 merchant ship rules did not suit small racing yachts, but it had been an easy way of creating rules and boxes to tick quickly, however inappropriate some were. But we had to comply or we could not sail the boats, so we bought the ridiculous mobile fire pumps for each of the boats: a stirrup pump, a garden hose with nozzle plus a bucket filled with sea water. It would, of course, never be used in practice as it would take too long to set up, the contents of the bucket would be flung straight at whatever fire had occurred. We rather missed the old Board of Trade, which had been replaced by the MCA, as it had been manned by ships' masters as surveyors who knew their business and what was practical.

The last boat was delivered from the builders two weeks before the start. They had done well to complete all eight in less than a year. Her paying crew, full of enthusiasm and led by Spud, worked flat out to help us get her ready in time and they made it for the start on 16 October 1996. We paraded the fleet in front of the Hoe, disrupted briefly by a motor yacht chartered by BT that ran right through the parade, and then got the fleet away through the eastern side of the Plymouth breakwater. William and I shook hands. We had got there, built eight boats, equipped them, worked out a race route and trained the crews in under a year. Now we had to get them around the world. The adventure that was to dominate the next two decades of our lives had begun.

We did not have a sponsor for the event so money was tight. We scraped money together to keep the fleet sailing and the crews fed and William sold a couple of his motorbikes to pay for food on one occasion, but we got the fleet around the world. It was not without incident. Two crew had to be got out of prison in Singapore because they had been over-celebrating. One crew took on an ex-French foreign legionnaire in the Seychelles and came second. Faced with reaching the limit on his credit card William put his last £500 on Red 19 on a roulette table in Singapore and came out with £8,000. This covered the looming sail repair bill with change left over. If that had not worked, we would have found some other way of dealing with the problem between us.

When our fleet arrived in Durban, we found the Point Yacht Club preparing to celebrate a Springboks win in the first Lions match of their rugby tour that year. The arrival of 120 British sailors to cheer on the Lions when *they* won was not the plan, but as a minor compensation their bar takings benefited. Their next match took place as we were sailing round to Cape Town. Spud and I decided that a deep low approaching the Cape would be best avoided so took the fleet into East London to avoid the gale and see the match, which the Lions won again. For the third match we were in Cape Town and I was bet a case of beer the Lions would win again. I took the bet and the Lions lost. The South Africans had eventually realised that they needed a kicker in their team!

As the race finished, William and I had to decide what to do next with this fleet of boats we owned. We had learned a great deal from the race and were beginning to gather a good team around us so it seemed senseless to lose the experience we had gained, plus what do you do with eight identical boats? The obvious thing was to run the race again, but when? It takes time to recruit the crews and the boats needed a re-fit. But we also realised that the usual four-yearly cycle for around the world races did not make financial sense. We had a small surplus at the end of the first race, which finished on 14 September 1997, but nothing like enough to keep the boats idle and not paying their way for three years. We decided on a two-year cycle and started recruiting for our next race to be run in 1998, a task not made easy by some negativity among yachting journalists.

To maximise income, we looked for additional work for the boats and advertised a voyage to Greenland. During the skipper recruitment I was told about a young 24-year-old named Alex Thomson, who was reported to be an excellent sailor and wanted to skipper. I was a little concerned at his youth, so decided to take him as my mate for a voyage to Greenland with two of our boats. Chris Bonington could not resist another chance to find unclaimed peaks and joined us, and I took Sue along because I wanted her to see the stark beauty of the country. This time we went to the fjords around Cape Farewell. It was blowing a bit when we got inside and I decided to anchor to an iceberg to prevent the ice pushing us onto a lee shore, on the basis that the berg would ground long before it got near the beach. Alex went across with the anchor and dug it in as best he could using an ice pick and then I went astern to ensure it would hold us. The anchor came flying back as if catapulted so that idea didn't work.

We eventually had to anchor and the following morning extricated ourselves from the ice with some difficulty. We got the boats through the ice to a small village called Aappilattoq, cut off for most of the year and served by a weekly helicopter. We stayed a few days, challenged the village to a game of football which we lost 11–1, I am still unsure how we scored the one. The village's winning celebrations went on into the next day! But then the ice closed in along the coast and we could not get out. We explored the fjords, which were largely clear of ice, went climbing and I went hunting with the locals. The village lived from hunting and fishing, a sealskin being worth £40 at that time. The occasional bounty of a polar bear could bring £10,000. Two Inuit brothers joined us for a while, bringing some welcome local knowledge. Alex and my godson, Ian Weatherall, were out fishing, with a style that would have earned 13 points from an East German judge, but yielded no results. One of the Inuit asked me what they were doing, which I thought seemed pretty obvious but he said they won't find any fish there. I asked where the fish were then and he pointed to a different part of the fjord. I told him to take the other dinghy and see what he could do and within an hour he was back with six lovely Arctic char, which provided a delicious dinner for everyone.

After three weeks trapped inside the fjords we got out through the coastal ice and ran into a Danish patrol boat who challenged us and told us not to go into the fjords on account of the ice. They did not believe that was where we had come from, until I asked them if they would take the two Inuit back to their village. We went north to Angmagssalik, the largest town on the east coast, threading our way in through the ice again. Here a number of crew were due to leave so we worked our way to the airport and one of our skippers flew in to relieve me so Sue and I could fly back via Reykjavik.

I had been impressed by Alex and was now sure he would be able to skipper a boat and command a crew of people a lot older than himself. He more than proved himself by winning the 1998/9 race and one of his crew in this race, Keith Mills, decided to back him subsequently. Alex went on to race in three Vendée Globe races, steadily improving his performance each time.

The only major change in our route for the second race was that we called at Nassau and Havana, Cuba, which was friendly but very old-fashioned. We also went back to Yokohama, to the Bayside Marina. In Cuba we moored the fleet in the Marina Hemingway, a marina village where work had stopped when Fidel Castro came to power. There was a yacht club there as well, run by an ex-Cuban navy captain who was very helpful and with whom I struck up a friendship. Cuba was run-down and a bit shabby, but it must have once been very attractive with its Spanish Colonial buildings and one can hope they may be restored before it is too late.

After Hawaii a block broke on the foredeck of one of the boats and a rope smashed into a crew's ankle, almost removing it. A doctor on one of the other yachts was hauled across in lumpy seas to tend to the injury and it was clear the casualty would have to be evacuated for hospitalisation. The nearest land was Johnston Atoll, used by the USA to dispose of some fairly unpleasant chemicals. The boat sailed there to find a manned heavy machine gun-mounted Humvee and the gunner asking people to keep out of his arcs of fire, which was pretty unnerving. We were not to know that the previous year someone had written a novel about terrorists arriving in a yacht to attack the atoll and the Americans were jumpy. However, they were very helpful once they appreciated that our crew were not terrorists and our casualty was flown back to Hawaii for proper hospital treatment. The doctor received a well-deserved commendation from the Royal Humane Society for his efforts.

By the 2000 race our reputation was becoming more established. Despite the doom and gloom from some of the media, we had run two successful races and more people were applying to participate. William and I were able to expand the team so we could put our heads above the parapet and start to think of where we wanted the business to go. Colin de Mowbray had started taking over some of my duties as race director in the previous race and now he took over the whole job which freed my time. This was when we decided that, just as football teams compete representing cities, why couldn't yachts? So each yacht represented a town or city. This led to other places along our route asking whether they could sponsor a boat and another income stream was created. The 2000 race started and finished at Portsmouth and was supported by *The Times* newspaper. It took a similar route to 1998, except we missed Shanghai as one boat had its generator room flooded so we returned the fleet to Yokohama to effect repairs and ran out of time. Instead of Shanghai we went to Okinawa, where my lack of any Japanese and concern at the danger of eating shellfish, meant I lost weight by eating nothing but Okinawa noodles for ten days.

Clipper was becoming increasingly busy as we grew the company but there were other activities going on that provided an interesting contrast. In 1994, I was invited to become a member of the new sports lottery group. The National Lottery was a great idea to raise money for various good causes, sport being one. I joined a group of sportspeople and our first task was to set up how we would work, supported by a good team. We met monthly to go through the applications for our grants and in the early days we had £25 million a month to give out to projects if they matched our criteria. One of our initial decisions concerned a new national stadium to replace the ageing one at Wembley. We provided the money to obtain the site and then a decision had to be made as to who was best placed to make it work commercially. The Football Association was an almost obvious choice. Sadly, political interference meant delays. You cannot have the Secretary of State and sports minister saying in July that the plans are brilliant, and then a new sports minister but the same Secretary of State saying in October that it would not work. It spooked the banks that were going to provide the funding. This led to a delay of two years before work started and that meant we lost the World Athletics Championships and put the costs of building up some £80 million.

An issue that concerned us was that it was all very well providing money for capital projects such as gyms, but they are not used effectively unless there are qualified trainers in place. So we asked Virginia Bottomley, the minister, if we could provide funding to pay for trainers. Her answer was practical: let's get the system going and look at this in a year. She contacted us before the year was out, having taken our point, and thereafter we the split the money between capital and revenue projects.

As a result of our work some of us were invited to join the Sports Council, which, after a hiatus, was chaired by the very effective footballer Trevor Brooking. Although there were a few political appointees, most of us came from the world of sport. It was a great group and we got on well, better than people expected. For one of our monthly meetings I was on my way from Paddington when our tube train was stopped due to a bomb threat. All the passengers were evacuated at Baker Street. To avoid being late I looked for a taxi and found myself in competition with Garth Crooks, another member. Garth was dressed in a brilliant array of clothing whereas I was in a business suit as I had to go on to the London Stock Exchange that afternoon. We could not have displayed a greater sartorial contrast, but outside of fashion we got on well and usually agreed on issues. One that particularly concerned us was the selling-off of school playing fields for development. Trevor Brooking went to see the prime minister who said he would deal with it, but nothing happened. The results are there for all of us to see some 20 years later when far too many of our young people are obese, a future drain on an already strained National Health Service.

It all came to an end when the Secretary of State, Tessa Jowell, decided to weed out the Sports Council and told us that nine of us were going to be retired, including our chairman. We had been too independent, it appeared, and changes had to be made to make the council more compliant with the political objectives of the new government. She asked us to attend a meeting and explained that she intended making changes. I pointed out that she had got rid of the entire audit committee and we were the people looking after the Wembley development. This had not been appreciated! Astonishingly, as a result, David Ross had his dismissal reversed.

Having been sacked, I thought I was in the clear but apparently not. I had been put on the group supervising a training rowing lake near Eton, a project initially budgeted at £6 million. It had reached £10 million when I joined and that is where it stayed until I left as every time they asked for more money I told them that it was public money for which I was responsible and I could not go back to the Sports Council for more. Of course, once I was sacked I had no authority, but it took four months before my resignation was accepted. The project cost £16 million in the end, and this just for a training lake, whereas at the time only £2.5 million had been allocated to the Weymouth sailing training centre, which we could all see would be the ideal place for any Olympic sailing and at the time sailing was Britain's most successful Olympic sport.

Naturally, *Suhaili* accompanied us wherever we moved. She went on display at the new Neptune Hall at the National Maritime Museum in Greenwich for a couple of years where I had become a trustee. But there was a problem with this as, being wooden, she needed to be kept moist. In the dry climate of the hall her planking began to shrink. I asked for water to be put in her bilges but was told this was not possible because of the risk of legionnaires' disease. I had been asked to sign her over to the museum permanently, but I could not bring myself to accept she would slowly fall to bits if she stayed where she was. She had been too much a part of my life to be deserted now.

The sad state of Sir Francis Chichester's *Gypsy Moth* at Greenwich and the even worse state of Sir Alec Rose's *Lively Lady*, which had been gifted to Portsmouth City Council, was a discouragement to allowing any official body ownership of boats. I took *Suhaili* back, re-commissioned her, and for a while she was on display, afloat, at the National Maritime Museum Cornwall in Falmouth until they wanted her moved. By then anyway it had become obvious that if she was to survive all of her Indian iron fastenings, the 1,400 bolts that hold the planks to the frames, would have to be renewed. Remarkably, they had lasted almost 50 years, but many were now rusted and some had failed completely. That task took up a lot of time over the next six years but was eventually finished in 2015 with the help of some willing volunteers.

There were other issues taking up my time as well. Many years ago while I was still at sea with British India I was asked whether I would like to be seconded to the Sail Training Association (STA) as mate aboard one of the two schooners, the *Sir Winston Churchill* and the *Malcolm Miller*. I agreed but then had to withdraw as my plans to sail around the world in *Suhaili* firmed up. However, it gave me an interest in the association so when I was invited to become its president in 1993 I did not take too much persuading.

The STA was a two-headed organisation – part was international, the bit that runs the Tall Ships Races, at that time sponsored by Cutty Sark whisky, and the other was largely national, a shipping company if you like, operating two schooners that took young people between the ages of 16 and 25 for a two-week taste of the tall ships experience. These youngsters performed all the duties of the crew around the vessels, from peeling potatoes, keeping a lookout, steering and climbing aloft to handle the square sails. For many it was their first time away from home and they suffered a form of benign deprivation without TV, videos or Mother making their beds and tidying up after them. The shock was such for some that the ships kept clear of ports with railway stations for the first five days in each voyage as many would go home given the chance. But at the end of a voyage nearly all were asking how they could stay aboard. The short experience made them more self-confident, more empathetic of the needs of others and they learnt the advantages of being in a team. Above all they learnt that they could do things they thought were difficult or impossible. It was far more about character development than teaching sailing.

My first not very happy trip with the ships was the 1994 Tall Ships Race to Corunna, when I sailed as navigator aboard the *Sir Winston Churchill*. The ship was a mess, more like a Lebanese tramp ship than the smart training ship she should have been. The crew seemed to have little knowledge of sailing and even less interest in it. The bosun, whose task was to supervise the youngsters up the mast, had refused to go aloft for eight years and had not been sacked – that gave me sleepless nights. The engines were switched on the moment sailing became difficult, a poor example to set the youngsters. It was hardly surprising therefore that we did not finish the race, but motored into Corunna.

It was obvious that urgent action was needed, but the crew's response to the state of the ships was to claim they had no time for maintenance. Remembering my own experience in the merchant navy I could not agree, but we needed to find a way of changing the culture of mediocrity that seemed to have crept into the organisation. George Cooper, head of the operational side of the RNLI and, like myself, an ex-merchant navy man and reservist, set about introducing the necessary changes with the active support of the council of trustees and within a short time the effects began to show. By 1998, the ships were sailing nearly full and the STA was the largest single provider of Royal Yachting Association Competent Crew Certificates in the country.

An annual conference decided the routes of the Tall Ships Race but the board was entirely British, supported by a committee made up from representatives of all the various international sail training organisations. Since only a small proportion of the annual fleets were British, this seemed wrong so I began to ease Brits off the board and replace them with representatives from other participating nations to strengthen its credibility, particularly as there was already resentment among our international participants that the STA ran the races and also had two vessels that competed in them. In suggesting this change I was encouraged by our patron, the Duke of Edinburgh, who gave me sound advice stemming from the experience of internationalising of the Duke of Edinburgh's Award scheme. Further changes were required, however, as there was a lack of business experience on the board, so I introduced Nigel Rowe as deputy chairman and later, after the sad death of Robin Duchesne, he took over as chairman.

The schooners were excellent sea boats. We took the *Malcolm Miller* to Spitzbergen in 1996, achieving speeds of up to 14 knots and providing a wonderful opportunity to explore this ice-ringed archipelago. But the two schooners were getting on, they had given 30 years of service and the older boats are the more expensive they are to maintain. The Lloyds' surveys differed each year, making it impossible to budget for the costs that might be necessary during the annual maintenance period. The time had come to seek replacements and we planned a new barquentine.

However, two brand-new first-rate sailing ship hulls became available in Germany as a result of a liquidation. Receivers, on the whole, are clever at accounts but don't always know the value of anything. Giles Pritchard-Gordon, a ship-owning member of our council, conducted a ruthless and speedy negotiation and we got the pair for £1.3 million. The money for the completion of the hulls took longer to raise, but Giles knew the Niarchos shipping magnate family and we persuaded them to provide half of the £11 million we needed and we obtained matching finance from Lottery funding. The hulls were towed round to Appledore in Devon and work commenced to turn them into two smart brigs, each capable of taking 52 young trainees. Initially the brigs gave us a few problems but once these difficulties were dealt with, they proved lovely vessels to sail. Our main problem was that they were costing close to a million pounds a year each to operate and they needed to be full to cover these costs.

As we wrestled with this problem Sue was diagnosed with ovarian cancer and my total attention had to be on her, so I had to retire. I gave a year's notice to the council so they could find a replacement. Lord Greenway took over but some members of the committee decided that to support the brigs they would raid the fund I had been putting together from the Tall Ships Race surplus, which had been earmarked to provide bursaries for young people in all the vessels in the races. Nigel Rowe was dismissed as chairman of the races board and there was uproar from the international contingent, who brought him back as chairman of the new International Sail Training Association and they set about organising their own races. Without the vessels the STA Tall Ships Race folded.

It was when I got home from seeing the Clipper Race through Okinawa in 2001 that I found Sue suffering. She never complained usually, but this time she was obviously unwell. She had seen the doctor three times but the treatment suggested was not achieving anything and her stomach had swollen to an enormous size, so I took her to Torbay Hospital for another opinion. Cancer had been around us for years, it was striking friends and acquaintances with alarming frequency. So far it had missed us, but not this time.

The hospital soon diagnosed ovarian cancer stage 3, fairly advanced and much harder to treat as a result. Cancer had finally struck the one person who meant the whole world to me. I was numb with shock and fright for a short time and then a determination to try to beat this horror surfaced. Sue's first operation took place quickly. Nine litres of liquid surrounding the tumour had to be drained from her stomach before they could operate. Why had that swelling not been an indication of the possibility that she had cancer? I was told that ovarian cancer was hard to diagnose. I waited while the operation took place and was then allowed into the recovery room. Sue was horrifyingly white initially, but the two nurses on duty never left her side as she slowly regained her colour. Their confidence worked on me and when Sue was taken back to the ward I left and drove home to two worried and unfed dogs.

Next morning, I drove to the hospital as soon as I was allowed entry to find a bleary-eyed Sue conscious but on a lot of pain relief, which was to be expected. For the next couple of days, I spent as long as was sensible with her, she was very tired, but another worry was that she could not eat anything. Four young doctors visited to try to sort out the problem but had no solution. Then the no-nonsense Scottish sister came in and said that in previous cases they had used a certain treatment and shouldn't they try that? The doctors agreed, relieved that someone seemed to know what to do, and of course it worked. Experience is so undervalued against paper qualifications.

As soon as possible I got Sue home to Torbryan and then she had to start her courses of chemotherapy. The cancer markers came down so the chemo seemed to be working and eventually they stated that the cancer was eliminated. We took off for a holiday in Cuba, spending a couple of nights in Havana, staying at the hotel Ernest Hemingway had lived in and exploring the old city. It gave me a chance to meet up with my friend, the ex-navy captain, but he was not allowed to take us to his house so we had to eat together in restaurants. After two days in Havana, we were driven to a beach resort on the north-west coast for what we had planned as a chance to just relax in the sun. On the way we could watch the sugar being harvested using old-fashioned equipment and even carts. It was sad to see the main export product of the country being harvested so inefficiently.

When we arrived at our resort our chalet was what we had hoped for, right on the beach looking north to a reef almost a mile away. We settled in and then returned to the restaurant for our dinner. We soon discovered that the menu was pretty basic, based largely on black beans, but that first night we assumed that this was that day's menu, not realising that it did not change from one day to the next. When we returned to our chalet we found that our deck chairs had disappeared. Ours were the only coloured ones so it was easy to find them when I walked up the beach. They had been taken by some German tourists so I took them back. The next morning I awoke early, still suffering from jet lag, and went outside to smoke a cigar just as three Germans came down the beach looking for 'their' deck chairs. I sat and looked at them as they walked past 'my' deck chairs!

Apart from the basic food and the lack of variety, the resort was delightful. Although most people only stayed a couple of days we stayed for eleven, sailing out in a Hobie Cat and canoe-ing around the island, relaxing in the sun. What we did not appreciate was that our lengthy stay was considered suspicious. After two days, some rather hard-looking fellows arrived who showed a peculiar interest in our activities and we left them to work it out for themselves. Clearly they thought we were acting as spies for the USA and our swimming, sailing and canoeing was actually us reconnoitring potential beach landing zones so we needed to be watched.

It had been a lovely break. Sue looked suntanned and well and I hoped that this might be a good omen. Sadly, it was not to be. Within two months a CAT scan showed that the cancer was back and she had to endure more chemotherapy. I was distraught. We had to find a cure, but of course there is no cure, which I refused to accept. In desperation we went over to the Dana-Farber Cancer Institute in Boston for further tests, but they discovered that the cancer had spread to her liver – a very bad sign. They gave us some suggestions of therapies which might work and on our return the Torbay hospital tried them, but their effect was only ever temporary.

By October I think Sue had had enough. She had put up stoically with so much for more than two years and could not cope with any further treatment. She could not even take the liquid food that was recommended. I watched her shrink through lack of nourishment and felt so frustrated that there was nothing I could do to help her. In mid-November we drove out to Dartmoor for the last time. She did not have the energy to leave the car and exercise the dogs, one of her favourite activities. I can still remember our driving back and looking at the sun shining through the golden autumn trees, not wanting to think that she would never see that sight again. It was downhill from there.

We lay in bed together to watch England win the Rugby World Cup, something that delighted us both, but two days later she went into a hospice. She was now on morphine all the time, a relief as it removed her suffering. I called the family because as she drifted in and out of consciousness I wanted her to know we were all there with her, to know how much she meant to us all. By the Friday we knew she had not long to go and she died just after midday with her family around her. It is shattering to watch one's love slowly leave this life. I was stunned. I don't deal in emotions much, but I drove out to Dartmoor on my own. I wanted to be alone with my raw grief and I have never felt so lonely. The person who I had grown up with, who had supported me through thick and thin, with whom I had shared so much, loved and trusted as my best friend, had been taken from me. I was desolate and angry. Why pick on her? For Sue the suffering thankfully was over, but for those who are left behind without her the suffering goes on.

After the funeral Sara had to go back home to her family, leaving me alone. I was fine in most respects. There is a system you have to deal with to record the death and obtain probate, which keeps you busy. You go into it mechanically but the bureaucracy forces you into a regime, probably a good thing as it gives you something practical to deal with. However, it was probably the worst time of my life and having to return to a now empty house was miserable. A house is a home when it is welcoming and your loved one is there in it, but it feels so desperately quiet when they are gone. Shortly afterwards, Mother died aged 96, so I lost the two most influential people in my life in the space of a couple of months.

17

THREE DOGS IN ACTION

Despite Sue's ill health, I still had other concerns. The 2002/3 Clipper race had followed very much the same route as before but sponsorship was increasing, enabling us to spend more on promotion. After four races our boats, although strong and capable of many more voyages, were looking dated. Yacht design was changing quite rapidly and our fleet needed to look more like the latest ocean racers. The business was now in profit, successful enough to encourage the financiers to make such a major investment and we could see our way forward, so we decided the time was right to build a new and larger fleet.

We looked around for a designer and contacted Ed Dubois, who quickly understood what we wanted – a racy-looking boat, strong and seaworthy, capable of being sailed by amateur crews. He produced a beautiful 68-footer and we enquired around the world for a price. During this time, I went on a business trip to China and met up with a company making powerboats at the Shanghai Boat Show. They were called Double Happiness, the world's leading manufacturer of table tennis equipment, but they also owned a boatyard just outside

Shanghai. Negotiations commenced and we signed a contract for ten of the Dubois boats.

We had to put off the next race by a year to allow them to be built and delivered, which made money tight for a while, so William and I stopped drawing a salary to ease cashflow and see us through. In addition, we negotiated loans from Lloyds Bank to cover the period. One sponsor payment was late, putting us at our limit for a short time and Lloyds agreed to extend the loans, but only if the loan rates on all our borrowings were increased, which seemed harsh. After all, if you have a cashflow issue the one thing you don't need is someone charging you more. The money came through three weeks later, but the higher interest rate remained. Lloyds appeared surprised when the moment we had paid off the loans we changed banks! Loyalty has to work both ways.

The new fleet had a few problems to begin with. The designer had produced the plans and it was up to specialist engineers to draw up the building specification. These engineers had said the skegs did not need the reinforcement of the steel 'T' piece I had asked for as they could achieve much greater strength using Glass Reinforced Plastic. When we collected the first boat from Felixstowe and tried to sail it back to Gosport the rudder would not turn as the kegs were moving too much, so we had to fit the 'T' pieces after all, stiffen them and after that their steering was excellent.

From a sailing perspective the ten Dubois 68s appeared a success with the crews from the start. They were built for 20 crew so income rose considerably. We quickly paid off the bank loans and then began to expand the team to provide better marketing. This also enabled us to look at making a film of each race to make available to crews as a memento and help to promote our port sponsors. It was shown by quite a few TV stations around the world, who liked the idea of ordinary people doing something extraordinary with their lives. As the company expanded we also recruited our own maintenance team and flew them around the ports to ensure that the boats were kept in working order. When someone suggested that this was expensive we could point to the high boatyard costs in most of the countries we visited, the variable quality of the work and the fact that our team knew the boats, meaning the work was carried out more speedily, effectively and with continuity.

Our biggest and totally unexpected problem came as the fleet approached the Philippines and was due to a mistake by the engineers. William and I were on our way to Bilbao when we got the message that one of the boats had serious leaks around its keel. We instructed another boat to accompany them in case the crew had to be evacuated and to both head for the nearest port, Subic Bay. By the time we arrived in Bilbao three hours later, we received messages that two other boats had the same problem. There was obviously a fleet-wide fault with the boats, so we ordered the entire fleet to stop racing and take it easy to get to Subic Bay. The problem soon became obvious. The engineers who had designed the lay-up of the hulls had not drawn out a gradual taper from the solid area of the bottom of the hull, designed to hold the keel bolts, into the rest of the hull. The resulting abrupt connection with the foam sandwich was the weak point and this was where the hulls were cracking. Such a sharp divide was bound to crack and eventually it did. The fact that a number of other yachts built around the world at the same time had the same error and actually lost their keels was little compensation to us.

We got all the boats safely to Subic Bay, but were faced with the problem that our boats were not safe and we could not possibly carry on with the race in those circumstances. Inevitably there were plenty of comments in the media that Clipper was finished and we would never sort the issue out. That was their considered view, based on the contention that bad news sells a story, but William and I had other ideas. William flew out to Subic Bay to take charge of the problem on site. I remained behind to try to get the engineers to come up with a solution that would be acceptable to the authorities, which of course they were nervous about due to it being their error and potential liability. They dithered so I called Bill Green, with whom I had sailed on *Yeoman XX*, and asked him to come and meet the engineers and talk about laminating, about which he knew more than most. With Bill's common sense approach we eventually got a solution, although it took two weeks to get it signed off by the officials. William went to work, assisted by four of Bill's best laminating foremen whom we flew out to provide expertise. William was in his element. Assisted by Justin Haller, our engineer, and Adam Wheeler, another engineer working with us at the time, they worked 20-hour days to maintain momentum. One minute William was driving a huge fork lift truck with a nine-ton keel hanging on the end, the next he was chasing up the 70 locals he had hired to help get the work completed under the expert supervision of Bill's people.

We told the crews we would pay for their return home or they could go off and explore for eight weeks. The costs were horrendous and unfortunately the engineers went out of business so there was no chance of recovering anything from them. We lost a skipper while the repairs were taking place, who believed that we could not possibly deal with the problem. In fact, within seven weeks we had cut out the bottoms of each of the boats, tapered the connection to the rest of the hulls and completely re-laminated them. With the official surveyor there to check the work as it was completed we were ready to continue the race.

Nearly all the crew returned, however one skipper told us he was ready but at the same time was saying to his crew that he had told us the boat had not passed survey and they were being forced to sail in unsafe boats. It was not true, we had the certificates, but naturally the crew were concerned. Sadly, journalists picked up his complaint and believed it and we lost a sponsor as a result. The skipper swiftly departed his boat at the next port before I arrived to sack him. Although we had lost eight weeks, we managed to complete the race with our now much stronger boats, which never gave trouble again.

This was the first race where we reversed our route. Instead of going westward around the world, we went eastabout. The advantage this brought was that it took the fleet to Australia after Cape Town, which put the boats into the Southern Ocean. This leg, through the Roaring Forties, one of the toughest from a weather point of view, has proved very popular and always fills up quickly. We still had to avoid Cape Horn as it did not fit into our schedule and would have meant a winter rounding, so we continued to pass through the Panama Canal. Traffic can be held up there, but by using a local agent we usually get the boats through within three to four days.

It has not always been easy. On one occasion we were awaiting delivery of a new gearbox for one of the boat engines and, inevitably, it was delayed. Rather than hold up the fleet, Justin

Haller removed a gearbox from a boat that had already been through and ran it back to the Pacific side in a taxi, fitted it to the last boat so it could transit and remain with the fleet. By the time it rejoined on the Atlantic side the other gearbox had arrived and could be fitted so the fleet was able to sail together on schedule. Waiting for the rest of the fleet to transit, a crew member on one of the boats decided to go swimming. Our rigger, Greg North, was up the mast and looked out across at a nearby sandbank. He called down to the swimmer to stop what he was doing and make his way quickly to the bank the other side and get out of the water fast – Greg had spotted a large crocodile on the sand bank!

The City of Hull sponsored the start of the second Clipper race with the 68s in 2007/8, supported by Yorkshire Forward. I had not seen the city since 1959 and was amazed at how it had transformed with the help of an active council. Crowds of hundreds of thousands of people came down to view the boats at the start and there was a £9 million benefit to the local economy.

Yorkshire Forward had established a Clipper steering group with the aim of maximising the impact of the sponsorship of both the Hull and Humber yacht and the Clipper events in Hull. This group was chaired by a local businessman, Jim Dick OBE. He was also keen to ensure that young people could benefit from the fantastic opportunities and in partnership with Hull City Council he came up with an initiative that would enable ten young people from disadvantaged backgrounds to each do a leg of the race. As part of the Wilberforce 2007 commemorations marking the bicentennial of the abolition of slavery, they would also carry the Fight for Freedom anti-slavery petition calling for an end to modern-day slavery around the world.

The young people went through the same training as the rest of the crews. Our training had increased from a mandatory three weeks to four weeks as our boats became larger. Its primary purpose is to make people safe on the boats and ensure they adopt the same procedures and descriptions of equipment around the deck. At some point they are likely to have to perform an operation at night or in bad weather and that is not the time to be asking what to do. In many ways, those who have never sailed before are easier to teach as we don't have to remove bad habits.

Basic boat knowledge and simple procedures take up the first week. This gets built on with sail trimming the second week, leading onto spinnaker drills and then short races between boats for the final week so people learn how trimming effects speed. The loss of a skipper on another racing boat in the Solent led us to undertake tests with a dummy to see how a body is dragged alongside a boat and it did not behave as we expected. Instead of floating on its back it was face down, which would quickly lead to drowning. So we developed systems for stopping the boats quickly and different lengths of tethers on safety harnesses. The dummy made man overboard recovery so much more realistic that we supplied one to each of the boats. The youngsters from Hull quickly realised that they could perform as well as anyone else on the boat, even senior businessmen, and it gave them confidence, which, after my STA experience, perhaps I was the least surprised at the huge change it effected in them. All found jobs quickly afterwards or went into further education and all are still doing well. The experience of being on the same level as outwardly successful people had opened their eyes to the potential of a better future for themselves and they all grasped the opportunity.

Jim Dick, being a keen sailor himself, couldn't resist the opportunity to take a leg of the race. It was during this leg in the middle of the south Atlantic when Jim had a conversation with the skipper Danny Watson about the amazing impact this experience had had on the young people. On completing his leg, Jim returned to Hull and in partnership with Dave Bertholini of the local authority, put together the plans and secured the funding for a follow-up scheme. This was called CatZero and its aim was to take disadvantaged young people from Hull for a three-month training course, which included two weeks sailing on a large yacht, with Alan Johnson MP and myself as the patrons. It has been a huge success with more than 1,500 young people being involved and 65 per cent finding employment afterwards.

CatZero is now an award-winning charity and in its tenth year, going from strength to strength working across the Yorkshire area and has developed its programmes to work with all ages and with full families. It is still run by Jim, Dave and Danny and has been identified nationally as demonstrating best practice in a number of areas. CatZero is an outstanding legacy of the Clipper Race programme.

In 2007, I was invited to become the president of the Cruising Association for its centenary. Based in Limehouse Basin in London, it has a strong international membership who campaign on behalf of cruising sailors and share information about pilotage, ports, charges, costs of fuel and where the best services are to be found. I did not feel honoured for long. A quick look at the accounts showed the association had about five months to live unless drastic measures were taken. I had not taken on the position to preside over its demise and I had some luck in Stuart Bradley, who was elected my vice-president. I had someone who I could work with and we called an immediate council meeting. Drastic action was necessary but first we had to analyse the situation to see where costs could be cut and income increased.

The association owned its own headquarters building but it was soon obvious that money was being wasted and there were savings to be made. Some, such as a telephone rental bill for a contract that had expired nearly three years before but was still being paid, were easy. Expensive hire agreements were cancelled and items were bought instead of being rented as and when money became available. Membership stood at around 3,500 but these figures did not tie up with the subscription income, which led to a thorough review of all finances.

The loss of some £43,000 a year on the bar/catering operation led to that business being leased out, cutting a large amount of the loss and creating a small profit for the association. Items like books with no reference to sailing which, we discovered later, had been bought to provide sound muffling when the association was headquartered near Baker Street Underground station, were disposed of. This allowed a reorganisation of the use of the building and created valuable space which we were able to rent out. With Desmond Scott joining Stuart and myself, as well as some strong support from other members of the council and a small army of volunteers, by December 2008 we were able to report a surplus of £17,000, a turnaround of £72,000. Rental from the vacated space soon increased this surplus. I agreed to stay on an extra year to allow our changes to settle in and then Stuart was elected president in my place to continue the good work.

It is interesting to see how morale changes when word gets around that something is being done about a problem. Membership had been declining, but the moment people realised that action was being taken to sort out the finances the numbers steadied and then, as the finances went the right way, began to rise. Stuart was able to phone me in 2010 to tell me the debts and overdraft were paid off and we were achieving a surplus, allowing the association to expand its services, develop its website, and make other use of the internet. The association's membership now exceeds 6,000 and I am proud to be its patron.

BBC Radio Solent covers probably the densest area of maritime activity anywhere. The Solent is not just a haven for yachting, it has the container terminal and cruise liners at Southampton as well as the ferries and navy in Portsmouth. In 2007 Mia Costello, the controller, undertook a survey to see if there was an appetite for a programme focusing on the local marine scene and the answer was a resounding yes. The name chosen was H2O and she asked if I wanted to be involved. We would go out every Friday evening between April and September. The first programme was broadcast in April 2008 and I was presenting with Shelley Jory Leigh, Britain's female powerboat champion, and Neil Sackley as the producer, engineer, reporter and presenter.

Having never presented a programme before, it took us one or two shows to get the timing right, vital in a live programme. The chemistry between us was right from the start and as we became more confident we started doing outside broadcasts. This led us to visit some of the less accessible features along the coast, varying from the Needles and Portland Bill lighthouse, the finale of Cowes week, the Olympic sailing from Weymouth of course, to sitting in a container crane in Southampton docks. I think the programme worked because of the interaction between the three of us and the genuine interest we had in the subjects. Neil put it rather well when he said: 'It worked because you and I had never powerboated; Shelley and I hadn't sailed; and you and Shelley hadn't done radio. So we taught each other our respective jobs.' When Shelley or I were away we had able substitutes in Dee Caffari, Geoff Holt, Tracey Clarke and Matt Sheahan, so the expertise was maintained.

Our most ambitious project was to enter the Cowes Torquay Powerboat race, the most prestigious powerboat race in Britain, over a distance of a little more than 200 miles. This was Shelley's territory, so she drove and I navigated while Neil worked his magic behind us to get reports through. We borrowed a Scorpion RIB with about 700 horsepower, which seems a lot but not in this arena. In fact, we had the lowest horsepower in the fleet, with a top speed of 53 knots. To me, the most vital factor was the weather as the wave direction and size would dictate how well we could maintain our speed. I memorised the distances, for example if you go inside Lyme Bay between Torbay and Portland Bill, it is eight miles further than the straight line, or about 11 minutes at the top speed we could make. There was no point in writing anything down as the vibration when going flat out made even picking the right button on the plotter a lottery.

The wind was south-westerly as we started. In this race and perhaps in powerboat racing in general, the boats start when going flat out and a flag is lowered, not the fine time and distance calculations which sailors are used to. Off we went and once through the Needles we started to bounce quite a lot. I asked Shelley to aim inside St Alban's Head where there was a bit of a lee so the waves were smaller and we could maintain a better speed. Then we went close into the Head and aimed for Weymouth to enjoy the lee created by Portland Bill. This allowed us to maintain an average of 50 knots. As we went around Portland, the most powerful boat in the fleet and ultimate winner *Cinzano* was just in front of us so I don't know what he had been doing. Now across Lyme Bay there was no choice but to head straight into the wind and waves so our speed lessened. The larger *Cinzano* disappeared ahead, but there weren't many other boats about. Where had they gone?

We speeded up as we got into the lee of Devon and then a large RIB went past us as if we were stopped. Shelley was upset, but I pointed out that the question to ask was why, with that speed advantage, he was behind us at this stage. On rounding the mark off Torquay it disappeared into Lyme Bay which seemed a mistake as it added those eight miles to its distance, whereas we went straight for Portland Bill and rounded it with them in sight. Now we had to go in towards Poole and then back to the Needles channel. As we sped up the Solent there were no other boats in sight, so we assumed they had all finished. But as we approached Egypt Point near Cowes I looked behind and there was the grey RIB again, going flat out, but our lead was too great for him to close before we crossed the finish line. Where had he been? We finished fourth overall and first in our class, a real credit to Shelley's driving. I had enjoyed the race. It had been an interesting experience, but I was in no hurry to do it again!

Chris Carnegy succeeded Mia and recommissioned the

show and we went on for a further six years, completing 204 programmes in total and winning a finalist award at the prestigious New York Festivals, which celebrates the world's best radio programmes and promotions. We were recognised in the sport and recreation category for the programme we made about Bart's Bash, the charity set up in memory of Bart Simpson, sadly drowned in an America's Cup capsize. However, just as we won this award a new controller arrived and decided to close the programme, believing Neil's skills would be better used in news and since no replacement was suggested we were dropped. It was a sad end to the only programme in Britain, which maintains it is a seafaring nation, that actually covered maritime matters.

In 2008 I received a phone call asking whether I would like to participate in a BBC TV programme with John Simpson and Sir Ranulph Fiennes to be called *The Three Dogs*, we being the dogs. The concept was that each of us would show the other two what we did, each demonstration being a separate TV programme. Ran would teach us how to travel in the Arctic, John would demonstrate the life of a war reporter and I would take them both around Cape Horn. It was irresistible. Ran and I had met some years before when, with Chris Bonington and Don Cameron, the balloonist, we had competed against each other on *The Krypton Factor*. Realising that Ran would be fit, I took off slowly in the obstacle course but was catching up a bit when he got the win. Chris won it overall, although for years I persuaded him that there were more mountaineering questions than sailing ones, but eventually had to admit that this was not true.

We were due to start in Afghanistan, but before we were allowed to go Ran and I had to complete a BBC hostile environment course. This involved in being kidnapped by some ex-Royal Marines, having hoods put over our heads and being interrogated. We did not have time to coordinate our stories, but Ran claimed to be a photographer and I a historian. We were marched into some woods and sat down. The marines kept calling me an old man and treating me as such so I behaved like one, stumbling with difficulty through the undergrowth. Their main interest was Ran, and I could hear guns being fired as they yelled at him. My guard did not want to miss the fun so he peremptorily ordered me to sit tight and not remove my hood and I heard his footsteps move away through the leaves. I left it a minute, raised the hood, found I was not being watched and ran off, causing consternation when my absence was discovered. The other part was dealing with the very realistic results of a serious accident with arms missing and blood pumping everywhere, but working as a team we dealt with the first aid required. An interesting experience.

Afghanistan was a place I had always wanted to visit, as my uncle had been the British minister there at the beginning of the Second World War. But while John and his team collected stories, Ran and I were locked up in a heavily guarded hotel and got bored. Eventually we escaped and headed for the souk to try to buy an authentic Martini–Henry rifle. We moved around a lot, never staying anywhere more than a few minutes, so that if the Taliban were warned they would have difficulty finding us. None of the rifles we examined was authentic as they had more modern sights and were probably made in Peshawar over the border in Pakistan. So we returned, past the machine gun posts at the entrance to the hotel, to be ticked off by the BBC security people who did not seem to understand that both of us had lived in these areas for years. Ran spoke Arabic and I Hindi, so we could understand what was being said one way or another.

We were allowed out under guard and met President Hamid Karzai and interviewed a failed suicide bomber. He was a young Pakistani who had been told by his village *mullah* that the foreigners were converting Afghan males to Christianity and raping their women and it was his duty to blow up as many of them as he could, guaranteeing him 72 virgins in a land of milk and honey in the afterlife. He got as far as the border, ran into the Afghan border police, asked them where the foreigners were so he could blow them up and was arrested. We felt sorry for him, a rather pathetic figure who had been manipulated, but never found out what happened to him.

The next part of the programme was to drive down to Jalalabad and we were told we were going in a convoy with the speaker of the Afghan parliament. That sounded all right as there would be plenty of guards, but we were going through a notoriously dangerous area where 11 French soldiers had been captured and beheaded recently and we did not think that two BBC armed guards was sufficient, so Ran and I threw health and safety back at them and said it was too dangerous. Consternation at this was not included in the programme. Eventually we agreed, but only after we had an AK-47 and five magazines each placed under our seats, just in case!

The journey was uneventful and we arrived at the governor's guesthouse in Jalalabad without incident. With that as our base, we visited the Khyber Pass, where the traffic has to change from driving on the left to the right, causing chaos with the trucks;

attended a meeting with headsmen of local villages, complaining that aid agencies ran around in new 4x4 vehicles and where was a tractor that could improve their lives, given all the aid that was flooding into the country; and visited a village that probably had not changed in a century, apart from the installation of a solitary phone line.

The following day we drove in convoy, escorted by 60 border police, to the Tora Bora hills, where Osama bin Laden had been holed up until he was winkled out by Special Forces. We camped at an outpost on top of a hill surrounded, we were told, by Taliban-sympathetic villages. Our only protection was a single band of barbed wire and our escort. The colonel's first action was to fire his Russian recoilless rifle at a nearby mountain to show he meant business. Impressive though this was, I could not help feeling that he was also announcing our presence to any Taliban within a radius of 15 miles. We spent the night there, Ran lying out among the stars as it reminded him of Muscat. John and I, after a cigar and glass of whisky and long discussion about Kipling, went to bed in the bunker.

The next day the colonel was going to take us back the way we had come, but we pointed out that the Taliban had had all night to mine that road and it might be better to choose another route so were relieved when he agreed. We arrived back in Jalalabad safely, watching the drones returning to the local US controlled airport from whatever mission they had been on. They set out with two Hellfire missiles, but it was rare they were both there when they returned. The next day we passed through the US Army checkpoints and boarded a rugged Russian aircraft for the flight back to Kabul, there being no escort available to take us back along the road. Looking down on the bald, brown mountains, it was easy to imagine British troops toiling along the paths below in the punitive expeditions organised at the height of Empire and I did not envy them.

Our first programme was completed. It had been a fascinating experience and we were sorry it was over. Although bare and treacherous, Afghanistan does have appeal and we would have liked to have seen more but the security situation did not allow for tourists.

Our next expedition was in January 2009 to Iqaluit in the Canadian north. The temperature was frequently down to minus 40, so covering skin and wrapping up well was essential, although we noticed the local Inuit wore much lighter clothing. The plan was to tow pulks (small sledges) across Frobisher Bay, at this time of the year frozen over, and camp where necessary. We were dropped off by motorised sledges, set up our pulks, put on skis and set off with me doing the navigation. Towards five in the evening, we stopped to set up our tents and settled in. This is where John, attending to a call of nature, left his gloves off for a minute and got frostnip. Fortunately, John's frostnip did not develop and he recovered completely but our doctor, Chris van Tulleken decided to pull him out, however much John protested. It could have been me, but I doubt it would have been Ran.

Ran had had a series of heart attacks, and I was certainly capable of lifting more than him, but as we pulked along together, me in the lead as navigator, I thought I could out-pace him. For half an hour I pushed the pace, and then a voice from right behind me asked whether I was OK. I increased the pace, beginning to get puffed and after an hour the voice right behind enquired again. After a further 15 minutes I stopped for a rest, panting, with Ran looking totally at ease. His stamina was impressive.

The BBC health and safety people had decreed that Ran and I were not to be allowed to light a spirit stove unless supervised, as if we had not lived with these things all our lives. Their supervisor put his head into our tent later to show us how to light one and discovered it flaming nicely and Ran and I enjoying a whisky together. He was told to clear off! That night the wind blew up and the tent began to collapse. Ran was up like a shot, fully clothed and onto the problem instantly. Not being able to find my gloves, without which frostbite would have disabled me as well, I was only ready to join him by the time he had everything under control. There are hard lessons to be learned in this freezing environment and I was glad I was travelling with one of the world's most experienced polar adventurers who could pass on his knowledge.

The final expedition was to Cape Horn. BBC health and safety decreed we must do their sea survival course and when I explained I had done one two years before stated that if I did not do theirs they would not certify me as safe to go around Cape Horn. I wish I could have got that comment in writing! We flew to Ushuaia in Argentina to join Skip Novak, who was going to take us westward down the Beagle Channel and then out into Drake Passage to sail east and around Cape Horn. First we had to call at Puerto Williams, the Chilean navy's post on the southern side of the channel for our permit. Chile and Argentina eye each other warily across the Beagle Channel and very few vessels are allowed into Chilean waters, but we had received permission. We sailed by day and anchored at night.

One evening in a sheltered bay, having put ropes out to hold the boat safely, we went ashore and barbecued a sheep for supper.

The following day we continued to explore, noting the way the glaciers were receding even here, a sad contradiction to those who claim there is no global warming. Finally, after our third night at anchor in the wonderful barren surroundings where few trees grow much taller than hip height, we headed out into the Southern Ocean. As we picked up the swell, Ran suddenly started making terrible noises and I thought he was having another heart attack, but it was just seasickness. Fortunately, the wind did not exceed 30 knots and we were soon running towards the Cape itself. We anchored behind the island and the next day decided to visit the lonely outpost there that maintains the lighthouse and keeps a listening watch only to find three cruise liners loafing around. We waited for them to become impatient and depart and took the dinghy ashore bearing fresh fruit and meat for the Chilean petty officer who manned the island with his family. It is a long posting and they were educating their two daughters via the internet. We paid our respects at the Cape Horn memorial to all the seamen who have lost their lives here, being careful to keep to the marked paths as the island is mined against an Argentine attack.

The whole programme from concept to broadcast had been enormous fun and was well received. Ran, John and I had hit it off from the start and became good friends. There was even talk of further expeditions, but the BBC said they did not want programmes about old men and that killed it off.

Despite these distractions, Clipper was still my main focus. Back at Clipper HQ, which had moved to Gosport, re-fits and training were underway in the spring of 2010 for our next race, following the same route as before. But in this race we lost a boat. The skipper had ignored the instructions to keep well clear of obstacles in the Indonesian archipelago which is badly surveyed and hit a rocky outcrop in the Sunda Strait. This was where the advantage of a fleet sailing in close company showed its benefits, with the boats never far apart we had another boat on site within 20 minutes. We told them to get the crew to safety and then tell us the situation. The information coming back was not good and we had to accept that the boat was a total loss, being ground to pieces by the waves. It had all been so unnecessary. On the crew's arrival in Singapore, I asked the skipper if he had looked at the chart and he told me he had but the light on the rock was not working. I pointed out that the chart stated 'Light extinguished'! He had clearly not looked closely enough at the chart and that could have cost lives.

Our MCA compliance surveyors reacted in a panic. They wanted an additional qualified person added to the crew and denied they had any knowledge of how we manned the boats, and this after 14 years of doing our surveys. This was just not credible and caused some problems, which we eventually resolved with the MCA.

I was more concerned at the instructions we had received from the same surveyor on how the rigging should be tuned. As the boat heels over the leeward rigging goes slack but ours were seriously slack. The slack rigging behaves like a paper clip which, when it is bent a few times, will eventually break. Having slack shrouds might work in the Solent where if a mast breaks it is a short motor to harbour, but is thoroughly danger-ous on a long oceanic voyage. I tried to explain this, but was told to just obey the instruction by the Jersey registry and if I tightened the rigging to remove this slackness our compliance certificates would be withdrawn, making it illegal to sail. The result was inevitable: rigging broke and two of our boats were dismasted. It was lucky no one was hurt.

It took time to have two new masts made and get them out to the dismasted boats so they could rejoin the race by Panama and was not without some bizarre difficulties. One set of new masts arrived at Los Angeles airport and there were eight hours to get them across to the other side of the airport to load onto the next aircraft. We rang the agent to tell her how important this was and she told us she only employed the 'best of the best', but she had lit a candle for us. Her candle must have flickered and gone out, because despite her 'best of the best', our masts missed their connection and we lost another valuable week.

This incident led to us removing the boats from the Jersey register as we could not go forward with them if they were going to force us to do something that we knew was unsafe and they would not listen. There had been no commercial benefits to having the boats registered in Jersey, except that the state and many locals were supporting us and had become good friends.

We ran the Velux 5 Oceans again in 2010, from La Rochelle, with Dave Adams as race director once more. We had problems with the French sailing authorities and IMOCA (the International Mono-hull Open Class Association) who encouraged the Barcelona World Race to move so they clashed with us. The International Sailing Federation Oceanic committee, of which I was a member, was keen to avoid this sort of behaviour but appeared powerless to stop the move. Inevitably it meant our entry list was reduced. Our efforts to encourage more sailors into solo around-the-world racing by limiting entries to boats built before 2003, which are a lot cheaper to buy so they could gain experience and establish their reputations, did not bring in the numbers we had hoped.

The route was slightly different this time. After the first stop in Cape Town, the boats called at Wellington in New Zealand, where I took time out to visit my cousin Dr Nigel Rankin in Auckland, have lunch with some ex-BI friends and take the railway back down to Wellington which was well worth the trouble. The next stop was the delightful Punta del Este in Uruguay, followed by Charleston, USA, and back to La Rochelle. The winner, with just four boats finishing, was the American Brad Van Liew in just over 118 days, a very creditable time for a voyage that is longer than the route for a non-stop circumnavigation. Second was Canadian Derek Hatfield taking 12 days longer. But clearly we could not continue to run races for a class of boats that seemed hell-bent on trying to disrupt us. William and I decided we had done enough to try to keep the race going and told Michael Rasmussen of Velux that we could not justify the sponsorship costs for another event as we could no longer gather sufficient entries to make it a worthwhile investment for them. I hated walking away from the Open 60 Class which we had set up in 1983 with the BOC Challenge, but the French grip on IMOCA was jealously guarded.

Once the Velux Race was over it was time to focus on the next Clipper Race where training was in full swing. The race is all about bringing crew to recognise their potential by making them face a challenging environment. More people have climbed Mount Everest than have sailed around the world, which puts around the world sailing into focus. Just over 200 people have sailed solo around the south of each of the three Capes of Good Hope, Leeuwin and the Horn, whereas more than 600 people have gone into space. It is a character-building experience and for many it is life changing. Having achieved something special with a circumnavigation, they usually feel confident to take on greater challenges. They have painted their lives with bright colours, not pastel shades, and that brightness is like a drug and they want more of it.

Our practical objective is to turn out a really good, safe all-round ocean sailor. That means giving responsibility. We choose a mixture of people for each boat when selecting the crews: age, experience, gender were all in the mix to try to create equal teams. The other objective is to give each professional skipper the right people to support them. Of course we did not always get it right, as some who did well in training did not perform so well when faced with the isolation and the immensity of being on an ocean voyage.

This applied to the skippers as well, and sometimes, reluctantly, we had to make changes. It is not easy being the skipper of a boat with an amateur crew. It requires remarkable qualities of leadership, patience, teaching and encouragement while ensuring that the boat is running properly and safely. Those skippers who have got their boats around the world with Clipper have achieved something special.

As our financial position improved, in the early days we had been persuaded to float on AIM on the stock market in 1999 – an interesting experience. For this they requested that we appoint a non-executive director and we were very lucky that Bob Dench agreed. His knowledge of the City was invaluable and he brought a lot of sage wisdom to our discussions. The initial share price reflected our balance sheet value at 73 pence per share, but we did not fit any of the usual stock market categories. Were we a sport, an event, a sporting event or a package holiday business? The lack of a clear market identity meant that the share price was marked down every time any business in adjacent categories had a problem. While it did not overly concern us, as we were not seeking investment, it was annoying to see the value of our now-profitable company being constantly written down. Eventually, the share price reached the point where we had more money in the bank than our value on AIM and we decided we had had enough. We notified the stock market, made an offer and bought our company back.

We de-listed in May 2009 and made an offer to the other shareholders of 5 pence in November. By February 2010 we had 90 per cent acceptances, but one shareholder was closing in on the magic 10 per cent which could have blocked us and with it came demands for a place on the board. Firstly, we did not need his investment and secondly we already had an excellent non-executive. Another outside director with no knowledge of the business would have been an unnecessary distraction. So we doubled the authorised share capital without pre-emption rights and he gave up and we bought him out.

2011/12 was our eighth Clipper Race and it was time to start planning to upgrade the fleet again. The Dubois 68 boats had done us proud, but after eight years of yacht development they were looking dated. They were not the same style as the new boats coming into service for around the world racing, like the latest Volvo fleet and Open 60s, which was what people expected. This time we went to Tony Castro for a design, not because we were unhappy with Ed Dubois but we thought a change would be a good idea.

Our remit was simple: we wanted something that looked modern but would be safe and fast for our amateur sailors. This inevitably meant that the boats would be heavier than the lightweight flyers that the professionals were using, but that did not matter as our race was between a fleet of identical boats where the performance would be down solely to the crews. He came up with a 70-foot-long design, more akin to the modern wedge shape and with firm chines aft. Our maintenance team had expanded to cope with the additional work and as we had a very good group it made sense to get them to do the design work for the layout of the engine room and to fit the generator and water makers, seeing as they would be the ones who had to get at them. Their plans certainly made maintenance easier, an important consideration when the schedule can be tight and time in ports limited.

Again we sought quotes from around the world and again settled on China, but this time in Qingdao. Work started on the moulds but we soon realised that the yard was having difficulties because of its management and our supervisor started to send us warning of the work not going ahead according to plan. It came to a head and we decided to move the moulds and the one mould-ing completed so far to another yard to complete the project. While the hulls and fit-out took place in China, the equipment was largely British and we sent items such as engines, winches, generators, etc. out to be fitted. The boats were shipped back to the UK without their keels, masts and rigs, which were built in Britain and attached in Hamble. We discovered some problems with the gunwales on some of the boats where there appeared to be large voids where the resin had been vacuumed badly. We had the entire fleet surveyed and, where necessary, the bad parts cut out and re-laminated in Hamble as we could not afford to have anything in the fleet that might create a problem at sea.

The first race with the 70s was in 2013 and left on time from London, parading down the Thames and starting out from Southend pier. I was pleased see all the boats set spinnakers as they headed for the North Foreland, a good omen for a competitive event.

We made some slight changes to the route to enable us to go via Sydney in Australia towards the middle of December and enter the whole fleet in the classic Sydney to Hobart race, the southern hemisphere equivalent of the Fastnet race. We had already placed two of the Dubois boats out in Sydney as Australians were our second largest national group of crews and it made sense to allow them, and others from Asia, to train at home. We entered these boats along with the 70 fleet into the race. Of course our 70-foot boats were stored for an around the world race, with food aboard for three weeks, so were not competitive with the out-and-out racers that made up the bulk of the contestants, but they finished in a close group near the middle of the results on handicap. It was a good result in the circumstances.

I navigated one of the 68s to keep my hand in and discovered, to considerable surprise, that as we entered the Derwent river in Tasmania we were lying second among the 14 Clipper boats. I reflected that this was not very clever marketing of the new fleet, which were certainly a lot faster off the wind but fractionally slower to windward. In the two subsequent Sydney to Hobart races we have done, when I have again navigated a

68, I have never managed to beat so many, coming only about halfway through the Clipper fleet. But the experience spices up the race and gives great satisfaction to the crews of the boats that do beat me.

The race basically followed our usual route from Australia, calling at Qingdao in China again. One of the key factors when planning these routes is the requirements of the ports and sponsors, and the need to keep to a tight schedule. Everyone knows that sailing boat speeds cannot be predicted with the accuracy of powered vessels. The old saying was that sailing boats have destinations, not estimated times of arrival. However, the arrangements for berthing 12 large yachts requires quite a lot of planning, so calculating the ETAs is important, and in southeast Asia this means fitting in with Chinese New Year. China has become a great favourite with the Clipper Race and Qingdao our most enduring sponsor. The welcome is fantastic and our hosts go out of their way to provide the facilities we require. They also supply crews and the race has now given more than 70 Chinese sailors the experience of an ocean crossing, an experience they take back to their country to pass on.

From China there is the long voyage across the north Pacific to the US west coast, this time San Francisco again. This leg is underestimated as the northern Pacific can be just as atrocious as the Southern Ocean and is a real test for boats and crews. One of the boats was pooped by a breaking wave, injuring a crew member who was evacuated by the US Coastguard. Another crew member, Andrew Taylor, was washed overboard on this leg and was lucky to be found alive nearly two hours later. His dry suit saved his life by allowing time for the boat to conduct a thorough search of the water. Andrew had an

Automatic Identification System (AIS) beacon but switched it to test and not transmit by mistake, which is why it took so long to find him. He only realised his error after an hour when he saw his boat turn away on one of the legs of its search pattern for him.

Sean McCarter, the skipper, was very determined not to lose a member of his crew and did a brilliant job in searching and finding Andrew. The beacon saved him in the end and we immediately fitted beacons to all the boat's dan buoys, long poles that can float with a flag and are thrown into the sea whenever someone goes overside to assist in finding them. For the next race they were attached to everyone's lifejackets. The range of the beacons is advertised as four miles but we found just over two miles was more likely in large seas, but this is good enough if a proper search pattern is mounted. What did surprise us was the speed at which the casualty drifted, nearly two knots, which is an important consideration when planning a search.

As we finished the first race and started preparations for the second with the 70s, I spotted a gap of time as the team had the re-fits and training well under control. So I decided it was time to get some more solo racing and entered the French Route du Rhum in 2014 with my Open 60 *Grey Power*. It is a race from St Malo to Guadeloupe, which I had done in 1982 and usually involved a beat out to Finisterre across the Bay of Biscay and then a trade wind belt across to the West Indies. Tactically it is interesting as the route to take depends on the positioning of the Azores high pressure system. My start was slow, *Grey Power* is built for downwind flying, and I was well down the fleet when I passed Ushant. But in the Bay of Biscay I got a more free wind and the boat became long-legged. I slowly reeled in the boats in front, making one tactical gybe south to avoid a southward movement of the high pressure system that paid off, and as we approached the finish I was up to third in my class and closing. Sadly, I ran out of track and that was where I finished.

It had been wonderful being back in the solo circuit. Although there were only a few in the race from my racing days in the 1980s there were plenty of very good newcomers. At the finish, I visited some local schools who had been following me and then picked up friends Alan Emtage and Michael Rhodes to sail down to Grenada where we hauled out at Jason Fletcher's Grenada marina until the following summer. My greatest surprise came in being awarded the UK Yachtsman of the Year trophy for the fourth time, only, I think, because not much else had happened in sailing that year!

Dilip Donde and Josh Warren joined me the next May and we recommissioned the boat in Grenada and sailed her up to Newport in the USA via Bermuda and Province Town. There David Aisher and Bernard Gallay joined for the joint Royal Yacht Squadron and New York Yacht Club Atlantic Race. I made a mistake with the weather early on and we lost time and distance, finishing only third in class, but it had been fun racing with friends. Bernard, who now runs a very successful brokerage in the south of France, subsequently received an offer for *Grey Power* and I sold her. She was becoming just a bit too much of a handful and I knew I was not sailing her as hard as I used to in my sixties, which was frustrating. So it was time to choose something more manageable and capable of longer voyages in more comfort as I entered my late seventies.

*

For the 2015/16 Clipper race we started once more from London and our first stop once again was Rio de Janeiro. Sadly we lost a crew member, Andrew Ashman, who stepped into the danger area by the main sheet and was most likely struck forcibly on the side of the head when the boat crash gybed. It was our first death and shook us all badly, not least because it was so unnecessary. Crew are trained to avoid this zone, or crawl beneath the main sheet track, which is safe, if they have to move through it. We directed the boat to Oporto and I was pleased that the entire crew, obviously shaken, were supporting each other and decided together they would continue.

While in Rio de Janeiro we had five crew and supporters mugged, which caused some problems for the authorities with the Olympic Games coming, but fortunately no one was seriously hurt. One of the boats had lost its decals and went ashore on its way to be hauled out down the coast. I took another boat with Jay and Greg and we surfed into the beach in a dinghy, capsizing as we did so. The boat was lying on its side just below high water level and beam on. Our first task was to turn her round so her bow was facing into the waves. We took the anchor in the dinghy and capsized. We capsized the second time as well. On the third attempt we lashed everything in the dinghy and when it capsized the anchor and chain remained inside so we carried on swimming it out to the full length of its anchor chain. We took the weight on the chain from the bow, but nothing moved as the keel was firmly embedded in the sand.

There was nothing for it but to dig the keel free and having no shovels we used pots and pans from the boat to move about ten tons of sand. With a messenger lead from the anchor cable to one of the coffee grinders, we eventually got the bow round.

This stopped the boat from being driven further up the beach and meant that when a tow arrived the boat could be pulled clear easily. We camped ashore, making a small shelter out of plastic sheeting lying on the beach and burning driftwood for a fire. Another boat came down to collect Jay and Greg, who were needed for maintenance on the rest of the fleet and to get a message to William that all I now needed was a tug. Our roles were reversed from when we dealt with the keel problem with the 68s. He was already negotiating with the authorities, agents, the Brazilian navy and the underwriters, but things don't happen fast in Brazil and it was five days before he got clearance for the tug to come down to us.

In the meantime, another 70 came down and I asked it to try to tow the beached boat off at high water. It went wrong from the start. The boat drifted down the beach so it was not pulling straight out to sea and then caught the tow line around its propeller. Its anchor was deployed too late and very quickly I had two boats on the beach, a complete disaster. We now had ten people in the camp ashore. When the tug finally arrived, I swam out and went aboard to discuss a plan with the captain. He spoke no English, I no Portuguese, but within ten minutes by drawing on scraps of paper we had a plan. We took a messenger ashore and then hauled in his long tow rope, securing it around the keel, as that has the strongest fixings to the hull and where it went the hull would follow. The boat came off easily and was taken to a yard some miles away for haul out, survey and repairs to its rudder. The next day the tug returned and we soon had the other boat afloat. We had been incredibly lucky. The only damage was two rudders which were speedily fixed and the two boats started off together a day behind the rest of the fleet and caught up in Cape Town.

The Pacific leg again proved tough and we lost another crew member, Sarah Young, overside, after her tether hadn't been clipped to the safety points around the boat. She was recovered, a credit to the crew, but regrettably did not survive. It was another tragic and avoidable loss and a stark reminder of the importance of safety equipment. The following year we lost another boat, which quite unnecessarily sailed too close to the coast south of Cape Town and went ashore. The SNRI, South Africa's equivalent of the RNLI, got everyone off safely very quickly, but the boat could not be recovered as it had gone ashore on the beach of a game reserve and we were not allowed to take heavy equipment down to free it.

In this race too, we lost another life. Simon Speirs had gone overside but his harness clip failed and he fell into the sea. He was recovered but could not be revived. The failure of the clip puzzled us all as they are top of the range and can take a direct pull of 2,000kg, but investigation showed that the clip had caught on something and the pull had been sideways and the catch had failed. This was the first time such an accident had occurred with these type of clips as far as anyone knew and research started immediately on how to build a clip that was stronger to pulls from all directions, not just in a straight line.

Despite these sad losses, Clipper continues to thrive having given more than 5,000 people from 46 different nationalities a taste of ocean racing, a very different game to weekend round-the-cans sailing. The balance between British sailors and those from other countries has slowly changed to the point that now the British are in the minority. We became involved with the government's 'Britain is GREAT' campaign, promoting what the country has to offer, with William being made one of its ambassadors and eventually receiving a well-deserved OBE.

Racing across oceans is an extreme sport, especially when those oceans include the Southern Ocean and north Pacific, but the sea can be dangerous anywhere and must never be taken casually. A little bit of apprehension before a long voyage is no bad thing if it makes a person run through everything and check that the boat and its crew are fully ready for the adventure. However, the rewards are immeasurable. Nothing can compare with sailing through the trades with a warm blue sea, sunshine and a good breeze. Writing this, as I sail *Suhaili* down to Falmouth to celebrate the 50th anniversary of my departure in the *Sunday Times* Golden Globe Race, escorted by 17 small boats that are preparing to replicate that voyage, solo and nonstop, one can reflect upon a life that has not always been easy but has usually been interesting.

Acknowledgements

Inevitably in an adventurous life spanning almost 80 years there are so many who have contributed to my development in different ways and I apologise to those who have assisted me through life but cannot be included. They range from friends at school, schoolmasters, some loved (some not) shipmates from many vessels during my 14 years at sea in the Merchant Navy, and those in the Royal Navy. Crews I have sailed with over the years in the oceans of the world, climbers, adventurers, business friends and colleagues who have shared my fear, frustrations and ultimately satisfaction.

To all who have shared my life with me in all its different aspects, I give appreciative thanks. If you are not mentioned, you are not forgotten and your friendship is something I still treasure. My recollections of our time together will always be a warm memory as I hope they will be for you.

Of course there were huge sacrifices by my family as I wandered off on some voyage or expedition, from a worried mother when I set off around the world in 1968, a worried but supportive father, brothers, all of whom had to bear the long silence when I could not make contact and many thought I was lost at sea. Later, an incredibly supportive wife who put up with my dreams and helped turn them into reality.

Finally to Fran Jessop, who turned my rambling memories into something readable.